Identity Analytics

Analytics for Identity and Access Management

Nilesh Bhoyar

Apress®

Identity Analytics: Analytics for Identity and Access Management

Nilesh Bhoyar
Livingston, NJ, USA

ISBN-13 (pbk): 979-8-8688-1744-1 ISBN-13 (electronic): 979-8-8688-1745-8
https://doi.org/10.1007/979-8-8688-1745-8

Copyright © 2025 by Nilesh Bhoyar

This work is subject to copyright. All rights are reserved by the Publisher, whether the whole or part of the material is concerned, specifically the rights of translation, reprinting, reuse of illustrations, recitation, broadcasting, reproduction on microfilms or in any other physical way, and transmission or information storage and retrieval, electronic adaptation, computer software, or by similar or dissimilar methodology now known or hereafter developed.

Trademarked names, logos, and images may appear in this book. Rather than use a trademark symbol with every occurrence of a trademarked name, logo, or image we use the names, logos, and images only in an editorial fashion and to the benefit of the trademark owner, with no intention of infringement of the trademark.

The use in this publication of trade names, trademarks, service marks, and similar terms, even if they are not identified as such, is not to be taken as an expression of opinion as to whether or not they are subject to proprietary rights.

While the advice and information in this book are believed to be true and accurate at the date of publication, neither the authors nor the editors nor the publisher can accept any legal responsibility for any errors or omissions that may be made. The publisher makes no warranty, express or implied, with respect to the material contained herein.

Managing Director, Apress Media LLC: Welmoed Spahr
Acquisitions Editor: Susan McDermott
Coordinating Editor: Jessica Vakili

Cover designed by eStudioCalamar

Distributed to the book trade worldwide by Springer Science+Business Media New York, 1 New York Plaza, New York, NY 10004. Phone 1-800-SPRINGER, fax (201) 348-4505, e-mail orders-ny@springer-sbm.com, or visit www.springeronline.com. Apress Media, LLC is a Delaware LLC and the sole member (owner) is Springer Science + Business Media Finance Inc (SSBM Finance Inc). SSBM Finance Inc is a **Delaware** corporation.

For information on translations, please e-mail booktranslations@springernature.com; for reprint, paperback, or audio rights, please e-mail bookpermissions@springernature.com.

Apress titles may be purchased in bulk for academic, corporate, or promotional use. eBook versions and licenses are also available for most titles. For more information, reference our Print and eBook Bulk Sales web page at http://www.apress.com/bulk-sales.

Any source code or other supplementary material referenced by the author in this book is available to readers on GitHub (https://github.com/Apress). For more detailed information, please visit https://www.apress.com/gp/services/source-code.

If disposing of this product, please recycle the paper

To my wife, Seema, and my daughters, Shubhada and Aaradhya, for all the vacations I missed but dream to make up for.

Table of Contents

About the Author xi

About the Technical Reviewer xiii

Introduction xv

Chapter 1: Introduction to Identity and Access Management 1

    Authentication and Authorization in IAM 1

    Privileged Access Management 5

    Cloud Infrastructure Entitlement Management(CIEM) 7

    Accounting and Governance 8

    Summary 10

    References 11

Chapter 2: Fundamentals of Identity Analytics 13

    What Is Identity Analytics? 14

    Capability Maturity Model 16

        Level 1: Initial 16

        Level 2: Managed 17

        Level 3: Defined 18

        Level 4: Quantitatively Managed 19

        Level 5: Optimizing 20

    Three Phases of Advancements in Identity Analytics 21

    Identity Analytics and Value Proposition 22

        Identity Analytics and Risk Reduction 23

        Identity Analytics and Automation 24

    Identity Analytics and the Rest of the Cyber 26

    Summary 27

    References 28

TABLE OF CONTENTS

Chapter 3: Data Preparation 29
    Where Do We Find the Data We Need? 30
    Why Has Access to Our Assets? 31
        Key Entities 32
        Answering "Who" 36
    What Do They Have Access To? 41
        Understanding Application 41
        Impact of Identity Governance on Access Control 43
        Answering "What" 44
    How Are Our Assets Being Used? 47
        Data Inputs 47
        360° View of Access 50
    Summary 57
    References 58

Chapter 4: Risk-Aware Metrics 59
    Metrics in Depth 60
    Key Metrics in IAM 62
    Metric Implementation 72
        Step 1: Business Requirements 73
        Step 2: Designing Performance and Risk Indicators with Thresholds 75
        Step 3: Data Model and System Designs 79
        Step 4: Metric Consumption 82
        Step 5: Review and Refresh 84
    Metric Alerting 86
        Configuring Alerts: Two Main Approaches 87
    Summary 88
    References 89

Chapter 5: Risk-Based Access Management 91

Challenges with Existing Risk-Scoring Solutions 92
Risk Scoring 92
    The Importance of Risk Scoring 92
    Approaches to Risk Scoring 93
    Risk Scoring Scoping 95
Risk Scoring Algorithms and Methodologies 98
    Rule-Based Risk Scoring 98
    Examples of Rule-Based Implementation 98
    Advantages of Rule-Based Scoring 99
    Challenges of Rule-Based Scoring 99
    Weighted Risk Scoring 99
    Sample Implementation Details 100
    Machine Learning-Based Methods 103
    Hybrid Approach 104
Risk Scoring Implementations 105
    The Role of Risk Scores in the Identity Life Cycle 106
    Risk Scoring: Real-Time or Not? 106
    Static vs. Dynamic Risk Scoring 107
Identity Risk Scores 108
    Identity Static Risk Scores 108
    Identity Dynamic Risk Scores 108
    System Architecture 109
Summary 112
References 113

Chapter 6: Identity Threat Detection and Response 115

SIEM: Core Concepts 116
ITDR: Core Concepts 117
    ITDR Implementation Outcomes 118
ITDR and SIEM Integration 119
ITDR and UEBA 119

TABLE OF CONTENTS

    Solution Design for ITDR 120

        Credential Access via Password Spraying/Phishing 120

        Lateral Movement 122

        Data Exfiltration 123

        Active Directory(AD) 124

        System Architecture 126

    Summary 130

    References 131

Chapter 7: Analytics for Cloud Access Management 133

    Cloud Access Management 135

    Data Foundation 136

        Answering Who? 137

        Answering What? 140

        Table: identity_policy_permission_map 145

        Answering How? 146

        Correlated Identity Activity Table 147

        Multicloud Considerations 148

    Detection Mechanisms 151

        1. Compliance Failure Detections 151

        2. Specification-Based Detections 151

        3. Behavioral Detections 151

    ITDR Integration 152

    Summary 152

    References 153

Chapter 8: Analytics for Regulatory Reporting 155

    What Are the Regulatory Requirements? 155

    NIST 800-53 in Depth 157

        AC-2 (1–12): Account Management—Manage Identity Life Cycle 158

        AC-2 (13): Account Management—Manage Identity Life Cycle (High-Risk Accounts) 158

        AC-5: Separation of Duties (SOD) 159

        AC-6: Least Privilege 159

System Design Reporting	162
Inputs	163
Data Processing	164
Outputs	166
Summary	167
References	168

Chapter 9: Machine Learning Techniques in Identity Analytics ... 169

Introduction to Machine Learning	170
Why Machine Learning for IAM?	171
Key Machine Learning Techniques in IAM	172
Common Machine Learning Use Cases Across IAM	173
Role Mining or Rule Mining for Policies	173
Access Recommendations	175
Access Anomaly Detection	176
Peer Group Analysis	178
Risk Scoring and Prioritization	180
Implementation Details	184
Inputs	184
Engines	185
Usage	186
Summary	186
References	187

Chapter 10: GenAI for IAM ... 189

Understanding ML, AI, and GenAI	190
IAM Vendor Perspective on GenAI	191
IAM Use Cases	193
Sample Implementation Details	196
Use Case 1: Generate Access Descriptions	196

TABLE OF CONTENTS

    Use Case 2: Access Chatbot for Governance and Risk 198

        Key Considerations 200

  Summary 202

  References 203

Chapter 11: Identity Analytics for Zero Trust 205

  Introduction 205

  What Is Zero Trust? 206

  Role of Identity Analytics in ZT Maturity 208

    Identity 208

    Device 209

    Network 210

    Applications and Workloads 210

    Data 211

    Identity Analytics Capabilities to Support ZT Architecture 211

  Deep Dive into Dynamic Authorization 212

    Limitations of Traditional Authorization 213

    Limitations of Traditional Authentication 214

  Foundational Data Services 217

    Policy Authoring at Scale 217

    Policy Accuracy and Validation 218

    Trust Algorithms and Behavior Monitoring 219

  Summary 222

  References 222

Index 225

About the Author

Nilesh Bhoyar is an accomplished data science and engineering leader with 18 years of experience in developing data-driven solutions for complex business challenges within financial services, supply chain, and cybersecurity domains. His track record includes driving innovation, collaborating with executive teams, and leading high-performing units. Currently, Nilesh is Senior Director of the Cyber Identity Security Management team at Capital One. Nilesh is at the forefront of leveraging data, machine learning, and AI to proactively mitigate threats to critical infrastructure and applications.

About the Technical Reviewer

Massimo Nardone has more than 29 years of experience in information and cybersecurity for IT/OT/IoT/IIoT, web/mobile development, cloud, and IT architecture. His true IT passions are security and Android. He holds an MSc in computing science from the University of Salerno, Italy. Throughout his working career, he has held various positions, starting as a programming developer, and then a security teacher, PCI QSA, auditor, assessor, lead IT/OT/SCADA/cloud architect, CISO, BISO, executive, program director, OT/IoT/IIoT security competence leader, VP OT Security, etc. In his last working engagement, he worked as a seasoned cyber and information security executive, CISO, and OT, IoT, and IIoT security competence leader, helping many clients to develop and implement cyber, information, OT, and IoT security activities. He is currently working as Vice President of OT Security for SSH Communications Security. He is a co-author of numerous Apress books, including *Pro Spring Security*, *Pro JPA 2 in Java EE 8*, and *Pro Android Games*, and has reviewed more than 70 titles.

Introduction

In today's digital landscape, identity has become the new security perimeter. As organizations adopt cloud, hybrid, and distributed environments, the challenge of knowing *who has access to what* has grown more complex. Compromised credentials, misconfigured entitlements, and gaps in monitoring remain the leading causes of breaches. Traditional approaches to identity and access management (IAM)—focused on authentication and static authorization—are no longer enough. What is needed is **identity analytics**: a discipline that brings together data science, machine learning, and governance to secure identities, enforce Zero Trust, and drive compliance at scale.

This book is written to provide security leaders, architects, engineers, and data professionals with a comprehensive foundation in **identity analytics**. It covers not only the conceptual underpinnings but also the practical methods, metrics, and technologies required to implement an analytics-driven approach to IAM.

Who This Book Is For

- **CISOs and security leaders** who need a strategic view of how analytics can enhance IAM maturity, where investments should be made to reduce identity-driven risk.

- **Security architects and IAM engineers** who want practical guidance on implementing analytics into their existing access management platforms.

- **Data scientists and analysts** who are exploring machine learning and GenAI techniques in the context of identity analytics for cybersecurity.

- **Compliance and risk professionals** who must use identity analytics to monitor controls, measure performance, and optimize the regulatory engagements.

Whether you are building your first identity analytics program or advancing an existing Zero Trust initiative, this book provides both strategic insights and hands-on techniques.

INTRODUCTION

Structure of the Book

The book is organized into **11 chapters**, each addressing a core aspect of identity analytics:

- **Chapter 1: Introduction to Identity and Access Management**

    This chapter lays the groundwork by introducing IAM concepts, tracing their evolution, and highlighting the challenges that make analytics essential. It also looks at today's hybrid landscape—spanning both cloud and on-premises systems—and explains how identity management works differently in each.

- **Chapter 2: Fundamentals of Identity Analytics**

    This chapter defines the field of identity analytics, outlining its key inputs and outputs and showing how those outputs integrate with broader cybersecurity domains such as security operations and UEBA. Because data products are often expensive and their ROI unclear, it can be difficult to decide how much to invest and where. This chapter helps build that case through practical use cases.

- **Chapter 3: Data Preparation**

    This chapter is more technical, focusing on data models, data pipelines, and how they should be designed with the end goal in mind. It explains the purpose of each input and why it is needed. The chapter concludes with an example of graph analytics, which is becoming the industry standard for achieving complete access visibility.

- **Chapter 4: Risk-Aware Metrics**

    A foundational capability in identity analytics is the ability to measure both performance and risk. This chapter explains how KPIs and KRIs are defined and takes a holistic view of what makes certain metrics—and the dashboards built around them—effective in driving action. It also highlights the key metrics that are essential for managing an IAM program successfully.

- **Chapter 5: Risk-Based Access Management**

  Risk scoring is a critical area of cybersecurity. Defining what is considered risky drives much of an organization's strategy. While many vendor products offer risk-scoring capabilities, this chapter explains why organizations should develop their own risk analytics functions and how to build them. It also explores key algorithms and provides guidance on how to implement them effectively.

- **Chapter 6: Identity Threat Detection and Response**

  Identity Threat Detection and Response (ITDR) is a key emerging field that focuses on techniques for addressing threats related to identity posture. Identity threats often take longer to detect and remediate compared to other types of cyber risks. This chapter explores why that is the case and how organizations can overcome these challenges. It also examines the integrations and handshakes between existing SIEM platforms and broader security operations mechanisms.

- **Chapter 7: Analytics for Cloud Access Management**

  Most Fortune 500 companies now have a significant presence in the cloud, and some have completely eliminated their data centers. New companies are being born in the cloud, and with the rise of GenAI, this adoption is only accelerating. In the past two to three years, many major cyber incidents have been linked to cloud misconfigurations. This chapter highlights how identity analytics plays a critical role in maintaining a secure cloud posture.

- **Chapter 8: Analytics for Regulatory Reporting**

  When it comes to regulatory engagements and compliance, IAM is one of the most heavily scrutinized domains. This chapter reviews key regulatory frameworks such as NIST, GDPR, and HIPAA. It outlines the critical controls and related monitoring required to ensure their effectiveness. We also explore how advanced analytics methods can help automate these monitoring activities and strengthen compliance assurance.

- **Chapter 9: Machine Learning Techniques in Identity Analytics**

  This chapter explores the role of machine learning in identity analytics. We review classical ML approaches—such as role mining, anomaly detection, and peer group analysis—applied to identity data. The discussion covers data requirements, key algorithms, and practical guidance for implementing these methods at scale.

- **Chapter 10: GenAI for IAM**

  The most successful production GenAI use cases today are focused on back-office automation and optimizing IT-enabled processes. IAM is a prime problem space for such applications. In this chapter, we discuss how GenAI can play a significant role in addressing chronic manual decision-making challenges in IAM. We also examine implementation approaches using OpenAI algorithms.

- **Chapter 11: Analytics for Zero Trust**

  The identity pillar is a key component of implementing a Zero Trust architecture. In this chapter, we examine what this pillar looks like at an advanced maturity state. We also outline a road map and provide sample implementations of key foundational features to support it.

Final Note

The identity analytics road map I have given in this book is definitely not an easy journey, and IAM alone cannot drive it. Successful implementation of the technologies I have described requires solid engagement across the spectrum—from data platform leaders to cyber leaders with responsibilities across IAM, security operations, insider threat, business, and DevSecOps. Leaders need to be part of this journey. Unfortunately, too often the focus is on implementing IAM solutions that automate provisioning and deprovisioning of access, while reporting becomes an afterthought—resulting in too many manual operations and risks that cannot be measured.

To gain the full benefits of identity analytics, one does not need to wait until reaching the destination. With incremental progress, organizations should begin to see the benefits of modernization. The chapters ahead provide detailed guidance on the art of the possible and how to secure your systems in an era where the perimeter is no longer the network, but the identity.

CHAPTER 1

Introduction to Identity and Access Management

As I write this first chapter, cyberspace is reeling from another massive data breach affecting Snowflake customers.[1] Once again, we're confronted with familiar terms like compromised credentials, broken access controls, and missing multifactor authentication (MFA). Compromised credentials are the leading cause of data breaches today and, unfortunately, the hardest to detect. A staggering 84% of cyberattacks now involve identity-based techniques, and it takes an average of 277 days to contain such attacks.

Why is this the case? The answer lies in the lack of standardization. Without standardization, seemingly simple questions such as "Do we have all our critical assets enforcing multifactor authentication?" become difficult for organizations to answer. If you can't measure it, you can't manage it, and effective measurement requires a data-driven culture.

In this book, we will explore how to cultivate such a culture within access management programs. But before we dive deep, let's start with some basic definitions and key concepts related to identities.

Authentication and Authorization in IAM

Identity and Access Management (IAM)) fundamentally involves granting and revoking access. At first glance, this might seem straightforward, but there's much more complexity beneath the surface. Ensuring that the correct identity receives the appropriate level of access at the right time and for the right identity is crucial. This concept is known as the principle of least privilege.

CHAPTER 1 INTRODUCTION TO IDENTITY AND ACCESS MANAGEMENT

Achieving this ideal state of access management requires intricate system designs and the implementation of robust access management platforms on a large scale. But what exactly is an identity, and why don't we simply refer to it as a person? Let's learn this with an example, as shown in Figure 1-1.

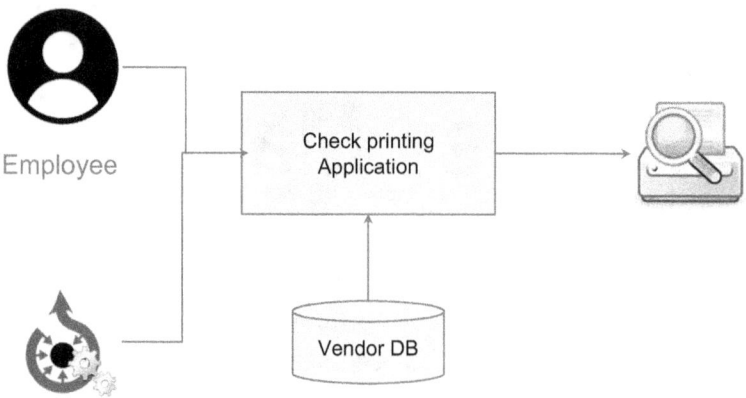

Figure 1-1. Typical Payment Processing Application

Company ABC Corp. has a check printing process for vendors. The check printing application operates in two modes: ad hoc printing and automated printing. Ad hoc printing is used when a vendor check needs to be issued at any time during the day, with an employee manually executing the operation. The automated process, on the other hand, uses robotic automation to print thousands of checks based on data from the vendor database.

An identity refers to the digital representation or profile of something that is recognized and managed within an organization's systems and applications.

- **Human Identities:** These identities represent people in the company who perform day-to-day activities that run the company. Now these people can be employees, contractors, or business partners. Typically, these identities are represented by employee IDs, employee numbers, etc. In the previous example, employees of check printing applications are human identities.

- **Non-human Identities:** These possess very similar characteristics to those of human identities (i.e., they can perform complex actions but are non-human). In the example discussed here, RPA Agent is a non-human identity. Non-human identities can be AI agents, chatbots, IoT devices, or any users who are used by application programs to perform certain tasks.

Now that we know identities, let's learn a few more concepts. What will happen if every human and machine identity in the company can access this check application? I think that would be pretty disastrous, and definitely, no company owner would want that. Hence, we have authentication and authorization management in IAM (see Figure 1-2).

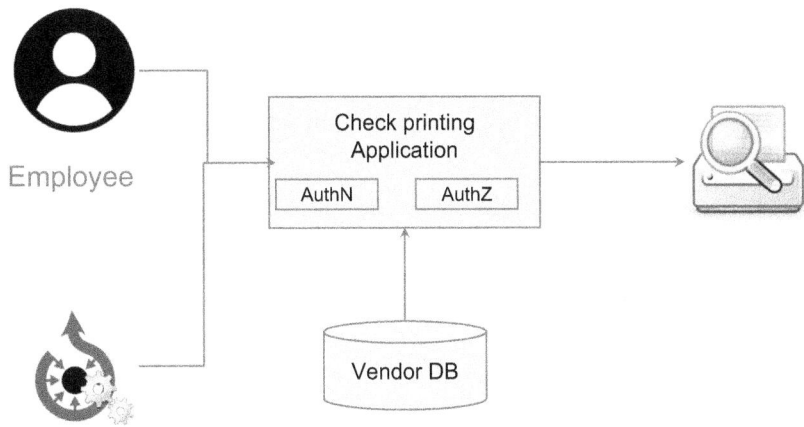

Figure 1-2. *Authentication and Authorization Flow*

Check printing applications (CPA) will have to confirm that the identity is the same as they claim to be: this process is called authentication. Authentication can be one step or multistep.

In one-step authentication, an application relies on a single method to verify identity; it is also known as single-factor authentication. There are numerous methods for single-step authentications:

- **Passwords**: Users enter a username and password to access their account. This is the most common form of one-step authentication.

- **Biometric Scans**: Users have to scan their fingerprints, retina, or facial recognition. Most smartphones come with these options now.

- **Personal Identification Numbers**: Users enter a numerical PIN to unlock a device or access a service, commonly used for ATM transactions or mobile device security.

CHAPTER 1   INTRODUCTION TO IDENTITY AND ACCESS MANAGEMENT

- **Voice Recognition**: Users speak a phrase that is analyzed and compared to a stored voice print, used in some phone systems and applications.

- **Pattern Unlock**: Users draw a pattern on a grid to unlock their device, commonly used on smartphones and tablets.

Multistep authentication, also known as multifactor authentication (MFA), is a security process that requires users to provide two or more verification factors to gain access to a resource such as an application. Many commercial applications are required to set up MFA nowadays.

Once authentication is completed, we need to verify if the identity has sufficient access or, in other words, is authorized to print the check at any given time. This verification process is known as authorization.

Authorization is the process of granting or denying specific permissions or access rights to authenticated users, applications, or systems. It determines what resources and actions an authenticated entity is allowed to access or perform within a system. Essentially, authorization answers the question, "What are you allowed to do?"

There are broadly three methods of implementing authorization:

- **Role-Based Access Control (RBAC):** Permissions are assigned to roles, and users are then assigned to these roles. For example, you can group all permissions required by developers in your company, such as access to GitHub, development environments, and developer training materials, into a "developer" role. Users assigned to this role will receive all the necessary access with a single assignment. RBAC works best in traditional corporate environments where job functions are clearly defined and change infrequently. Organizational structures in such settings are typically hierarchical, with higher levels inheriting permissions from lower-level groups. However, RBAC often leads to over-privileged access. Over time, roles tend to become bulky and accumulate permissions that are not necessary for certain job functions. In later chapters, we will explore approaches that make role definitions more dynamic—leveraging machine learning to minimize these issues. Role definitions can be made dynamic using machine learning to minimize such issues.

- **Attribute-Based Access Control (ABAC):** Access is controlled based on attributes assigned to users and assets. For instance, you might want only associates in the Accounts Payable department to have access to the check printing application. Attributes like department and job roles are used to enforce this control. ABAC works well in environments where organizational structures are dynamic and responsibilities change frequently. It supports access governance at a more granular level than role-based access. ABAC is also valuable in situations where additional context is needed to make access decisions—for example, allowing associates to print checks only during local business hours.

- **Policy-Based Access Control (PBAC):** This model uses policies to grant access. PBAC is gaining widespread attention with the adoption of the Zero Trust framework. For example, multiple policies can be applied at both the user and asset levels for the check printing application. A policy might include rules to verify that the device belongs to the company, is assigned to the correct user, is authorized to use the application, and that the risk score is associated with the user's activity. This is an advanced version of ABAC, where access is managed at a much more fine-grained level with deeper contextual awareness. Unlike ABAC, PBAC expresses and governs these attributes through centrally managed policy definition and evaluation systems. PBAC is particularly suitable for large-scale, multi-cloud, and highly regulated organizations.

Privileged Access Management

Privileged access refers to the permissions that allow users to perform operations beyond the capabilities of a regular user. Let's unpack this with our check printing application example (see Figure 1-3).

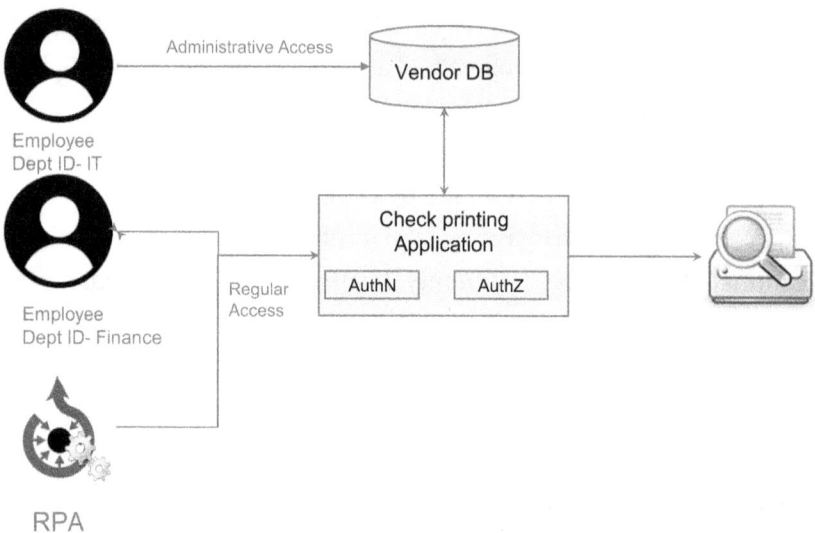

Figure 1-3. *Privileged Access*

Regular access allows users to perform routine tasks such as printing checks and handling other accounts payable operations. In contrast, administrative access to the vendor database provides IT associates with full read/write permissions for all table schemas. IT associates typically use these elevated permissions to fine-tune the database, implement new functionalities, or debug production issues.

However, administrative access extends beyond their primary job functions, enabling them to download sensitive vendor information such as TIN/EIN details and view all historical payments. When it comes to IT administrative permissions, privileged accounts can perform functions beyond standard job responsibilities. For example, they can install new software; add, modify, or delete existing accounts; and bypass the normal safety controls that are typically enforced for standard access. This level of access surpasses regular operational needs and, if misused, can severely disrupt business operations. There have been numerous incidents of misuse, including a notable case at Shopify.

Privileged Access Management (PAM) modules within Identity and Access Management (IAM) systems are designed to manage such high-sensitivity access. Given the nature of these permissions, there are stringent compliance and risk management requirements:

- **Enforce Least Privilege Principles**: Access should be granted at the minimum level necessary for users to perform their activities.

- **Use Behavior Monitoring**: Monitor access to detect deviations from regular usage patterns.
- **Avoid Perpetual Permissions**: Grant access only when needed and revoke it immediately after the task is completed.

These practices help ensure that privileged access is appropriately controlled and monitored, reducing the risk of misuse and enhancing overall security.

Cloud Infrastructure Entitlement Management(CIEM)

Cloud adoption has accelerated digital transformation, enabling engineering teams to adopt new services at record speed. The flexibility of spinning up new infrastructure, testing new technologies, and scaling infrastructure for production loads automatically has driven the next wave of innovation for enterprises.

Although this flexibility is advantageous, it has introduced new challenges, particularly in access management and overall security. Simple questions such as "Who has access to our most sensitive datasets?" have become difficult to answer due to the myriad data storage options, each with unique access management methods, unlike the on-premises world. For instance, in AWS, one can manage S3 bucket access using resource-based policies, IAM policies, or a combination of both. Consequently, the answer to who has access to the data is no longer stored in a single database table.

Let's take an example. AWS S3 access is broadly managed by IAM policies, resource-based policies, session policies, and organization policies (as shown in Figure 1-4). These policies are coded in JSON. Therefore, if one wants to know who has access to a specific bucket, the answer lies in summarizing the effective permissions across these four objects to determine the net permissions. Once we identify these net permissions, we can determine if a given identity has access to the particular S3 bucket.

CHAPTER 1   INTRODUCTION TO IDENTITY AND ACCESS MANAGEMENT

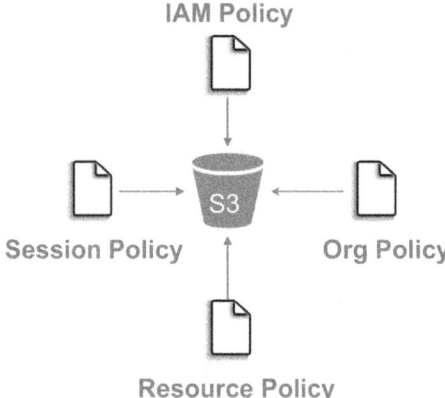

Figure 1-4. *Cloud Access Management*

We will explore this topic in depth in Chapter 11.

Accounting and Governance

Banks guarantee the safety and security of our assets, and hence, we trust them to guard those. However, trusting does not mean we won't verify bank balances, prior transactions, and review any suspicious activities. We trust our banks most of the time, but we do verify activities from time to time.

Access management is no different. There are several vendor applications typically used by companies to manage identity life cycle management, but installing and using a vendor application does not guarantee the safety of your company. If it were that simple, there would be no need for companies to purchase cyber insurance. Every company has its own uniqueness when it comes to how it manages access. After all, companies exist because they have some differentiator from their peers in terms of the services or products they sell.

Despite all the differences, the general guiding principles on how access should be managed are mostly the same. Luckily for us, these principles are well documented in governance documents such as NIST 800-53, CIS, ISO, and PCI-DSS, among others. Companies develop their own governance procedures based on these frameworks. Governance frameworks drive what needs to be monitored for compliance with that framework. Monitoring requirements dictate what should be accounted for and how discrepancies in regular accounting should be monitored.

Let's illustrate this with an example (see Figure 1-5). After all, what we are discussing here is fundamentally a data problem, and this book is all about it.

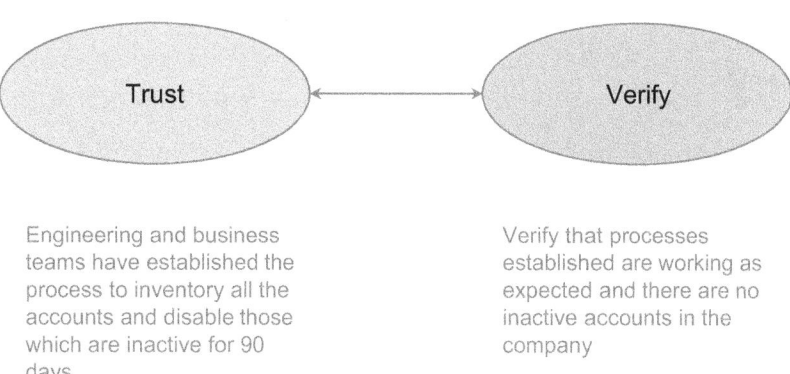

Figure 1-5. Governance Framework

Almost all the frameworks mentioned recommend disabling access when an account has been inactive for 90 days. If an attacker gains access to such an inactive account, they can exploit those privileges to compromise the system and potentially steal data or disrupt operations. Moreover, inactive accounts can be used as targets for brute-force attacks where attackers try to guess valid usernames and passwords by systematically trying out many different combinations. Inactive accounts are attractive targets because they may not be monitored as closely as active accounts.[2]

This requirement will be part of an organization's information standard requirements, and risk management teams will mandate that all application teams follow these guidelines. This activity will be federated with engineering teams within the organization, but adherence to these guidelines needs to be monitored centrally to ensure that people are doing what they say. In other words, trust teams with responsibilities but verify that they are indeed following these activities. Establishing these requirements is called governance, and monitoring whether all inactive accounts are being disabled is a key process in access accounting.

If you are part of a public company or a company in a highly regulated industry such as healthcare or pharmaceuticals, government regulators will verify your adherence to these standards, and you will have to prove such adherence. Typically, risk management professionals will work with identity analytics teams to document what tools and processes have been implemented for such detections. Effective monitoring is demonstrated through successful logs of monitoring jobs and associated documentation for any actions taken.

We will explore this topic in greater depth in Chapter 4.

Summary

In this opening chapter, we explored the complexities of Identity and Access Management (IAM) within the broader context of cybersecurity. The chapter highlights the critical role that compromised credentials play in the majority of cyberattacks, accounting for 84% of incidents.

Authentication and authorization are the foundational concepts in IAM. We discussed how managing identities—both human and non-human—is more complex than it initially appears. The principle of least privilege is emphasized as a core tenet of effective access management, requiring intricate system designs and robust IAM platforms.

Through a practical example, the chapter introduces the distinction between human and non-human identities, illustrating the need for precise authentication and authorization processes. We also introduced the advanced concepts in authentications such as MFA and ways it can be implemented. The chapter then delves into authorization models, including Role-Based Access Control (RBAC), Attribute-Based Access Control (ABAC), and Policy-Based Access Control (PBAC), explaining how each model helps manage and enforce access rights within an organization.

Additionally, the chapter introduces the concept of Privileged Access Management (PAM), which governs high-sensitivity access, such as administrative permissions for critical systems. We discussed methods organizations typically use to implement least privilege around such critical access.

The chapter concludes by discussing Cloud Infrastructure Entitlement Management (CIEM), emphasizing the challenges of managing access in cloud environments where different storage options and access management methods can complicate security efforts. We introduced some concepts such as effective permissions to understand the associated primary and secondary access patterns.

Finally, the chapter touches on the importance of accounting and governance in IAM. Adherence to governance standards is not just a matter of internal policy but is also subject to external regulatory scrutiny, particularly in highly regulated industries.

CHAPTER 1   INTRODUCTION TO IDENTITY AND ACCESS MANAGEMENT

This chapter establishes the foundation for the rest of the book, emphasizing that while numerous tools are available to secure identities, their true effectiveness can only be measured by fostering a data-driven culture within Identity and Access Management (IAM). Implementing such a culture is essential for ensuring the success and sustainability of IAM programs.

References

1. Matt Burgess. "The Snowflake Attack May Be Turning Into One of the Largest Data Breaches Ever," https://www.wired.com/story/snowflake-breach-advanced-auto-parts-lendingtree/

2. CrowdStrike Global Threat Report 2024. https://go.crowdstrike.com/rs/281-OBQ-266/images/GlobalThreatReport2024.pdf

3. IBM. Cost of a data breach 2024. https://www.ibm.com/downloads/documents/us-en/107a02e94948f4ec

4. Shruti Kulkarni and Alon Nachmany. "Understanding IAM and Authorization Management," https://cloudsecurityalliance.org/blog/2023/03/30/understanding-identity-and-access-management-iam-and-authorization-management

5. Microsoft. "What Is Privileged Access Management (PAM)?" https://www.microsoft.com/en-us/security/business/security-101/what-is-privileged-access-management-pam

6. Samantha Schwartz. "'Rogue' Employees Caused Shopify's Data Breach. What Makes an Insider a Threat?" https://www.ciodive.com/news/shopify-breach-security-insider-forrester/585823/

7. "Dormant Accounts: The Hidden Danger of Cyber Security," https://www.coretocloud.co.uk/dormant-accounts-the-hidden-danger-in-your-cyber-security/

8. Ken Spinner. "Inactive Accounts: The Key to Your Company's Sensitive Data," https://www.infosecurity-magazine.com/opinions/inactive-accounts-key-sensitive/

9. Mike Chapple. "Information Security and Privacy Quick Reference."

CHAPTER 2

Fundamentals of Identity Analytics

Despite being titled "fundamentals," this could be the most crucial chapter of the book. Here, we will delve into what identity analytics is, why it has been gaining attention from leaders, and what it can do for enterprises. This chapter will lay the groundwork for the use cases that Identity and Access Management (IAM) analytics teams need to support. These use cases will form the foundation for determining the types of data we need to curate, the data models we need to build, and the infrastructure required to support these efforts.

Since the 2021 OWASP Top 10 update, broken access control has been ranked as the number one risk, reflecting a significant shift in regulatory engagements. Gone are the days of simple probing questions such as

- What applications are used to manage access provisioning?
- What are your identity source providers?

Today, the questions are more advanced and scrutinize the efficacy of these tools and their proper utilization. Regulators now ask questions such as

- How many authentications go through multifactor authentication?
- How many associates have bulk download capabilities for sensitive customer data?

Answering these questions is challenging, as the answers often depend on various conditions. For instance, regarding the second question, it's unclear whether the inquiry pertains to human identities with the ability to download sensitive information from customer support portals or associates responsible for data analytics workloads.

Furthermore, while it might be straightforward to identify how someone can access enterprise analytical datasets, determining which datasets are genuinely sensitive without correct data tagging is much more difficult.

Frequently, organizations face massive ad hoc analysis exercises requiring inputs from multiple teams. Despite considerable effort, they may still find themselves with precise but not accurate answers. The primary reason for this is that most IAM implementations were not designed with an analytics-first approach. Typically, IAM programs focus on installing cool vendor products into the ecosystem without paying sufficient attention to measuring the efficacy of those tool implementations.

What Is Identity Analytics?

In the post-cloud era, we've witnessed a massive surge in digitization and automation, making the IT landscape more complex than ever. Applications are now built around microservices, with service identities enabling communication between these components. Even medium-sized organizations are tasked with managing thousands of human and machine identities.

Although Identity Governance and Administration (IGA) tools have evolved to help manage access more efficiently, a key challenge remains: How do we measure the effectiveness of these tools in truly securing the identity perimeter? This is where identity analytics comes into play. Identity analytics enhances IGA capabilities by providing insights into IAM operations, tooling, and access decisions, helping to reduce access risks in a measurable way. As the name suggests, identity analytics is the application of data analytics to manage and secure identities within an organization.

CHAPTER 2   FUNDAMENTALS OF IDENTITY ANALYTICS

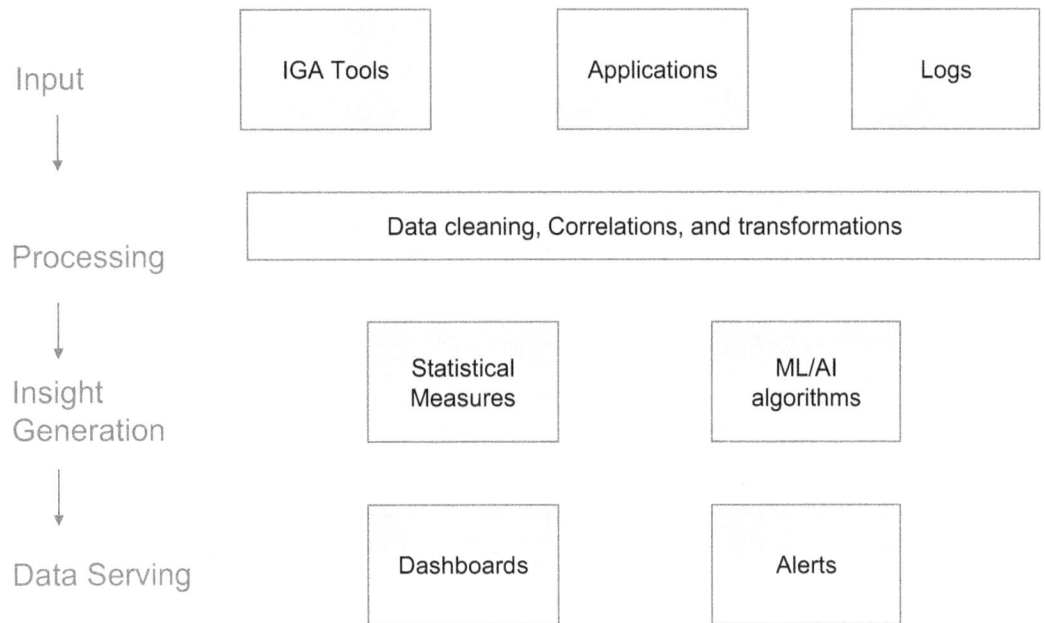

Figure 2-1. *High-Level Architecture*

Figure 2-1 highlights the key components of identity analytics, though this is not an exhaustive list. It gives a broad overview of what a typical identity analytics stack looks like.

1. **Input**: This refers to the datasets required to generate real-time intelligence for access decisions. Typically, these datasets include metadata from IGA tools, application user and role inventories, and activity logs from applications, IGA systems, and networks.

2. **Processing**: Data sourced from these systems is rarely ready for immediate use. It often requires processing to remove noise, enrich it with additional attributes (such as data from configuration management databases or CMDBs), and correlate logs so that we know which applications or assets these signals correspond to. The data processing layer handles this cleanup, transformation, and correlation of logs.

3. **Insight Generation**: This layer generates the signals needed for monitoring IAM operations and building risk-based awareness for access decisions. Algorithms applied here can range from simple

statistical measures, such as identifying terminated users who still have access, to more complex anomaly detection techniques like Random Forests for identifying keystroke irregularities.

4. **Data Serving**: This is the layer where users interact with the outputs of identity analytics. These outputs can range from simple dashboards to real-time alerts, depending on the needs of the user. The insight generation and data serving layers are highly dependent on the persona of the user. For example:

    a. An IAM executive may be interested in understanding how many applications aren't leveraging SSO (single sign-on) or MFA (multifactor authentication).

    b. A SOC (Security Operations Center) analyst, on the other hand, may be focused on detecting anomalies related to cloud identities.

Building an identity analytics capability doesn't happen overnight. Significant investment is needed upfront to set up the necessary infrastructure before organizations can start reaping the benefits. That said, not all organizations are at the same level of maturity when it comes to identity analytics, and in the following sections, we'll explore these varying maturity levels.

Capability Maturity Model

The Capability Maturity Model (CMM)[1] is a methodology used to develop and refine an organization's process maturity. Once the organization understands where they are with maturity levels, it is a bit easier to come up with continuous improvement road maps and measurable targets. We will map out this maturity model with identity analytics here.

Level 1: Initial

Outcomes

Here, outcomes are unpredictable and reactive. This level is often characterized by a chaotic or ad hoc approach to project management.

People

- Existing IAM Engineering teams wear the hat of data analytics when analytics support is required.
- Lack of funding/support for hiring analytical resources.

Capabilities

- No formal business requirements.
- Missing metric definitions for key IAM programs.
- Data gathering practices are not repeatable.

Technologies

- No data management and reporting capabilities.
- Data questions are answered based on transactional IAM systems.

Level 2: Managed

Outcomes:

Here, some metrics are defined, and the team is able to generate reports in an ad hoc fashion with manual activities.

People

- Team is typically borrowed from other teams during the regulatory engagements or internal audits.
- Some funding and support for analytical needs, but mostly it is on a needed basis.
- Knowledge silos and processes operated with people risk.

Capabilities

- Key metrics are defined.
- Data gathering practices are somewhat repeatable but not governed.
- Data standards and metadata dictionary are maintained only for governance- and compliance-related activities.

CHAPTER 2 FUNDAMENTALS OF IDENTITY ANALYTICS

Technologies

- Basic data management and reporting capabilities.
- Most of the reports are versioned and stored in spreadsheets.
- Data processing capabilities are limited to relational databases and for smaller volumes. Typically, historical records cannot be readily queried.
- Datasets are available but not correlated.

Level 3: Defined

Outcomes

Identity analytics operates as a key vertical in the IAM program, and analytical services are widely known to the leaders. Team members have a strong influence on the IAM program strategy.

People

- Formal IAM analytics teams with defined roles and responsibilities.
- The team consists mostly of data analysts.
- Sufficient funding and support for analytical resources.
- Team members have strong relationships with other data functions within the business and have all the new technologies and training available at their disposal.

Capabilities

- Well-defined metric definitions for all key IAM controls.
- Business requirements are well defined and confirmed by senior leadership.
- Important reports required for internal audits and external regulatory engagements are automated and readily available.
- Consistent and repeatable data gathering practices.

Technologies

- Advanced data management and reporting capabilities.
- Data governance practices are well documented, and employees are trained annually to follow them.
- Key reports are automatically generated but not daily refreshed.
- Too many reporting tools and dashboards, as every time there is a new requirement, a dashboard is created to satisfy that.

Level 4: Quantitatively Managed

Outcomes

Identity analytics services are used by the entire enterprise. Insider threat and CSOC teams have access to curated and correlated datasets, expediting their activities.

People

- The analytics team is highly advanced and consists of data engineers and data analytics with advanced statistical background.
- Ongoing professional development and advanced training.
- Strong organizational support and funding for analytics initiatives.

Capabilities

- Data integrations are documented, and they are monitored to guarantee accuracy and timeliness.
- Datasets are governed for compliance requirements such as GDPR and CCPA. Compliance requirements are monitored and enforced.
- The team has implemented some advanced statistical measures to detect ongoing threats, and those threats are automatically notified to the SOC and ITDR teams.
- All key metrics are documented and registered, and their definitions are regularly reviewed for accuracy. Dashboards governing those metrics are readily available for the leadership.

CHAPTER 2   FUNDAMENTALS OF IDENTITY ANALYTICS

Technologies

- Sophisticated data management, reporting, and visualization capabilities
- Advanced analytics platforms with predictive and prescriptive analytics features
- Seamless integration of IAM systems with comprehensive data analytics tools

Level 5: Optimizing

At this level, identity analytics is a central function not only for cybersecurity but for the entire enterprise. Continuous improvement of processes through predictive modeling allows the organization to anticipate trends, identify potential threats before they emerge, and consistently optimize identity management strategies.

People

- The team is comprised of data scientists and machine learning engineers with expert-level knowledge of IAM and IAM datasets.
- Associates are well-versed in the latest trends and technologies, ensuring they remain at the cutting edge.
- Strong relationships with IT, security, compliance, and business teams foster a culture of collaboration.
- Established relationships with other companies facilitate knowledge sharing and joint initiatives.

Capabilities

- Logs are enriched at the source, correlated, and made available in real time for ad hoc analysis and machine learning workloads.
- Predictive and prescriptive analytics are embedded into authentication and authorization activities, with access decisions largely automated and based on both static and dynamic datasets.
- Continuous monitoring of regulatory compliance ensures that deviations from baselines are detected and remedied automatically.

- Metrics are actionable and actively monitored to identify potential gaps and drive improvements.

Technologies

- Cloud adoption is fully realized, with auto-scaling infrastructure that supports the storage and real-time processing of massive data volumes.

- Products are developed as microservices, ensuring seamless integration with other cybersecurity solutions.

- Machine learning models are supported by an enterprise-wide ML platform that automates common tasks like model retraining, data pipeline monitoring, and model governance.

- Datasets are managed by an enterprise-wide data platform, allowing the team to scale effortlessly while focusing on innovation and continuous improvement without worrying about infrastructure upgrades or maintenance.

Three Phases of Advancements in Identity Analytics

Although the Capability Maturity Model (CMM) offers a valuable framework for benchmarking against industry standards, understanding maturity through the lens of actionable insights and operationalization is crucial for leaders. This approach provides a clear perspective on where an organization currently stands and helps chart a path forward. The following phases—Measure, Monitor, and Predict—offer a practical and simplified view for data practitioners.

1. **Measure**: The Measure phase is where organizations start by employing simple data queries designed to answer descriptive questions, often for audit purposes. These algorithms provide straightforward answers to essential questions, such as identifying the number of critical applications within the organization and determining who has access to them. Though basic, these insights form the foundation for understanding the current state of identity management, offering the initial clarity needed to build more advanced analytics.

2. **Monitor**: In the Monitor phase, organizations advance to more sophisticated algorithms that analyze correlations between access usage logs and identity information. This stage enables the reduction of potential security risks by eliminating unused access, identifying identities that aren't utilizing Multi-Factor Authentication (MFA), or spotting instances where MFA is bypassed. The effectiveness of these monitoring efforts is directly linked to measurable risk reduction, delivering a clear return on investment (ROI) and reinforcing the value of robust identity management practices.

3. **Predict**: The Predict phase represents the highest level of maturity in identity analytics. At this stage, organizations transition from merely identifying risks to implementing automated remediation strategies. Advanced algorithms process extensive volumes of data—such as access usage logs, network logs, and operating system logs—to detect deviations from normal behavior in real-time. This proactive approach not only mitigates risks but, in some cases, can eliminate them altogether, significantly enhancing the organization's security posture.

Identity Analytics and Value Proposition

If you've carefully read the previous sections, you might be wondering: if identity analytics holds such transformational potential, why haven't all companies embraced it from the outset? Why are there so many unique challenges and distinct issues with Identity and Access Management (IAM) implementations? The answer lies in the significant upfront investment required to implement identity analytics effectively.

Furthermore, there's a lack of comprehensive material that connects identity analytics with return on investment (ROI) in a way that resonates with both cybersecurity leadership and broader business executives. In this section, we aim to address these gaps and make a compelling case for the value of identity analytics.

Identity Analytics and Risk Reduction

Consider enterprises that utilize cutting-edge data warehousing solutions like Snowflake and have invested in top-tier IAM products. Despite this, many still remain unaware of lurking vulnerabilities in their authentication processes. Why? The absence of advanced analytical solutions renders it nearly impossible to measure and manage residual risk effectively.

The sophistication of an organization's identity analytics can be gauged by the complexity of the algorithms deployed within its ecosystem. As the complexity of these algorithms increases, so too do the associated costs, including the computational power and data requirements. However, the ROI in terms of risk reduction is substantial.

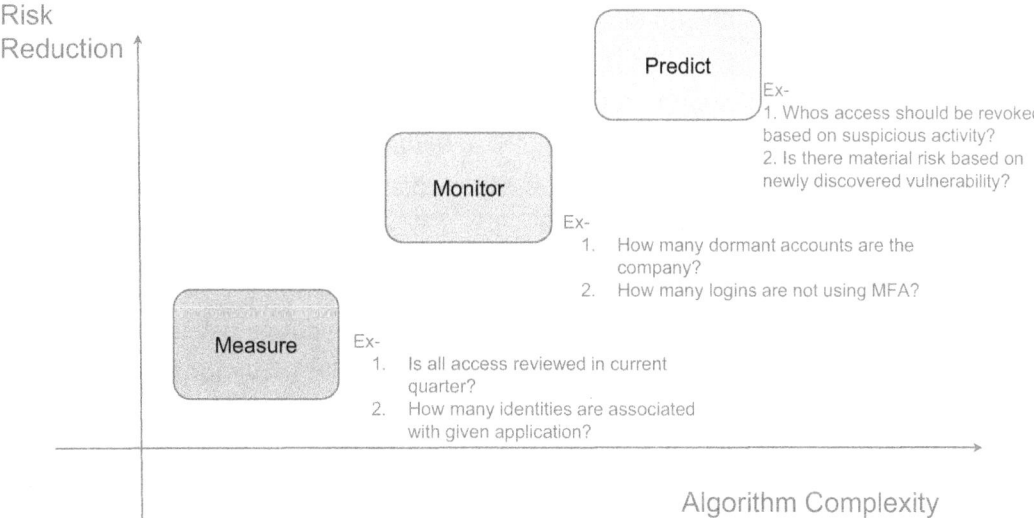

Figure 2-2. *Advanced Analytics and Risk Reduction*

The evolution of identity analytics can be categorized into three phases: Measure, Monitor, and Predict (see Figure 2-2). Let's delve deeper into each of these phases.

1. **Measure**

   At this stage, algorithms are primarily simple data queries designed to answer descriptive questions—often for audit purposes. These algorithms help organizations answer straightforward questions, such as identifying the number of critical applications and determining who has access to them.

CHAPTER 2   FUNDAMENTALS OF IDENTITY ANALYTICS

2. **Monitor**

    In the monitoring phase, algorithms become more sophisticated, relying on the correlation of access usage logs with identity information. This allows organizations to begin reducing their blast radius by, for example, eliminating unused access, identifying identities that aren't utilizing multifactor authentication (MFA), or identifying cases where MFA is being bypassed.

3. **Predict**

    The predictive phase represents the pinnacle of identity analytics. Here, organizations not only identify risks but also implement automated remediation strategies. Algorithms at this stage process massive volumes of access usage data, network logs, and operating system logs, correlating them to identify deviations from normal behavior in real time. This proactive approach allows organizations to not just mitigate risk but, in some cases, eliminate it altogether.

Data analysts can leverage algorithms to quantify and calculate risk reduction as capabilities progress through these phases, making it easier to demonstrate the importance of identity analytics to leadership and secure their buy-in.

Identity Analytics and Automation

Identity analytics holds the potential to revolutionize automation within IAM, bringing transformative changes across the board. Imagine an IAM environment where controls are monitored and managed automatically, where employees are productive from day one with immediate access provisioning, and where compliance efforts are streamlined through automated insights that simplify the drafting of compliance responses. These are not just theoretical possibilities—some organizations are already realizing these benefits through advanced identity analytics.

Just as with risk reduction, automation in IAM can be categorized into three phases, each offering broader automation and greater savings as organizations progress (see Figure 2-3).

CHAPTER 2　FUNDAMENTALS OF IDENTITY ANALYTICS

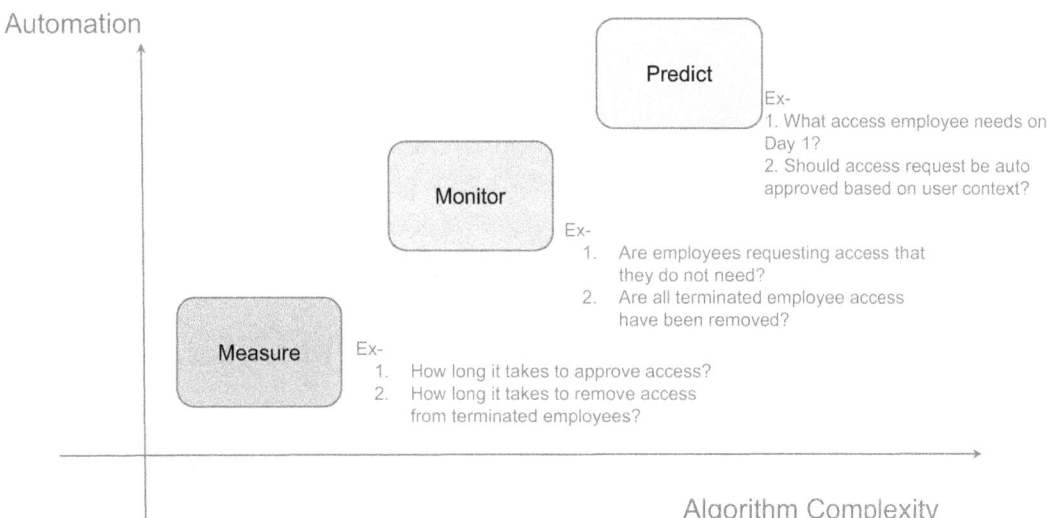

Figure 2-3. *Advanced Analytics and Optimization*

1. **Measure**

   In the measurement phase, organizations assess the efficiency of their existing processes and identify areas for improvement using solutions like Robotic Process Automation (RPA). For example, by identifying which applications take the longest to remove access after an employee's termination, organizations can develop targeted robotic automations to optimize these processes.

2. **Monitor**

   In this phase, organizations continuously monitor identity life cycle processes to identify suboptimal areas or recurring failures. These processes often involve multiple steps and complex system integrations. Effective monitoring enables organizations to address control failures proactively—failures that could be extremely costly if they occur during an external regulatory audit.

3. **Predict**

   As the name suggests, this phase leverages AI and machine learning to drive process automation. Organizations can replace costly manual controls, such as user access reviews, with automated decision-making for the majority of access rights. This reduces certification fatigue and returns thousands of productive hours back to the organization.

Traditionally, IAM is associated with manual, labor-intensive processes and controls that are notoriously difficult to implement. However, AI-enabled automation has the power to introduce large-scale efficiencies that extend beyond governance and compliance, positively impacting every individual within the organization. The potential for identity analytics to streamline and enhance IAM processes is immense, offering a compelling case for investment in advanced automation technologies.

Identity Analytics and the Rest of the Cyber

Common use cases among the cyber modules are highlighted in Figure 2-4.

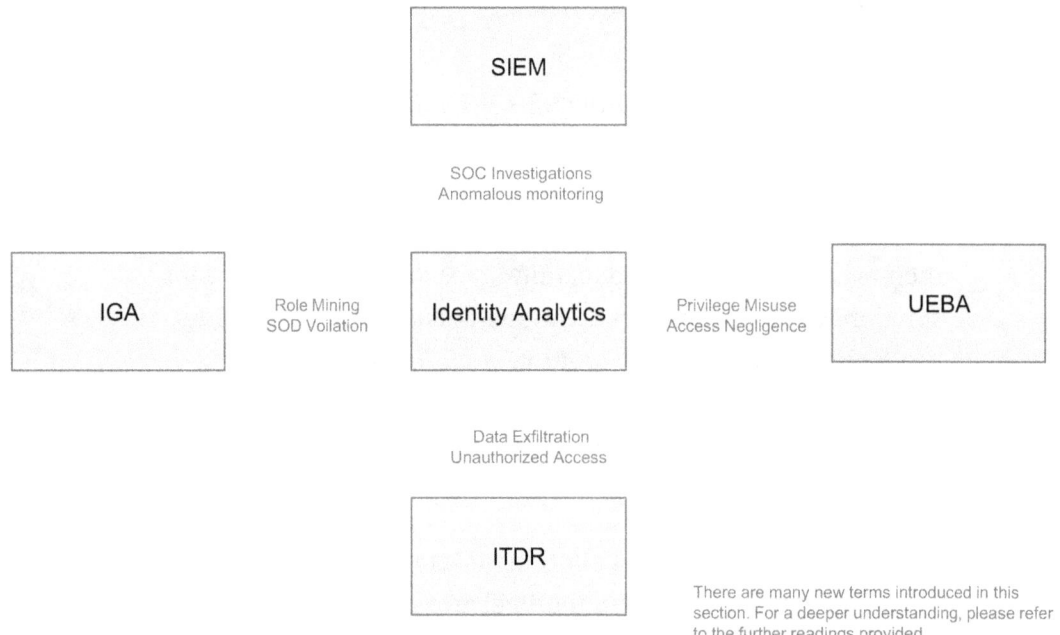

Figure 2-4. Identity Analytics and Other Cyber Capabilities

Identity analytics does not operate in isolation; it is deeply interconnected with other aspects of cybersecurity. In the visual above, I've highlighted key areas of integration to emphasize the synergies organizations can achieve across these programs. Ideally, these teams should collaborate, share strategies, and align on data curation and modeling approaches.

A common theme across these four areas is the need for correlated datasets that can track user actions, including the specific access used at any given time. Investments made by one team in this area should be strategic, ensuring that other teams do not need to duplicate efforts. This brings us to an exciting part of the book—how to curate data effectively to achieve these integrations. We will explore this in the next chapter.

Summary

Chapter 2 introduces **identity analytics** as a critical component of modern Identity and Access Management (IAM). It emphasizes why identity analytics is gaining traction among leaders and how it can transform enterprise security. This chapter provides the foundation for the IAM use cases that data analytics teams must support, outlining the types of data, models, and infrastructure required for an effective identity analytics program.

The chapter introduces the **Capability Maturity Model (CMM)** for identity analytics, outlining five levels of maturity:

- **Initial**: A chaotic, ad hoc approach where analytics support is reactive and unstructured.

- **Managed**: Some metrics are defined, and reports are manually generated during audits, but processes are not repeatable.

- **Defined**: Analytics becomes a key vertical within IAM, with formal teams and established roles, metrics, and processes.

- **Quantitatively Managed**: Advanced data integration and compliance monitoring, with automated threat detection and reporting.

- **Optimizing**: Identity analytics is embedded enterprise-wide, using predictive models and automation to enhance IAM and security strategies.

The chapter also introduces three phases of advancement in identity analytics.

- **Measure**: Basic data queries answer foundational questions, such as determining which users have access to critical systems.

- **Monitor**: More advanced analytics correlate access logs with identity data to reduce risk, identify unused access, and monitor MFA compliance.

- **Predict**: Advanced algorithms enable real-time risk detection and automated remediation, allowing organizations to address potential threats before they manifest.

Finally, the chapter explores the value proposition of identity analytics, highlighting its role in **risk reduction, automation, and integration with broader cybersecurity functions**. By automating processes and enhancing IAM governance, identity analytics improves operational efficiency, security, and regulatory compliance.

References

1. Sarah K. White. "What Is CMMI? A Model For Optimizing Development Process." https://www.cio.com/article/274530/cmmi-explained.html

2. Proofpoint. UEBA. https://www.proofpoint.com/us/threat-reference/user-entity-behavior-analytics-ueba

3. Microsoft. "What Is SIEM?" https://www.microsoft.com/en-us/security/business/security-101/what-is-siem

4. Pamela Armstead. "What Is Identity Governance Administration?" https://www.okta.com/blog/2020/10/identity-governance-and-administration/

5. SailPoint. Role Mining Guide. https://documentation.sailpoint.com/identityiq/help/rolemgmt/role_mining.html

6. James Maude and Alex Leemon. "What Is Identity Threat Detection & Response (ITDR) and Why Is It Important?" https://www.beyondtrust.com/blog/entry/what-is-identity-threat-detection-response-itdr-and-why-is-it-important

7. Lori Robinson. "Utilize Identity Analytics to Improve IGA Processes and Reduce Risk." https://www.gartner.com/en/documents/3830964

CHAPTER 3

Data Preparation

As of the writing of this book (Fall 2024), the top ten companies in the S&P 500 account for nearly 40% of the market capitalization,[1] dwarfing the contributions of the remaining 490 companies. A quick Google search reveals that these companies have established unique data foundations early on, allowing them to become market disruptors.

When it comes to targeting customers with products they can't refuse, two critical elements come into play: data coverage and data depth.

- **Data Coverage**: This refers to the breadth of data collected, encompassing various attributes about customers. It also extends to geographical reach, meaning the ability to gather customer data from across the globe. For example, Meta[2] has 3.37 billion active users—more than half of the global population—giving them unparalleled insight into customer behaviors worldwide and providing them with unrestricted revenue-generation capabilities.

- **Data Depth**: This refers to the richness and granularity of the data collected. It provides fine-grained insights into customer behavior. For instance, Meta's four key platforms—Facebook, Instagram, WhatsApp, and Threads—offer deep insights into what users like, how they react, and what triggers a chain effect, enabling highly targeted advertisements.

These tech giants—Amazon, Google, Meta, Microsoft, and Netflix—haven't just developed technologies to harness vast amounts of data; they've also built capabilities to clean, process, and generate insights in real time. This is a massive advantage.

The reason for discussing these data advantages is to draw a parallel for enterprises, especially regarding cybersecurity. If an enterprise can build massive data processing platforms that inventory all human and machine identities and capture data in depth, it can monitor behavior and gain unique advantages against threats. Such organizations can not only react quickly to emerging threats but also predict them. Despite the availability of numerous vendor products in the cybersecurity field, accurate threat prediction remains elusive because each business is unique, and this uniqueness translates into unique system architectures, making threat detection inherently challenging.

I propose a data-first approach to Identity and Access Management (IAM). By prioritizing data collection and transformation to understand existing threats, organizations can then focus on buying or building the products that genuinely help prevent those threats.

Where Do We Find the Data We Need?

Before we look at where we find the data we need, we need to understand what we are looking to answer at a very high level (see Figure 3-1).

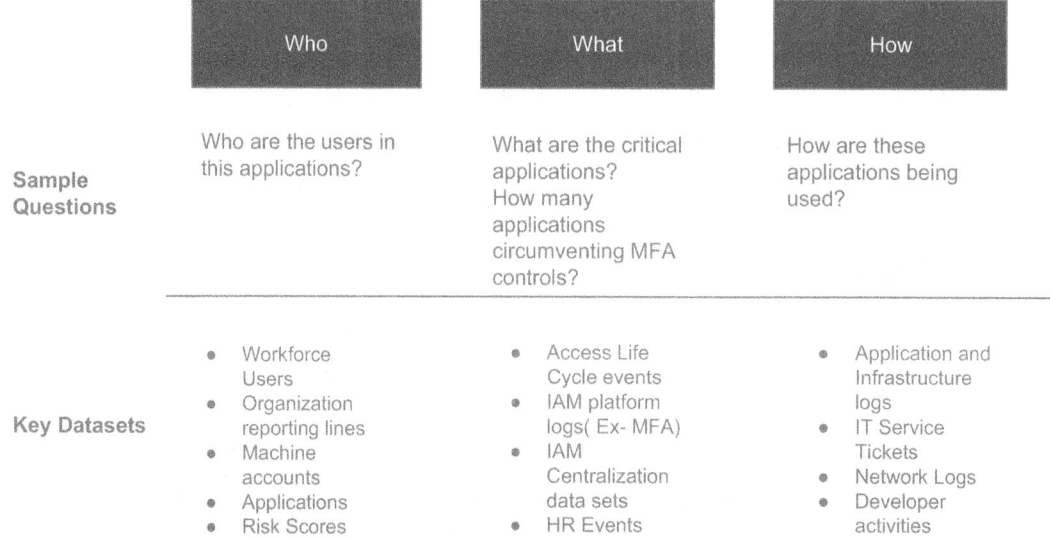

Figure 3-1. Key Questions To Answer

In this section, we outline the types of questions we should be able to answer and the corresponding data needed to do so. This list is by no means exhaustive, but it should provide a clear understanding of the minimum requirements:

- **Who**: This question addresses who has access to our system. By knowing the definitive list of actors within the system, it becomes easier to define the identity perimeter—we can establish an allowed list of individuals who are authorized to operate within our ecosystem.

- **What**: This question focuses on what these actors are permitted to access within the ecosystem. These inquiries are primarily driven by asset inventory and help determine the resources available to each actor.

- **How**: This question examines how these assets are being utilized by the actors within the organization. It involves correlating user activities with application events, which helps us define a baseline for normal behavior.

When considering the above questions and the associated datasets, it becomes clear that the sources of truth for these answers vary by organization. This variability limits the effectiveness of any vendor product in delivering the desired outcomes. For instance, workforce identities depend heavily on how an organization onboards new associates. Many large companies, especially those that have grown through acquisitions, often have multiple sources of truth for these datasets. It's unrealistic to expect any vendor to build connectors for all such applications. This reinforces the argument made in earlier sections regarding the need for enterprises to invest in their own data platforms. By doing so, they can gather a variety of data sources and easily correlate them to enable intelligence gathering. Such investments lay the foundation for successfully implementing vendor capabilities, should the organization choose to do so.

In the latter part of this chapter, we will continue to reference the visual framework discussed here. We will also explore how we can progress in our journey, identify the necessary datasets, and review the available technical tools to develop these solutions.

Why Has Access to Our Assets?

To enable advanced analytics for IAM, it is important to capture deep contextual information about identity. As organizations gather more identity-related attributes, they can achieve greater automation and risk reduction, as discussed in the previous chapter.

CHAPTER 3   DATA PREPARATION

Measure	Monitor	Predict
Questions: Who are the users in the system?	Who is attempting to access resources from locations outside standard business boundaries?	Who might pose a future security risk due to unusual access patterns?
Key Datasets: <ul><li>Workforce Users</li><li>Organization reporting lines</li></ul>	<ul><li>User Geo information</li><li>User Risk scores</li></ul>	<ul><li>User Geo velocity</li><li>User Keystrokes</li></ul>

Key Entities

The key data entities to capture for building context around identities include the identities themselves, their attributes, and the activity logs associated with their behaviors.

Identity

As previously discussed, the concept of "doers" within an organization encompasses both human and machine identities, each playing a critical role in the enterprise.

> **Human Identities:** The primary focus here is on employees, including contracted associates. These identities are typically sourced from the company's HR systems. Organizations often have multiple HR systems, each assigning unique IDs to individuals within that system. These unique identifiers can complicate efforts to correlate information across the enterprise, particularly when attempting to link actions or access to specific "Actors." Additionally, understanding the organizational hierarchy, including reporting structures, is crucial for ensuring correct approval processes and access controls. To address the challenges of multiple HR systems, it may be necessary to create a consolidated, unique identifier that unifies data across these disparate sources.

> **Machine Identities:** Machine identities represent non-human actors within the system—these are system accounts used for application integration or to perform batch operations. Although these identities are not tied to a person in the traditional sense, it is essential to identify the human owner responsible for each machine identity. Knowing the owner is crucial because, in the event of an issue, it's important to know whom to contact for resolution.

Many readers might find that existing Identity Governance and Administration (IGA) systems already provide some degree of integration with identity stores across the company. This can serve as a valuable starting point, particularly for human identities, where HR system integration is often sufficient. However, curating a comprehensive inventory of machine identities typically requires enabling numerous integrations, far more complex than those needed for human identities.

Identity Attributes

Knowing just information on who the employees are and an identity listing is not enough, though. To answer all our questions, we need several other attributes. Let's discuss those here and possible data sources for them.

HR Events

Knowing in-depth information on employment helps in many ways. This information includes dates on hiring, re-hiring, termination, promotion, etc. Most of this information can be curated from initial data pulled from HR systems when we try to formulate the identity information.

We also need information on re-organizations/re-alignments, as these tend to drive the types of access one needs in that organization.

Job Details

What associates do in the company determines the type of access they might need; for example, an associate in a software engineering role has very different access needs from an associate in medicine research. Knowing their job role, their expertise levels, and what the current projects they are working on helps us determine the optimal access needs. Possible data source information includes supplementary HR systems storing more enriched datasets around jobs and skills, JIRA boards, GitHub collaborations, project systems information, etc.

Device Information

It is important to know if associates are using the same device that is assigned to them; this is applicable for laptops as well as mobile devices. Typically, such information is stored in the asset inventory. We should store this information in the system.

User Keystrokes

Keystrokes are helpful in monitoring key logging, and they are important to understand if there is a malicious user on the platform. These are logs, so we will have to build a streaming infrastructure to capture this and create an SQL interface.

Risk Scores

Risk scores are a really involved subject, which we will cover in subsequent chapters. But to give high-level information here, these represent how risky the identity is. Risk can be calculated based on static information such as what access users have and can also be computed in a dynamic fashion based on user activity. There are many vendor offerings that offer this service as well.

Summary

In summary, at a high level, we have seven key entities, with **HumanIdentity** at the center of this structure (see Figure 3-2). The diagram provides a conceptual overview of how to think about creating tables and establishing their relationships. The size and complexity of these tables will vary depending on the data sources you integrate.

CHAPTER 3   DATA PREPARATION

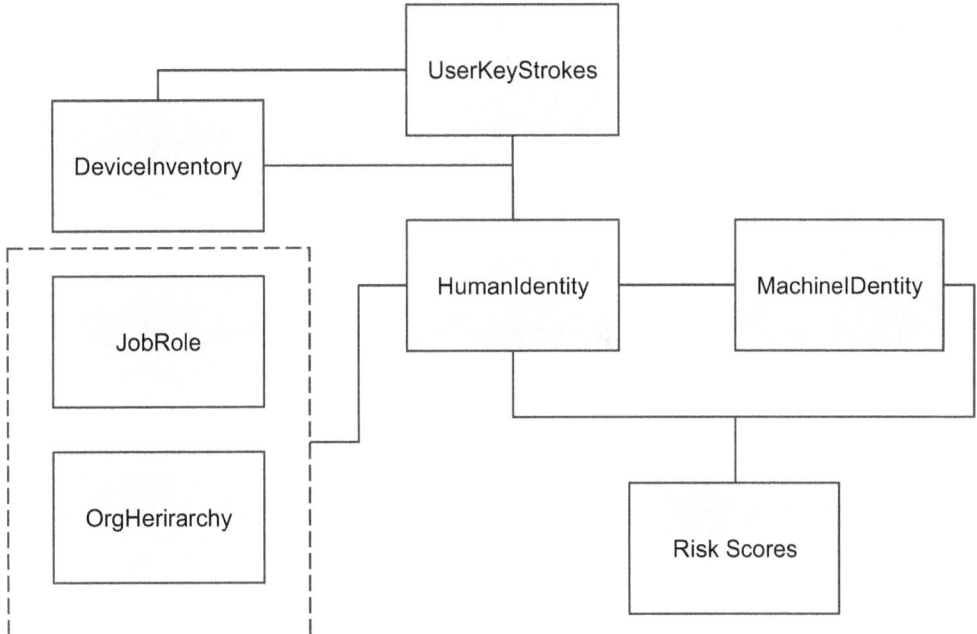

Figure 3-2. *Identity Risk Scores*

The key attributes shown in each entity are meant to guide you, though your datasets may be more comprehensive and enable broader use cases.

Key Points

- **Human and Machine Identities:** These are interconnected through an ownership relationship, where one human identity can own multiple machine identities.

- **Risk Scores:** These are calculated for both human and machine identities, helping to assess potential vulnerabilities.

- **Job Role Information:** This entity includes both static information, such as job titles, and dynamic information, such as ongoing projects.

- **User Keystrokes:** These are linked to both devices and human identities. It's crucial to know which device captured the keystrokes and to whom the data pertains.

CHAPTER 3 DATA PREPARATION

Answering "Who"

Now that we know which key identity attributes are required, let's focus on how to bring this data together and what kinds of data models are needed to support analytical use cases.

Identity Attribute Data Ingestion

System architecture in Figure 3-3 illustrates key components that organizations need to build from data ingestion to data storage.

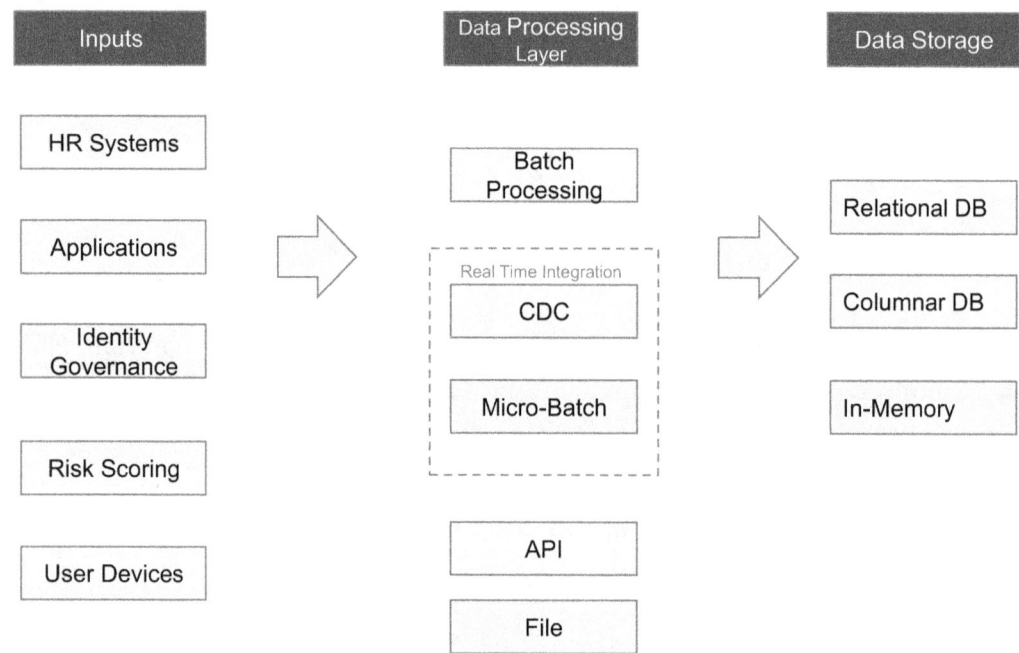

Figure 3-3. *High-Level Data Processing Architecture*

Data Inputs

These are the core elements of our data models, as they provide the foundational information that correlates with all other datasets.

- **Human Identities**: HR systems are the primary source of human identities and related events. These systems track employees and contractors, providing the necessary data to manage access and identities within the organization.

- **Applications**: This category includes business applications within the enterprise, ranging from locally developed apps to SaaS platforms and third-party applications installed in the company. Managing users and tracking access details—such as roles and permissions—across potentially thousands of applications is a challenging task. Fortunately, some vendor products are leveraging AI to address this complexity.

- **Identity Governance**: Today, most organizations already have Identity Governance and Administration (IGA) systems in place. These systems typically manage access grants across various business applications. An IGA system often includes access discovery features, which can significantly accelerate the establishment of a foundational identity analytics stack by leveraging existing IGA connectivity. While this approach may introduce some limitations in accuracy, it enables a faster setup of core identity analytics elements. Additionally, IGA systems provide workflow insights, showing how access is provisioned and deprovisioned within applications—a crucial aspect of ensuring proper governance.

- **Risk Scoring**: Risk scoring assesses how risky an identity is. Many IGA products come with built-in risk scoring capabilities. However, third-party risk scores can be limiting, leading some organizations to develop their own scoring systems. We will explore this in more detail in Chapter 6.

- **User Devices**: This includes laptops, mobile devices, and other assets that associates use to perform their daily activities. Asset inventories within the enterprise typically serve as the source of this information.

Data Processing Layer

Batch Processing: This traditional method processes large volumes of data in bulk at scheduled intervals. It is well-suited for non-time-sensitive data. This can be a good option for user devices, identity HR tables, and some of the application datasets that tend to have less user change movement over time. Hourly scanning for such information using batch programs can be good enough for analytical purposes. These are easier to set up.

Real-Time Integration with Direct DB Connect: For time-sensitive or rapidly changing data, real-time integration is crucial. This is achieved through two mechanisms:

- **Change Data Capture (CDC)**: This method captures and tracks changes in data sources in real time, ensuring that the system reflects the most up-to-date information.

- **Micro-Batch Processing**: A compromise between real-time and batch processing, micro-batching processes small batches of data at frequent intervals, balancing timeliness with processing efficiency.

API Integration: Many SaaS and third-party applications offer API options for integration, enabling real-time data exchange in some cases. With the widespread adoption of microservices architecture, even custom, homegrown applications can provide API options, making integration more seamless and efficient.

File-Based Integration: Despite advancements in software engineering, there are situations where direct database or API integration is not feasible. For example, some SaaS applications may lack an API option, or legacy mainframe applications may be installed in local data centers without modern integration capabilities. In such cases, file-based batch integration can be an effective alternative.

Data Storage

The data storage component has been expanded to include multiple types of databases, reflecting the diverse nature of the data being handled. One can implement these storage options based on the analytical and operational needs.

- **Relational Databases**: These continue to serve structured data that require complex querying and transactional integrity. This might be a good choice for small-sized enterprises, but typically, they are limited to large enterprises as they are not optimal for large-scale read-heavy operations. There are well-known DB engines in this category–MySQL, Oracle, Postgres, etc. Major public cloud providers offer all of these.

- **Columnar Databases**: Optimized for analytical queries, these databases efficiently handle large volumes of data, especially for tasks that involve scanning vast amounts of data. These are an ideal choice considering the identity analytical stack tends to be read-heavy with vast amounts of data. Amazon Redshift, ClickHouse, and Google BigQuery are some of the good products available in this category.

- **In-Memory Storage**: This fast storage option is crucial for real-time analytics, enabling the system to quickly retrieve and process data with minimal latency, which is essential for time-sensitive identity management tasks. A good use case for these databases is if we enable integration of identity analytics with the authentication infrastructure. If we consider insights in authentication decisions, then we need superfast data retrieval for optimal user experience.

User Behavioral Datasets

Traditional detection and mitigation systems are designed to ingest data into SIEM platforms and then apply rules on those logs to determine whether suspicious activity is occurring. While these approaches work reasonably well for monitoring networks, they are far more limited when applied to identities—particularly when trying to detect rogue insider activity.

What is needed instead is the ability to correlate identities with their activities and establish a baseline of normal behavior. Deviations from this baseline, often referred to as *drift from normal behavior*, are a key method of detection. This approach is known as **UEBA—User Entity Behavior Analytics**.

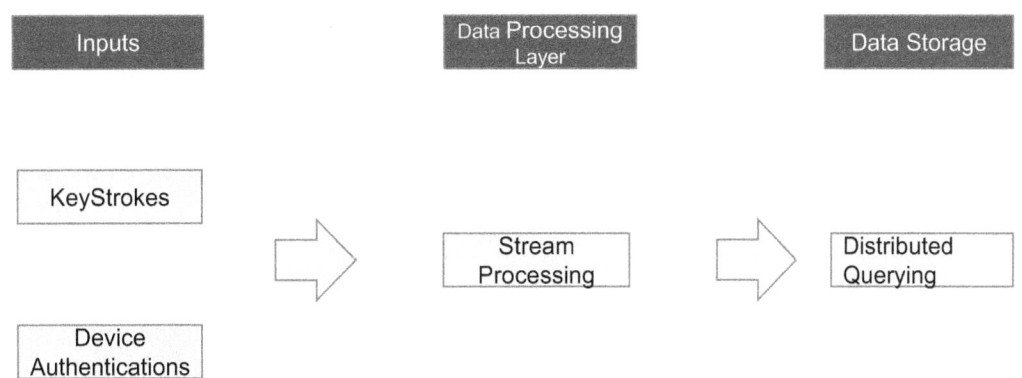

Figure 3-4. High-Level Data Processing Architecture for UEBA

CHAPTER 3　DATA PREPARATION

Figure 3-4 represents an architecture for processing and analyzing user behavioral datasets in real time, focusing on two key types of input: **keystrokes** and **device authentications**. These inputs are essential for monitoring user behavior; we will add more datasets as we cover other sections.

Data Inputs

- **Keystrokes**: This dataset captures every key pressed by the user, providing granular insights into user actions. Keystroke data is often used for detecting patterns, establishing baseline profiles, and identifying unusual typing behaviors that might indicate compromised accounts.

- **Device Authentications**: This involves logging information about devices being used to access the system, including successful and failed authentication attempts. Tracking device authentication helps in identifying unauthorized access attempts and understanding user access patterns across different devices.

- One can use log ingestion agents such as Logstash or Fluentd at this stage.

Data Processing Layer

- The data collected from these inputs is then processed in real time using a **Stream Processing** engine. Stream Processing allows for the continuous analysis of data as it flows through the system, enabling immediate insights and responses.

- Apache Spark streaming, Apache Flink, and Apache Kafka are possible technologies that can be used in this space. There are vendor offerings for similar open stack technologies.

Data Storage

- After processing, the data is stored using **distributed querying** systems, which allow for the efficient retrieval and analysis of large volumes of data distributed across multiple servers or locations.

- Distributed querying enables scalable analytics on the processed data, facilitating complex queries at much lower cost. We can save tons of investments with zero copy and zero transfer options, i.e., data can be enriched at local log storage places such as AWS S3 buckets and queried right from there, saving tons of compute that would have been required to transfer these datasets.

- Apache Trino, Apache Hive, and Apache Iceberg are some of the good options for this. Similar to other layers, there are vendor offerings for these products; popular ones are Snowflake and Databricks.

What Do They Have Access To?
Understanding Application

Complexity of the discussion is going to become a bit more complex from here; to help the user grasp more understanding of the datasets, we will briefly cover when we say what the user has access to involves what.

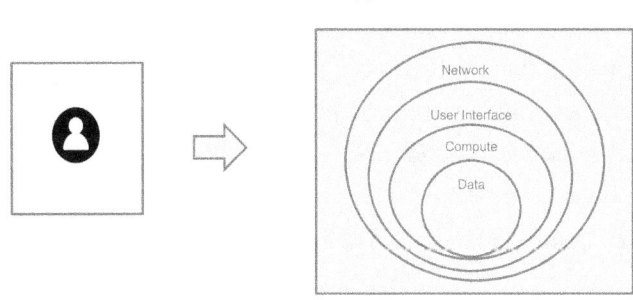

Figure 3-5. *Application Architecture*

CHAPTER 3   DATA PREPARATION

Typically, an application has four layers to it: network, user interface, compute, and data (see Figure 3-5). Complexity at each layer depends upon how complex the application is; not all apps are made in the same way.

- **Network Layer:** The network layer consists of how the application is being configured, whether it is an internal application or users can access via the public internet. Architecture at this layer depends upon several factors such as who manages the internet, cloud adoption, general risk appetite of the enterprise, etc. Typically, app developers and network engineers have access to this layer.

- **User Interface:** The user interface defines how users are accessing this application. Most of the time, it is a web interface or a desktop application if it is for a business user. User interface can also have just an API, and that is how services are being exposed from an application.

- **Compute:** Mostly, applications are hosted on a server. Servers execute all the back-end services that provide the information users need in "user interface" layers.

- **Data:** As the name implies, this layer is responsible for storing all information associated with the application, including records of user interactions. Because this data is often the organization's most valuable asset, this layer is the primary target for attackers attempting to breach the application.

Now, when we say an employee has access to the application, that access very well could be the access to one of these layers, depending on the role. For instance, if an associate is a database admin or a data engineer, then most likely the associate has access to the data layer in the application. I said most likely, as there might be a case where direct access to the database is not allowed, and the only way one can get access to the data is via API in application layers.

If an employee is an infrastructure engineer, then most likely the employee can have access to the compute layer of an application. So summary of the discussion is that identity can have access to all or one of the layers in the application. Hence, if someone asks, "Identity has access to what?", if we are discussing the application access, we need information on all these layers to determine that answer.

CHAPTER 3 DATA PREPARATION

Impact of Identity Governance on Access Control

How an employee gains access to systems significantly influences what they can ultimately access within the organization. Figure 3-6 depicts a typical Identity Governance and Administration (IGA) system. These systems provide a crucial interface for users to request access to the application layers discussed previously. Although not mandatory for access management, IGA systems offer essential functionalities that streamline and enhance the efficiency of managing access across the enterprise.

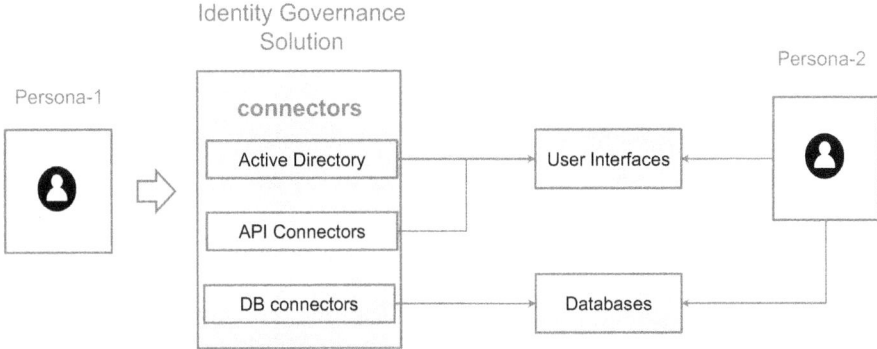

Figure 3-6. *Access Managed via IGA Solutions*

Users can be granted access to applications with or without the support of an IGA system, and this difference is pivotal in understanding the scope of their access.

For **Persona-1**, access is managed through an IGA system. In this scenario, if we examine what Persona-1 has access to, we observe that their permissions are tied to Active Directory groups, API connectors, and database access groups. These elements serve as intermediaries, governing the pathways that enable the user to interact with actual user interfaces and databases. The use of these intermediaries ensures that access is governed by predefined policies and roles and is continuously monitored, thereby reinforcing security and compliance.

On the other hand, **Persona-2** operates without such intermediaries. This user has direct access to applications and databases, bypassing the controls and oversight provided by an IGA system. While this might simplify access, it also introduces challenges in managing permissions and increases the risk of unauthorized access, as there is no centralized mechanism to enforce policies or monitor access.

If asked what Persona-1 has access to, the answer would include not only the list of applications and databases but also the intermediary components required to reach these applications, such as Active Directory groups or database groups managed within the IGA system.

In contrast, the answer for Persona-2 would be simpler: a direct list of applications and database groups that the employee can access without going through any intermediaries.

With the previous discussion, I think we are in a position to uncover data models and pipelines we need to bring all data required to answer "What" in identity analytics.

Answering "What"

Figure 3-7 depicts a high-level data processing architecture capturing information on resources, corresponding accesses in IGA solutions, and other contextual information.

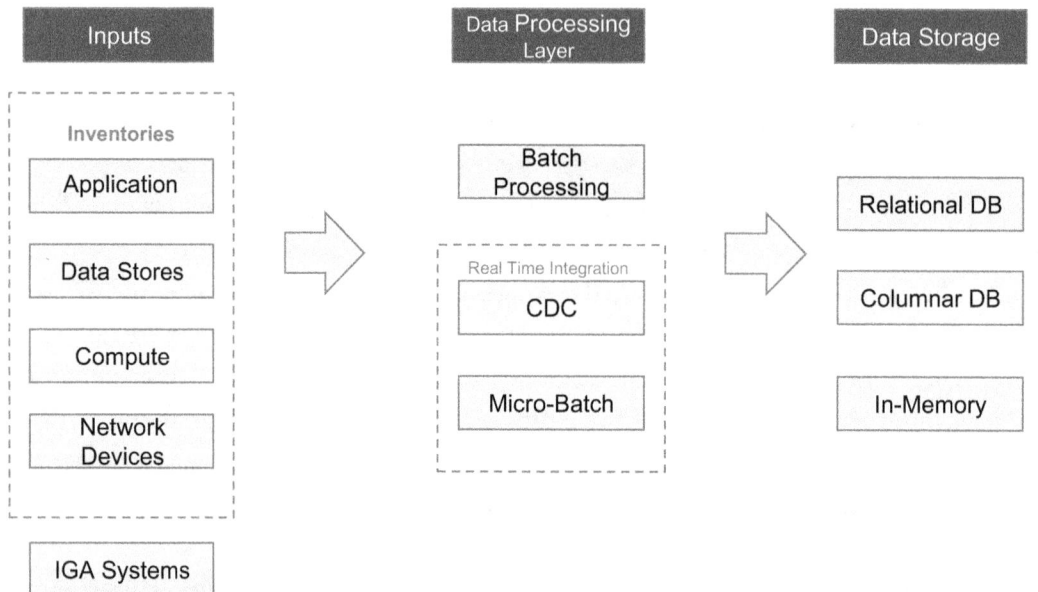

Figure 3-7. *High-Level Data Processing*

Data Inputs

To answer what users have access to, we need an asset inventory in the company. Most companies should have home-grown or vendor products to build such asset inventories. Until the time we do know what exists in the company, one can define how to secure those assets. Asset management is the most foundational capability in cyber programs, and typically, enterprises would have this well-defined and curated.

Asset Inventories

Asset inventory management is fundamental to any cybersecurity program. By maintaining a connected and comprehensive asset inventory, an enterprise gains a clear view of its IT landscape, enabling continuous monitoring of infrastructure. This clarity is essential for swiftly investigating cyber incidents, as it allows the organization to quickly assess the impact and identify which systems require urgent attention.

In addition, asset inventories help organizations track vulnerabilities within their platforms and promptly identify the personnel responsible for addressing them. Typically, these inventories are managed through systems known as Configuration Management Databases (CMDBs). Several vendors, such as ServiceNow, IBM, and BMC, offer solutions that support this critical function.

- **Applications, UIs, and APIs:** These are all the user interface apps available in the company. These can be desktop apps, web UIs, plugins, admin portals for the network devices, APIs, etc. There are ways to discover these in the company and inventory them. Most technologies available today give precise information on these, but the accuracy is hard to achieve; hence, many asset platforms provide self-registration of an asset as well.

- **Data Stores:** These are all the data stores in the company. Data stores can be SQL, non-SQL, block storage, content management systems such as SharePoint, data lakes, and data warehouses. Data store access can be direct via SQL query interface, or it can be an API interface via applications.

- **Compute:** With cloud computing, computers have evolved. There are server and serverless options. Serverless component access will be discussed in detail when we go through cloud environments. Compute consists of servers in local data centers, cloud services such as AWS EC2, GCP compute machine, and Azure virtual machines, etc.; there are many more, but we need an inventory system for all of them.

- **Network Devices:** Network devices are critical components that connect applications to consumers and ensure seamless communication across the network. These include switches, load balancers, firewalls, intrusion detection systems (IDS), modems, routers, network hubs, cloud security groups, and more. These devices play a pivotal role in defining the network perimeter and are typically managed through dedicated admin portals. Asset discovery tools are used to identify and monitor these devices, with some requiring manual registration. Given their significant impact on the network's security and functionality, asset management programs prioritize these devices as high-priority assets.

IGA Systems

Identity Governance and Administration (IGA) systems are critical tools that manage user identities and their access to various applications and resources within an organization. These systems include components like user provisioning, role management, access requests, and compliance reporting. Information can be pulled via API or direct DB connections from these systems. We can pull datasets such as identities, associated access subscriptions, roles, role permissions, access requests, access certifications, and other datasets related to identity life cycle management programs.

Data Pipelines

Both CMDB and IGA systems typically offer direct DB connectivity for the batch option, and they also provide APIs.

Looking at the volume, it is ideal to get one time load from the batch and then use the API for the delta loads. One can also implement change pointers on these databases and enable more real-time integration if such an option does not violate this party's agreement with the software vendor providing these datasets.

Data Storage

Despite their large size, they can be stored in SQL databases. However, while these databases are capable of handling vast volumes of data, they come with certain limitations.

One of the key challenges is related to cyber investigations, which often require extensive historical data to be retained for querying. This necessity significantly increases the size of the datasets, making them cumbersome and difficult to query efficiently. Additionally, these large datasets are rarely used in isolation; they are often joined with other datasets, such as identity records and log files, further complicating the querying process.

To overcome these limitations, leveraging a distributed querying engine can be advantageous. This approach allows for efficient querying of large historical datasets without the performance constraints typically associated with SQL databases. A practical strategy would be to use SQL databases for data that requires real-time processing and alerting capabilities while employing a distributed querying infrastructure for managing and analyzing historical snapshots.

How Are Our Assets Being Used?

Knowing what users are doing on their endpoints is just as important as understanding what is happening within the application. Logs associated with user activity in the application, application network traffic, and the volume of API calls all play an important role in understanding how the application is being used.

Data Inputs

To know how identities are using the application, we need to correlate logs with datasets curated in prior sections. Figure 3-8 illustrates the architecture required to ingest and store such logs.

CHAPTER 3   DATA PREPARATION

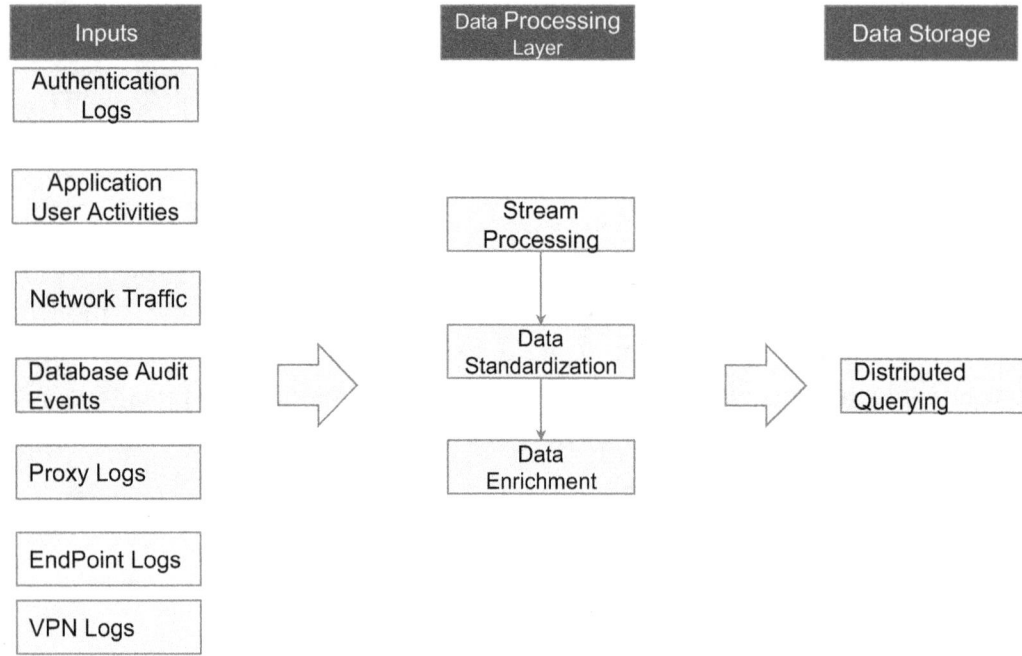

Figure 3-8. Data Processing for Application Activities

Data Inputs

The **Inputs** section on the left side of the diagram represents the diverse range of logs that are crucial for identity analytics:

- **Authentication Logs:** These logs track login attempts, including successful and failed attempts, providing insights into user access patterns and potential unauthorized access attempts. These logs can be ingested from SSO and MFA systems such as PingID, Okta, Duo Security, and IBM Security Verify.

- **Application User Activities:** These are the application logs for user activity sessions. Logs give us fine-grained user activities that can be correlated with user access to understand rogue access.

- **Network Traffic:** This captures data related to user interactions across the network, including data transfers and connections. Monitoring network traffic helps identify unauthorized access or data exfiltration attempts. Network logs can also be used to plot inter-application communication and understand the baseline profiles for applications from a networking standpoint.

- **Database Audit Events:** Logs that document activities within databases, such as queries, data modifications, and admin activities that include new user profiles and permissions. These activities are useful to understand normal usage patterns and also possible unauthorized usage by authorized users.

- **Proxy Logs:** These logs track web activity, including the websites users access and the data they transmit. They are useful in identifying suspicious behavior, such as attempts to bypass security controls.

- **Endpoint Logs:** Logs from user devices (e.g., laptops, desktops, mobile devices) that capture software usage, security incidents, and system changes, helping in tracking activities on individual endpoints.

- **VPN Logs:** Logs that document remote access sessions through Virtual Private Networks (VPNs), helping to monitor and secure access to internal systems from remote locations.

Data Processing Layer

The **data processing layer** is where the collected logs undergo real-time analysis through **Stream Processing**. This layer is responsible for

- **Stream Processing:** Real-time processing of incoming data streams allows for immediate detection of suspicious behavior. By continuously analyzing data as it is generated, the system can identify potential security threats, unusual patterns, and anomalies in user behavior. This layer is crucial for implementing dynamic and responsive identity analytics, ensuring that any irregularities are flagged and acted upon promptly.

- **Data Standardization**: Unfortunately, there is little to no standardization on how logs are being generated; hence, they are not easy to understand. We need a data transformation layer to convert these varieties of logs into a standardized format so that we can quickly understand who is doing what with that resource.

- **Data Enrichment:** Even though not every log will be enriched, without knowing the application name of the server generating suspicious IP traffic, it is hard to know what is happening in the system and with whom one needs to talk to verify that traffic. Hence, there needs to be a data enrichment layer that attaches metadata to these logs.

- Ideally, the identity analytics team should work with the data governance function and enforce maximum standardization and enrichment at the data source itself, but it is not possible all the time due to limitations such as a vendor application not allowing customization.

Data Storage

The processed data is then stored in the **data storage** layer, where it can be queried and analyzed further:

- **Distributed Querying:** The data is stored in a distributed querying infrastructure, which allows for efficient and scalable analysis across large datasets.

- Cyber analysts are typically proficient in SQL skills. Enabling infrastructure that gives them an option to join these desperate data sources not only improves threat detection SLAs but also improves the accuracy of those threats.

360° View of Access

In this section, let's combine all the intelligence we have gathered in prior sections to come up with a data analysis layer.

CHAPTER 3 DATA PREPARATION

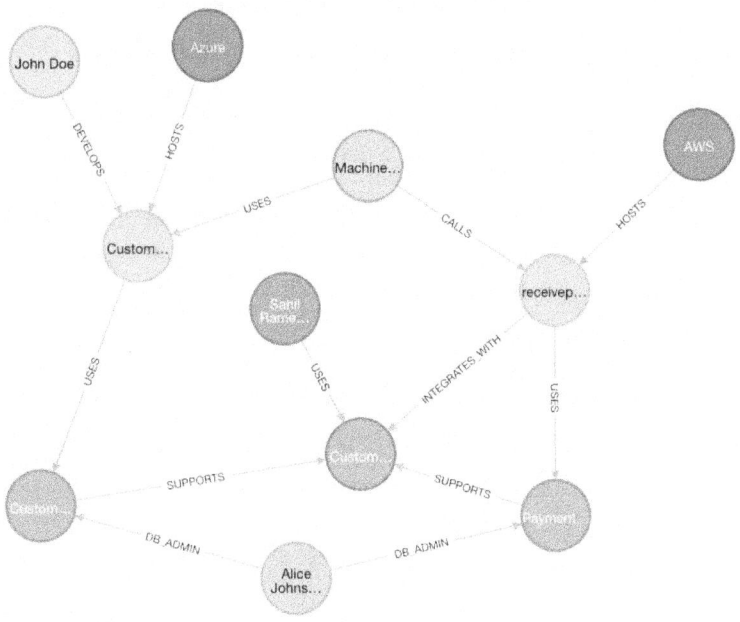

Figure 3-9. Access Relationships

By now, you might have noticed that while these datasets are interconnected, analyzing them individually can be both time-consuming and challenging when trying to capture the complete picture. It's akin to viewing a house from different windows, attempting to piece together its entire layout. While this approach might work in some scenarios, there's a high chance of missing finer details.

The best solution is to create a graph analytics layer that integrates all these attributes. Below, I've provided a mock-up example of such a graph (see Figure 3-9).

In this example, we've created a graph that describes the assets, identities, and access involved in a customer payment web portal. This example captures the key components, though in reality, there could be many more elements. I've kept it simpler for the sake of clarity and understanding.

At the core of the system is the **CustomerPayments** application, which was created on January 1, 2024. This application is crucial for handling customer transactions and is supported by two key databases: **CustomerDB** and **PaymentsDB**.

51

- **CustomerDB** is a SQL database powered by MySQL, created on June 1, 2023, specifically tailored to manage customer-related data.

- **PaymentsDB** is a NoSQL database powered by MongoDB, created on July 1, 2023, and is used for processing payment-related information.

Application and database nodes like these can be generated using CMDB (Configuration Management Database) inventories, ensuring that all critical components are accurately represented.

Two APIs are integral to this system:

- The **receivepayment** API, hosted on a Linux server with AWS as the cloud provider, integrates seamlessly with the **CustomerPayments** application. It utilizes **PaymentsDB** as its back end, connecting via a secure REST endpoint. This API is essential for processing incoming payment transactions.

- The **CustomerUpdate** API, hosted on a Windows server with Azure as the cloud provider, connects to **CustomerDB**. This API is responsible for updating customer information and ensuring that the data remains accurate and up-to-date.

These nodes can be generated from CMDB datasets, while the relationships between these components can be established through IGA (Identity Governance and Administration) logs. IGA logs help identify which system accounts the API uses and what profiles are being used to access the database. For instance, **Machine-123** is a system identity that interacts with both APIs. This connection can be validated using network logs, providing a comprehensive view of the data flow.

The system also includes roles for various personnel:

- **John Doe**, a Software Engineer hired on May 15, 2022, actively maintains the **CustomerUpdate** API. His contributions are critical, with the latest update recorded on February 5, 2024. Platform and software engineers like John have access to the application code, APIs, and servers for development purposes. These nodes and edges can be generated using IGA datasets, with properties derived from OS-level logs and GitHub activity, reflecting their interactions with the source code.

CHAPTER 3   DATA PREPARATION

- **Alice Johnson**, a Data Engineer, though currently inactive, plays a pivotal role as the Database Administrator for both **CustomerDB** and **PaymentsDB**. Her last logged-in activities were on March 1 and March 2, 2024, respectively. Data Engineers and DBAs have access to both databases for regular maintenance and enhancements. These nodes and edges can be created using IGA datasets, with properties sourced from database audit logs.

- **Sahil Ramesh**, a Business User specializing in Payment Receivables, uses the **CustomerPayments** application regularly. His last login was recorded on March 12, 2024. Business users like Sahil have direct access to the application, and their access profiles, including the last login time, are critical attributes for understanding how they interact with the system. These nodes can be generated from identity datasets, with edges determined by combining IGA datasets with application logs.

In addition to these human users, the system also incorporates a **machine identity** named **Machine-123**. This machine identity has access to both APIs, performing essential automated tasks. It last logged in on March 10, 2024, and had its password last rotated on February 28, 2024. Machine identities can be sourced from IGA systems or from privilege access management systems, depending on how IAM (Identity and Access Management) solutions have been architected.

By integrating knowledge from the key datasets we've discussed in previous sections, this graph provides a powerful tool for answering complex questions such as

- **Who has access to an asset but is not utilizing it?** For instance, last logins represented in edges between associates and their assets can highlight users who are not consistently using their access.

- **What are the assets associated with a user or application?** Simple graph queries can reveal the relationships between associates and assets, providing clarity on how resources are being utilized.

- **Which access points are enabling lateral movement?** Without a graph, one might mistakenly assume that John Doe has access only to the **CustomerUpdate** API. However, by analyzing the connections, it becomes clear that John can potentially gain access to the **receivepayment** API through credentials managed by **Machine-123**.

53

CHAPTER 3   DATA PREPARATION

As we can see, visualizing all access datasets in one comprehensive graph is incredibly powerful. It can unlock the potential for detecting and preemptively mitigating access-related risks. In the upcoming chapters, we'll delve deeper into this graph and apply data science techniques to perform more complex analytics.

Source Code

The source code below generates the graph we discussed in Figure 3-9.

```
// Delete all existing nodes and relationships
MATCH (n)
DETACH DELETE n;

// Create the Application node
CREATE (app:Application {AppName: "CustomerPayments", AppCreated: '2024-01-01'});

// Create Database nodes with additional attributes
CREATE (db1:Database {DBName: "CustomerDB", DBType: "SQL", CreationDate: '2023-06-01', DBEngine: "MySQL"});
CREATE (db2:Database {DBName: "PaymentsDB", DBType: "NoSQL", CreationDate: '2023-07-01', DBEngine: "MongoDB"});

// Create relationships with attributes between the Database nodes and the Application node
MATCH (app:Application {AppName: "CustomerPayments"})
MATCH (db1:Database {DBName: "CustomerDB"})
CREATE (db1)-[:SUPPORTS {used_for: "Production"}]->(app);

//Attach Payment
MATCH (app:Application {AppName: "CustomerPayments"})
MATCH (db2:Database {DBName: "PaymentsDB"})
MERGE (db2)-[:SUPPORTS {used_for: "Production"}]->(app);

// Create the API node with its properties
CREATE (api:API {APIName: "receivepayment", GitHubLink: "https://github.com/your-repo/receivepayment"});

// Connect the API node to the existing Application node
MATCH (api:API {APIName: "receivepayment"})
```

CHAPTER 3   DATA PREPARATION

```
MATCH (app:Application {AppName: "CustomerPayments"})
CREATE (api)-[:INTEGRATES_WITH]->(app);

// connect the API Node to DB
MATCH (api:API {APIName: "receivepayment"})
MATCH (db:Database {DBName: "PaymentsDB"})
CREATE (api)-[:USES {rest_endpoint: "https://api.yourdomain.com/
receivepayment"}]->(db);

// Create a server node
CREATE (server:Server {OStype: "Linux", InstalledOn: "2024-01-10",
CloudProvider: "AWS"});

//Connect the Server Node to the API Node
MATCH (api:API {APIName: "receivepayment"})
MATCH (server:Server {OStype: "Linux"})
CREATE (server)-[:HOSTS {installed_on: "2024-01-10"}]->(api);

// Create the CustomerUpdate API node
CREATE (api2:API {APIName: "CustomerUpdate", GitHubLink: "https://github.
com/your-repo/customerupdate"});

// Create Server 2 node with its attributes
CREATE (server2:Server {OStype: "Windows", InstalledOn: "2024-01-15",
CloudProvider: "Azure"});

// Connect the CustomerUpdate API to CustomerDB
MATCH (api2:API {APIName: "CustomerUpdate"})
MATCH (db:Database {DBName: "CustomerDB"})
CREATE (api2)-[:USES {rest_endpoint: "https://api.yourdomain.com/
customerupdate"}]->(db);

// Connect the CustomerUpdate API to Server 2
MATCH (api2:API {APIName: "CustomerUpdate"})
MATCH (server2:Server {OStype: "Windows"})
CREATE (server2)-[:HOSTS {installed_on: "2024-01-15"}]->(api2);
```

CHAPTER 3   DATA PREPARATION

```
// Create the SoftwareEngineer node with its attributes
CREATE (se:SoftwareEngineer {EmployeeID: "SE12345", Name: "John Doe",
HiredOn: "2022-05-15", Active: 1, ManagerName: "Jane Smith", Email:
"johndoe@example.com"});

// Connect the SoftwareEngineer to the CustomerUpdate API
MATCH (se:SoftwareEngineer {EmployeeID: "SE12345"})
MATCH (api2:API {APIName: "CustomerUpdate"})
CREATE (se)-[:DEVELOPS {developer: "John Doe", last_change_on:
"2024-02-05"}]->(api2);

// Create the DataEngineer node with its attributes
CREATE (de:DataEngineer {EmployeeID: "DE67890", Name: "Alice Johnson",
Active: 0, ManagerName: "Jane Smith", Email: "alicejohnson@example.com"});

// Connect the DataEngineer to CustomerDB
MATCH (de:DataEngineer {EmployeeID: "DE67890"})
MATCH (db1:Database {DBName: "CustomerDB"})
CREATE (de)-[:DB_ADMIN {role_name: "Database Administrator", last_logged_
in: "2024-03-01"}]->(db1);

// Connect the DataEngineer to PaymentsDB
MATCH (de:DataEngineer {EmployeeID: "DE67890"})
MATCH (db2:Database {DBName: "PaymentsDB"})
CREATE (de)-[:DB_ADMIN {role_name: "Database Administrator", last_logged_
in: "2024-03-02"}]->(db2);

// Create the MachineIdentity node with its attributes
CREATE (mi:MachineIdentity {Name: "Machine-123", LastLogin: "2024-03-10",
LastPasswordRotate: "2024-02-28"});

// Connect the MachineIdentity to the receivepayment API as CALLS
MATCH (mi:MachineIdentity {Name: "Machine-123"})
MATCH (api1:API {APIName: "receivepayment"})
CREATE (mi)-[:CALLS]->(api1);

// Connect the MachineIdentity to the CustomerUpdate API as USES
MATCH (mi:MachineIdentity {Name: "Machine-123"})
```

```
MATCH (api2:API {APIName: "CustomerUpdate"})
CREATE (mi)-[:USES]->(api2);

// Create the BusinessUser node with its attributes
CREATE (bu:BusinessUser {Name: "Sahil Ramesh", LastLogin: "2024-03-12",
Type: "Payment Receivables"});

// Connect the BusinessUser to the CustomerPayments application
MATCH (bu:BusinessUser {Name: "Sahil Ramesh"})
MATCH (app:Application {AppName: "CustomerPayments"})
CREATE (bu)-[:USES]->(app);

// View the entire graph to confirm
MATCH (n)-[r]->(m)
RETURN n, r, m;
```

Summary

Chapter 3 focuses on the critical role of **data preparation** in building effective identity analytics systems. It begins by highlighting the importance of taking a **data-first approach** to Identity and Access Management (IAM).

The chapter identifies the key questions identity analytics needs to answer:

> **Who** has access to the system?
>
> **What** resources or assets can they access?
>
> **How** are they using their access?

The chapter introduces the **data processing pipeline**, detailing how data is gathered, cleaned, transformed, and stored for further analysis. This pipeline ensures that organizations can collect data from various sources, such as identity governance systems, application logs, and network logs, and process it for identity analytics.

It explains that gathering the right data from various sources—such as HR systems, application access logs, and device information—is essential. However, correlating this data across multiple systems is often a challenge for organizations, particularly those with complex infrastructures.

Finally, the chapter discusses the importance of integrating all the data into a **graph analytics model**. This model allows organizations to visualize how identities interact with applications, databases, and other resources, helping to answer important questions about access control and security risks. By doing so, companies can better detect and mitigate potential threats.

In summary, Chapter 3 emphasizes the importance of thorough data preparation and outlines the steps needed to build a strong foundation for identity analytics within an organization.

References

1. "Summer 2024 Snapshot of the S&P 500's Market Cap." https://seekingalpha.com/article/4703123-summer-2024-snapshot-of-sp500s-market-cap

2. Therese Poletti. "Meta's Daily Active Users Grow 7% to 3.27 Billion in June." https://www.marketwatch.com/livecoverage/meta-earnings-results-ai-q2-facebook-revenue-instagram/card/meta-s-daily-active-users-grow-7-to-3-27-billion-in-june-gjKp201nA4KJQuCNxeN3

3. SailPoint. "What Is Identity Governance and Administration (IGA)?" https://www.sailpoint.com/identity-library/identity-governance

4. Distributed Query. https://thirdeyedata.ai/presto-distributed-sql-query-engine-for-big-data/

5. "Build Modern Data Streaming Architectures on AWS." https://docs.aws.amazon.com/pdfs/whitepapers/latest/build-modern-data-streaming-analytics-architectures/build-modern-data-streaming-analytics-architectures.pdf#what-is-a-modern-streaming-data-architecture

6. "What Is IT Asset Inventory?" https://www.paloaltonetworks.com/cyberpedia/what-is-it-asset-inventory

CHAPTER 4

Risk-Aware Metrics

Before discussing how one can develop an effective IAM metrics program, I would like readers to understand why having the right metrics is so important.

The 2017 Equifax breach is often cited as a prime example of a failure in cybersecurity metrics. Although Equifax focused heavily on certain metrics, they overlooked critical ones, ultimately leading to a massive breach. The company had already invested significantly in cybersecurity programs but lacked essential metrics, such as the accuracy of IT asset inventories, the time taken to detect unauthorized access, and leading indicators for vulnerability management[1].

Despite these substantial investments, Equifax could not effectively identify assets with exploitable vulnerabilities, resulting in prolonged detection times for all impacted assets. The root cause of the breach was that a known vulnerability had yet to be patched in time. While Equifax had metrics to measure the number of new vulnerabilities detected, it lacked metrics to track whether these vulnerabilities were being managed promptly. They focused on measuring process performance but needed to have effective measures to assess residual risk, reflecting a lack of strong Key Risk Indicators (KRIs).

What Equifax experienced is unfortunately not unique to them; incorrect metrics driving unintended or suboptimal behaviors is a widespread issue across various domains, not just in cybersecurity. This problem is evident in the business world as well. For example, Wells Fargo[2] implemented a new performance metric for their sales associates under an initiative called "Gr-eight." The goal was to sell eight products per household, pushing a cross-selling metric that tracked the average number of financial products each customer held.

Wells Fargo's intense emphasis on this metric led to unrealistic targets for the sales team, fostering unethical behaviors among associates. In an effort to meet their targets, many employees engaged in questionable practices, ultimately leading to significant regulatory repercussions. This scandal severely damaged Wells Fargo's reputation, led to widespread job losses, and hindered the bank's growth.

In summary, while metrics are essential for keeping operations efficient and for measuring progress toward goals, using the wrong metrics can have severely negative effects, sometimes doing more harm than good. The right metrics must be chosen carefully to ensure they drive behaviors that align with the organization's ethical and operational objectives. In the context of Identity and Access Management (IAM), risk-aware metrics help assess, prioritize, and respond to identity-related threats by quantifying risk across users, devices, access patterns, and entitlements. These metrics are key enablers of risk-based authentication (RBA), Zero Trust, and adaptive access control.

Metrics in Depth

A metric is a quantifiable measurement of a product, process, or phenomenon that can be directly observed or calculated. It may be directly measured or derived from other measurements. For instance, metrics can include the number of new customers or the average number of logins to a website. Metrics are defined and tracked to measure different aspects of a business and are used to assess overall health. However, a standalone metric is rarely useful; typically, metrics are compared to baselines. In the examples above, we might compare new customer sign-ups with those of a competitor or against the number from last year to determine if our market presence is growing.

In business or management, metrics are classified based on what they measure. Broadly, they fall into one of four categories:

1. **Effectiveness**: These metrics assess whether an organization is achieving its intended outcomes. For example, if an organization aims to automate access provisioning, measuring the percentage of manual access requests over time can indicate progress toward this goal.

2. **Efficiency**: These metrics show how resources are being utilized. For instance, in evaluating access provisioning efficiency, we might measure the average time it takes for an associate to gain access once a request is initiated.

3. **Productivity**: These metrics measure output relative to input. An example could be the number of applications managed centrally by an Identity Governance and Administration (IGA) instance. Managing more applications centrally can reduce duplicated effort across the organization.

4. **Conformance**: These metrics indicate whether processes adhere to specific compliance standards. For example, if a standard requires multifactor authentication (MFA) for logins, tracking the percentage of logins without MFA can help measure compliance with these guidelines.

Metrics are essential for the operation and management of large-scale systems, providing a way to monitor system health and evaluate if the business is meeting its goals. These categories help clarify what is being measured and why. In the field of cybersecurity, metrics are often discussed in terms of KPIs (Key Performance Indicators) and KRIs (Key Risk Indicators).

In cybersecurity, metrics are primarily designed around risk reduction, making most metrics outcome-driven. Broadly, they can be classified as follows:

1. **Leading Indicators**: These metrics predict potential increases or decreases in risk. For example, tracking the percentage of past-due unpatched servers highlights potential vulnerabilities that could be exploited. These indicators are often referred to as Key Risk Indicators (KRIs) because they signify residual risks within the company.

2. **Lagging Indicators**: These metrics show how well an existing process or product is performing and reflect the outcomes of prior actions. They're typically known as Key Performance Indicators (KPIs) since they measure the effectiveness of processes or products. Lagging indicators are retrospective and reveal the results of actions taken based on KRIs.

We can establish a causal relationship between these indicators. Let's illustrate this with an example in Identity and Access Management (IAM).

Example: Ensuring the Security of Admin Passwords

Business Outcome: Prevent admin account passwords from being compromised. To achieve this, the best approach is to enforce strict password rotation and multifactor authentication (MFA) policies. Figure 4-1 demonstrates the relationship between performance metrics and this business outcome.

Metric: **% of Accounts with MFA Enabled** ➤ Business Outcome: **Passwords Protected**

However, strict policies may require exceptions. For instance, some vendor applications may not support MFA, preventing its enforcement. In such cases, companies typically have exception procedures. A KRI can be established to track this:

KRI: **% of Accounts with Exceptions for MFA** ➤ KPI: **% of Accounts with MFA Enabled** ➤ Outcome: **Passwords Protected**

This KRI-KPI pair provides insight into which risks are mitigated through MFA-enabled accounts and which are assumed through exceptions. If these percentages don't sum to 100%, unmanaged accounts might exist, representing a risk of password exposure. The higher this percentage, the greater the risk of potential breaches.

A KRI also helps to quantify the acceptable level of risk. Companies often establish thresholds to indicate tolerable levels of risk; if the KRI percentage surpasses this threshold, action may be required—such as avoiding vendor products that don't support MFA.

Understanding KPIs or KRIs in isolation is rarely sufficient. Their combination offers a comprehensive view of the risks associated with business outcomes and effective risk management strategies.

Case Study: Experian

Experian effectively tracked how quickly they detected new vulnerabilities, with solid KPI reporting. However, they lacked an associated KRI—specifically, tracking unresolved vulnerabilities past their due dates. Without a clear view of remediation rates, leadership had a false sense of security, believing their detection speed was sufficient without understanding the remediation gaps.

In summary, pairing KPIs and KRIs provides a balanced perspective on both performance and residual risk, enabling more informed, proactive risk management.

Key Metrics in IAM

Although the title mentions "key metrics," this can be somewhat misleading. It's not solely about identifying key metrics but rather about understanding the **business outcomes** we aim to achieve. These key business outcomes determine the processes we need to establish and optimize for greater effectiveness. The measurements of these processes then define the key metrics in Identity and Access Management (IAM). We can classify these key processes by major domains; this is how I would categorize them:

CHAPTER 4   RISK-AWARE METRICS

1. **Centralization**

   Centralization involves managing access through a unified platform, eliminating the need for federated processes and reducing inconsistencies across systems. This approach removes duplication and strengthens IAM controls, as processes are now managed through a robust, centrally governed system. For instance, multifactor authentication (MFA) can either be enabled at the individual application level or managed centrally. When MFA is centrally managed, it provides visibility into the protocols in use, ensuring correct configurations across the organization. By contrast, managing MFA individually across hundreds or thousands of applications makes it difficult to confirm consistent implementation and compliance.

2. **Authentication**

   Authentication is the foundational process that verifies users are who they claim to be. Metrics in this area help measure how effectively IAM reduces the risk of unauthorized access. These metrics track user authentication success rates, instances of failed access attempts, and the adoption of MFA, all of which provide insights into the effectiveness of the authentication framework.

3. **Authorization**

   The authorization layer ensures that users have the appropriate level of access based on their roles and responsibilities within the company. This layer governs access workflows, certifications, and other mechanisms to prevent over-privileged access. Metrics associated with authorization confirm that users have only the access they need, reducing the risk of unnecessary or excessive permissions in the environment.

4. **Privileged Access Management (PAM)**

   Privileged Access Management (PAM) is a specialized component within IAM that governs elevated permissions and access associated with sensitive applications and systems. PAM activities include session monitoring, password vaulting and rotation, privileged account discovery, and more. Metrics in this area are designed to ensure that privileged access is secure, compliant, and easy to manage for users with elevated permissions. In Privileged Access Management (PAM), **risk-aware metrics** strengthen security by detecting misuse or overuse of privileged credentials and highlighting accounts or activities that pose the greatest risk. They also support the enforcement of just-in-time and least privilege principles while enabling automated responses to abnormal behaviors.

5. **Cloud Identity and Access Management (CIAM)**

    As more organizations move to cloud environments, Cloud Identity and Access Management (CIAM) has become a critical focus. Whether your company is fully cloud-native or operates in a hybrid cloud environment, you are likely managing numerous cloud identities and addressing security concerns raised by internal audits or external regulators. Most access controls used for on-premises applications apply to the cloud as well. CIAM metrics help ensure that cloud environments are secure and that the principle of least privilege is effectively implemented.

6. **Governance, Risk, and Compliance (GRC)**

    A GRC program ensures that IAM procedures and processes comply with industry regulatory standards and effectively mitigate risk. Metrics associated with GRC confirm that IAM processes and products meet these standards, reducing risk exposure and supporting compliance efforts.

7. **Operational Analytics**

    Despite advancements in automation technologies like RPA and AI, many IAM processes remain manual. Operational metrics measure the effectiveness of these manual processes and assess the resilience of IAM applications, identifying any business disruptions caused by system downtimes. By tracking these metrics, organizations can ensure IAM processes remain reliable and continue to support business objectives efficiently.

Each of these domains provides vital insights into IAM's security, compliance, and operational efficiency. By using metrics to monitor each domain, organizations can identify areas for improvement and optimize their IAM frameworks to meet business goals effectively.

Table 4-1. KPI vs. KRI

Area	Business Outcomes	KPI	KRI	Relationship
Centralization	Achieve a centralized IAM system to reduce redundancy and streamline access governance.	Percentage of applications integrated with centralized IAM solutions. Example: MFA PingID	Percentage of applications sought for exceptions.	The performance indicator measures how effectively native applications are being integrated with centralized platforms, offering a clear view of progress. In contrast, the risk indicator highlights limitations or challenges that may obstruct this integration. A high-risk indicator often points to a substantial presence of legacy applications, which can lead to poorly managed federated access risks. It's important to note that a low performance indicator does not necessarily reflect underperformance by the integration team; rather, it may indicate constraints inherent in the integration process. A comprehensive understanding emerges only when both metrics are analyzed together, providing a balanced perspective on the performance achieved and the risks that remain in the integration efforts.

(*continued*)

Table 4-1. (*continued*)

Area	Business Outcomes	KPI	KRI	Relationship
Authentication	Strengthen authentication processes to enhance security and prevent unauthorized access.	Percentage of users enrolled in multifactor authentication (MFA).	Average number of times users receive MFA prompts.	Increased MFA enrollment (KPI) helps reduce the risk associated with compromised credentials. However, a significant rise in the number of daily MFA prompts can lead to **MFA fatigue**, increasing the likelihood of users falling victim to **MFA bombing attacks**. An example of this occurred during Uber's 2022 cyber incident, where repeated MFA prompts were exploited to gain unauthorized access. Monitoring this risk indicator (KRI) ensures that, while expanding MFA coverage to more users and applications, we are not causing undue fatigue that could weaken our security posture.

(*continued*)

Table 4-1. (*continued*)

Area	Business Outcomes	KPI	KRI	Relationship
Authorization	Ensure users have appropriate access levels, reducing over-privilege and maintaining compliance.	Average number of days it takes to complete the access request workflow.	Access request taking more than N days.	Delays in granting access beyond predefined thresholds introduce operational risks. Frustrated users may attempt to bypass access request workflows to obtain the access they need, which can escalate both compliance and cybersecurity risks.
Authorization	Ensure users have appropriate access levels, reducing over-privilege and maintaining compliance.	Access revocation rates in certifications (access reviews)	Access lines revoked in certifications but re-requested after the closing of the certification campaign.	Focusing solely on the KPI might lead leadership to believe that the organization is progressing toward a least-privilege state. However, if the KRI is increasing, it indicates that certification revocations were not legitimate and the underlying access risks remain unresolved.

(*continued*)

Table 4-1. (*continued*)

Area	Business Outcomes	KPI	KRI	Relationship
Authorization	Ensure users have appropriate access levels, reducing over-privilege and maintaining compliance.	Number of segregation duty policies configured.	Number of SOD (segregation of duty) violations.	An increasing trend in the KPI might create a false sense of confidence that segregation of duties (SOD) risks are being effectively mitigated. However, if the KRI is also rising—and at a rate higher than the KPI—it clearly indicates that the organization is falling behind in addressing these risks.
Privileged Access	Secure privileged accounts to prevent misuse and ensure authorized high-level access.	Percentage of privileged accounts with session monitoring.	Number of privileged accounts with third parties where monitoring logs are not available.	MFA on privileged accounts (KPI) reduces risks associated with unmonitored sessions (KRI), as unauthorized access attempts are deterred at the authentication level.
Privileged Access	Secure privileged accounts to prevent misuse and ensure authorized high-level access.	Percentage of accounts with automated password rotations.	% of accounts requiring manual rotations.	Manual password rotation is not only inefficient; it also means tons of misses and increasing risk of password compromise, as well as operational risk associated with account lockouts and API/Batch failures.

(*continued*)

Table 4-1. (*continued*)

Area	Business Outcomes	KPI	KRI	Relationship
Privileged Access	Secure privileged accounts to prevent misuse and ensure authorized high-level access.	Percentage of accounts with automated password rotations.	Percentage of non-expiring and non-rotation passwords.	While we want passwords to go away in favor of passwordless tools, they still exist. Rotating passwords is less risky compared to passwords that do not expire and change over the period.
Cloud IAM	Implement secure and compliant access controls for cloud resources to prevent unauthorized access.	Percentage of cloud assets integrated with enterprise IAM.	Number of cloud accounts with administrative privileges lacking IAM controls.	Integrating cloud assets with Identity and Access Management (IAM) as a Key Performance Indicator (KPI) helps reduce the number of unmanaged administrative accounts, which serve as a Key Risk Indicator (KRI). This approach enforces consistent security policies across cloud resources. For example, AWS API keys can pose a significant security risk if not rotated regularly or if hard-coded within the code base. Misconfigured cloud resources can expose these keys, leading to severe vulnerabilities. Numerous examples demonstrate how such misconfigurations have resulted in leaked API keys and massive data breaches.

(*continued*)

CHAPTER 4　RISK-AWARE METRICS

Table 4-1. (*continued*)

Area	Business Outcomes	KPI	KRI	Relationship
Governance	Ensure compliance with IAM policies, standards, and regulations, reducing audit findings.	Percentage of IAM controls tested as effective.	Percentage of IAM controls tested as ineffective compared to other cyber towers.	Knowing how IAM is performing with other cyber towers gives a sense of completeness and comfort if IAM is trending as other cyber towers and if identity risk is being taken seriously at the same level as that of network security; after all, identity is a new perimeter.
Operational View	Ensure efficient IAM operations for business continuity and rapid incident response.	Average time to resolve IAM-related incidents.	Frequency of incidents related to IAM misconfigurations.	Faster resolution times (KPI) prevent recurring misconfigurations (KRI), reducing the likelihood of repeated incidents and improving IAM operational resilience.

Table 4-1 highlights some of the key KPIs and KRIs in IAM (Identity and Access Management). The purpose of this section is to guide the reader on how to approach KPIs and their associated KRIs and how to craft a compelling data narrative for monthly or quarterly executive business reviews.

If I were tasked with developing a metrics program in IAM, I would take the following steps:

1. **Evaluate Current Measurements**

    Begin by reviewing the metrics currently being tracked. Compare them against the KPIs and KRIs listed in Table 4-1 to determine if the organization is already measuring these critical aspects. Identify any gaps or opportunities for improvement.

2. **Prioritize Critical Domains**

    If some KPIs or KRIs are not currently being tracked, prioritize addressing the most critical domain over the next six months. This prioritization should be done in collaboration with leadership, considering factors such as

    - Upcoming regulatory assessments
    - High-risk areas within the organization that need immediate attention

3. **Assess Additional Metrics**

    Examine metrics that are currently tracked but not listed in Table 4-1. Ask:

    - Why is this metric important?
    - Is there a KRI associated with this metric?
    - Can these metrics and KRIs be linked to demonstrate measurable risk reduction?

This structured approach ensures alignment between what is measured, what is prioritized, and how metrics and risks are communicated to stakeholders. It also helps create a coherent data-driven story that highlights progress and areas of concern effectively.

CHAPTER 4   RISK-AWARE METRICS

Metric Implementation

Let's start with a few simple but thought-provoking questions:

- How many times have you attended a presentation where the speaker had a compelling story to share, but the presentation fell apart because the audience questioned the metrics—either how they were calculated or their overall trustworthiness?

- How often have you seen someone struggle to explain a metric because the underlying calculation was too complex or the data quality was questionable?

- Have you ever faced the challenge of comparing metrics from this month to last month, only to realize that changing business conditions weren't reflected in the calculations, rendering the comparison meaningless?

- Have you encountered a dashboard with metrics that seemed "too good to be true," but no details were provided about how the dashboard was developed, when it was last updated, or whether exclusions influenced the interpretation of the data?

Chances are most readers have experienced at least one of these scenarios. If you haven't, consider yourself one of the luckiest data professionals on the planet. For the rest of us, these situations highlight common pitfalls in metric implementation.

In this section, I'll provide a road map for building a **strong and reliable metrics program**—one that avoids these pitfalls and ensures your metrics are both actionable and trustworthy.

Figure 4-1 illustrates the execution flow of a metrics program. The flow is designed as cyclic because the process is inherently **iterative and continuous**. While some steps may already be familiar to readers, this section provides valuable insights that can enhance your understanding. I encourage readers not to skip this discussion, as it offers important perspectives that could improve the effectiveness of your metrics program.

CHAPTER 4 RISK-AWARE METRICS

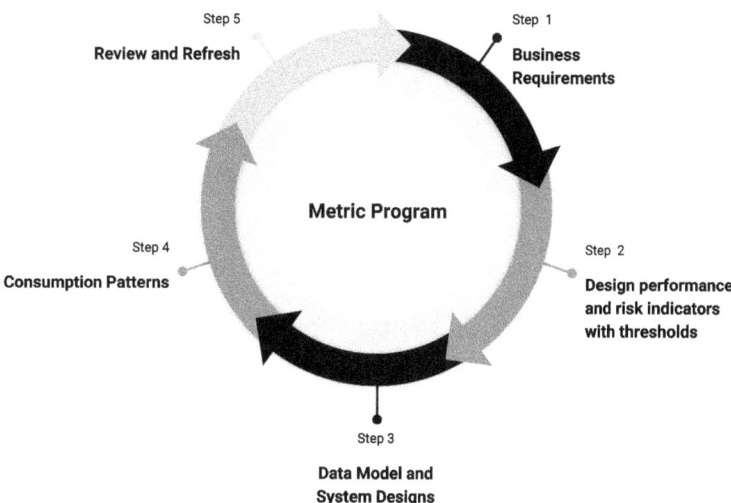

Figure 4-1. Metric Lifecycle

Step 1: Business Requirements

The only scenario where building a dashboard without clearly defined business requirements might be justified is during the business proposal phase. In this phase, the goal is to influence leadership by showcasing what a metrics program can achieve and surprising them with impactful data stories—even insights they might not have considered possible. For all other situations, it is essential to secure buy-in from key stakeholders about what matters to them and how it should be measured.

Identifying Stakeholders

The business requirements phase begins with identifying the relevant stakeholders. These typically include

1. **IAM/Cyber Leadership**

    These are the executive sponsors for the IAM program as a whole. They are responsible for committing to certain risk mitigation goals at the board level. They understand the leading risk vectors and what actions are necessary to manage them. Your role is to measure whether their vision is on track and provide data to support that journey.

73

2. **IAM/Cyber Operations**

    These teams execute the vision and strategy set by leadership. They include

    - **Engineering Teams:** Responsible for implementing IAM applications that manage IAM processes.

    - **Operations Teams:** Work with application teams to onboard native applications onto IAM platforms. Once onboarding is complete, they handle workflows for access requests, access reviews, terminations, certifications, secret rotations, session management, and more.

3. **Security Operations Center (SOC)**

    SOC teams monitor real-time activities for signs of unauthorized actions, vulnerabilities, or exploitation of IAM platforms. They consist of

    - **Detection Engineering and Operations Teams:** Monitor logs across native applications and IAM platforms to identify potential cyber risks.

    - **Insider Threat Teams:** Focus on identifying and mitigating risks originating from within the organization.

4. **Risk and Compliance Teams**

    These teams map regulatory standards (e.g., NIST 800-53) to security requirements for the organization. The resulting requirements are formalized as controls. These teams ensure business processes adhere to these controls and actively monitor for compliance.

5. **Internal/External Audit Teams**

    Audit teams validate whether engineering and operations teams are effectively fulfilling their responsibilities. Their goal is to identify gaps and ensure accountability through structured review processes.

6. **All Enterprise Employees**

   While IAM leadership bears most responsibilities, non-IAM associates play a vital role. For instance:

   - If SOC detects anomalous database activities, IAM teams collaborate with database engineers to determine if these activities are intentional or out-of-band.
   - Associates supporting databases need access to reporting tools to conduct effective investigations.

During this phase, product managers supporting the metrics program should document all measurements that stakeholders consider critical, important, or nice-to-have for their roles. Once these requirements are collected:

1. **Streamline the Requirements**

   Remove duplicates and align overlapping needs to avoid inefficiencies.

2. **Prioritize Key Processes**

   Create a ranked list of processes to monitor, how they should be measured, and clear timelines for when each process should be addressed.

This systematic approach ensures that the metrics program aligns with the organization's objectives, supports its stakeholders, and delivers actionable insights.

Step 2: Designing Performance and Risk Indicators with Thresholds

Once we identify the processes and products critical from a user's standpoint, the next step is to design performance and risk indicators with clearly defined thresholds. Thresholds are essential because they represent the organization's risk appetite—the level of risk the business is willing to accept. A metric without a threshold is often meaningless, as it fails to provide actionable context.

The outcome of this step is the creation of a metrics registry—a document or database that maps processes and products to their respective Key Performance Indicators (KPIs) and Key Risk Indicators (KRIs). This registry includes details such as the calculation methods, data sources, update frequency, and the ways metrics are consumed within the organization.

Attributes of a Metric Registry

1. Domain

The domain refers to the specific process or area within Identity and Access Management (IAM) to which the metric belongs. These domains are discussed in the earlier section on IAM key metrics.

2. Metric Name

The metric name should be self-explanatory. Anyone reading it should immediately understand what is being measured and why it is important. A clear name ensures alignment and avoids ambiguity in interpretation.

3. Metric ID

A unique metric ID helps identify and track the metric in a relational database. Storing metrics in such databases ensures they can be shared and reported easily while maintaining accuracy and consistency.

4. Metric Type

Metrics can be classified as leading or lagging indicators:

- **Leading indicators** predict future performance or risks.
- **Lagging indicators** measure past performance.

Additionally, understanding whether a metric is a KPI (measuring success) or a KRI (measuring risk) is critical for operationalizing these metrics into dashboards. This will be discussed further in the next section.

5. Stakeholder

The stakeholder is the individual or group responsible for the metric or the primary consumer of its insights. Identifying stakeholders ensures clarity about

- Who to consult if there are questions about data accuracy
- Who will act on the metric's insights
- Who owns the overall health of the metric

6. Calculation

The calculation method is one of the most critical attributes of a metric. For example, if a metric states that "95% of applications are managed via MFA," understanding how this is calculated is essential. Does it mean

- *Number of applications supporting MFA ÷ total applications?*
- *Number of active MFA URLs in logs ÷ total applications?*

The interpretation can vary significantly depending on the methodology, making it crucial to document the exact calculation process.

7. Data Sources

Metrics are only as reliable as their data sources. Understanding whether the data is

- **Automatically generated** (e.g., logs from processes).
- **Manually entered** (e.g., user-generated CSV files) is vital. Manual data may require additional validation due to its higher potential for inaccuracies.

8. Frequency

The frequency of updates determines how often the metric is refreshed. For example, if leadership receives a report based on data updated monthly, it's crucial to validate whether the situation has changed since the data was last collected.

9. Thresholds

As previously noted, metrics without thresholds lack actionable meaning. Leaders are responsible for defining thresholds, which should align with the organization's risk appetite. For instance, a threshold might specify that a critical metric falls within an acceptable range (e.g., "≥ 90% MFA compliance").

10. Exceptions

Cybersecurity often includes **exceptions** to deterministic rules. For example:

- A rule might flag applications not using MFA as a risk.
- However, there might be exceptions for applications without a user interface that rely solely on microservices managed by an API gateway.

Documenting these exceptions ensures clarity and reduces false alarms.

11. Location

Metrics should not only show the current state ("destination") but also provide actionable insights on how to achieve desired outcomes. The **location** attribute provides a direct path to where the metric data is stored or displayed.

12. Version

Metrics, like code, should have version control. Changes to metrics or dashboards should include

- Peer reviews
- Segregation of duties (SOD)
- Clear documentation linking the change to a business requirement

Treating metrics as code ensures traceability and prevents situations where dashboards are modified without clarity on who made the changes and why.

Step 3: Data Model and System Designs

I am consistently surprised by the amount of technical debt present in data analytics organizations. This debt often arises due to two main factors.

1. The Ever-Evolving Nature of the Data Field

The data landscape is constantly changing, with new technologies emerging rapidly. This continuous evolution can make it challenging for organizations to keep their systems up-to-date and maintain best practices.

2. Ad Hoc Dashboard Requirements

Data teams frequently receive requests for ad hoc dashboards, which are often built quickly without sufficient consideration for scalability or future-proofing. While these quick solutions may address immediate needs, they can create significant problems over time.

These quick wins often transform into substantial, ongoing burdens for data teams. Over time, they become a massive tax on resources, draining the team's energy and diverting focus away from building new features. What initially seemed like an efficient solution can grow into a barrier that hinders the team's ability to scale and innovate.

I cannot emphasize enough the importance of treating metrics and dashboards like software products. In software development, we have architects, system designers, and product managers who work together to build robust products. While these roles need not be filled by three separate individuals, it is crucial to adopt a delivery workflow that incorporates these functions.

Once we have identified performance and risk indicators, data engineers, architects, and product managers should collaboratively undertake the following steps.

1. Identify Data Sources

Locate all the data sources required to perform the calculations mentioned in the registry, including any exceptions. Understanding the full landscape of data inputs is essential for accurate and comprehensive analysis.

2. Design a Data Ingestion Framework

Develop a data ingestion framework that simplifies the process of incorporating new data sources, making it primarily configurable. Key characteristics of this framework should include

- **Ease of Integration**: Integrating new data sources should be straightforward, minimizing the effort required to expand the data pipeline.

- **Quality Checks**: Build data quality checks into the framework to ensure accuracy and timeliness. This allows data engineers to focus on developing transformations rather than repeatedly implementing duplicative checks for each new integration.

3. Build Libraries

Most of the transformations we need to perform are similar across different integrations. For example, we often need to enrich logs with application and asset inventory attributes or augment data sources with company-specific metadata. The technical team should design reusable libraries to facilitate easier integration in the future.

4. Decide on Technology Stack

Choose the programming languages, database types, and vendor tools that will form the foundation of your data system. I have frequently seen teams invest in duplicative technologies, leading to excessive time spent supporting those tools. Standardizing the technology stack can enhance efficiency and reduce maintenance overhead.

5. Develop Standardized Data Models

Implement standardized data models and entities to build foundational elements correctly from the start. While this might seem like a slow process when building the initial dashboard your customers need, investing in data model standardization ensures that, when you want to develop something new, you will already have enriched, verified data that is easy to use.

6. Design the Data System

Just as programming languages and system design have a significant impact on how a software product scales in the future, the selection of reporting tools, data curation processes, and transformation tools determines how a data metrics product will scale. Key design considerations include

- **Data Integration Tools**: Decide whether to use vendor tools for data interface designs (e.g., Ab Initio, Cognos, Alteryx, Talend) or to develop them from scratch using technologies like Python or Spark.

- **Data Storage**: Determine where source data should be enriched and where the final metrics should be stored. Options might include using DynamoDB for its resiliency in AWS or a relational database in a colocation environment. The choice depends on scaling needs and future requirements.

- **Reporting Tools**: Select appropriate reporting solutions, whether open source options like Apache Superset or vendor products such as Tableau, AWS QuickSight, or Microsoft Power BI. These decisions impact developer costs, productivity, and user experience.

7. Address Data Governance and Compliance

Ensure that data producers refresh data at regular intervals and that all data handling complies with standards such as GDPR and CCPA. Proper data governance is essential for legal compliance and maintaining trust with stakeholders.

8. Implement Monitoring

Establish monitoring of the overall infrastructure and data pipelines to ensure that the information being reported is reliable. Monitoring helps detect issues early and maintain the integrity of your data systems.

Designing data systems is an involved topic; there is a vast amount of literature to discuss this, but the attempt here is to convince the reader to treat identity analytics as a software product and build this with a correct foundation.

Step 4: Metric Consumption

Imagine this: A senior executive approaches a data analyst with a request to build a dashboard that could revolutionize how the business operates. The analyst dedicates countless hours, crafting a complex and visually stunning dashboard. The executive uses it for a board presentation, and it's a resounding success. The analyst receives accolades and even an award for creating this "killer dashboard."

Fast forward six months. The analyst receives an email from the engineering team asking whether the dashboard should be purged due to a lack of usage. Shocked and confused, the analyst wonders: *What went wrong?*

Though this story is fictional, it's a scenario that plays out frequently. Why does this happen? Several factors contribute to the decline in dashboard usage.

Why Dashboards Fall Out of Use

1. **The Newness Factor**

   Like viral videos or social media posts, dashboards often experience an initial surge of interest. Over time, as the novelty wears off, their usage declines. This pattern aligns with the **power-law distribution**, where only a few dashboards maintain high engagement over the long term.

2. **Changing Business Conditions**

   In fast-moving fields like IAM and cybersecurity, priorities shift constantly. A dashboard that once addressed a critical need may become irrelevant as new challenges and objectives emerge. When users no longer see value in the data points provided, they stop engaging.

3. **Unmet New Requirements**

   As users' needs evolve, dashboards must evolve with them. When dashboards fail to provide additional context or data that users require, they become inefficient tools. Users may turn to alternative methods to gather the information they need, reducing active engagement.

4. **Lack of Actionable Outputs**

   Dashboards that provide metrics without actionable insights are often ignored. For instance, a dashboard showing applications not using MFA is of limited use if there's no associated process for addressing these gaps. If outputs are not tied to actions or operationalized effectively, users have no reason to return to the dashboard.

Recommendations to Drive Dashboard Engagement

Dashboards remain the most common vehicle for metric reporting, but their value depends on how they are consumed. Here's how analytics teams can influence dashboard engagement:

1. **Don't Just Build Visualizations—Build Solutions**

   Metrics exist to measure something, but measurements alone don't solve problems. Analytics teams should collaborate with leadership and product management to design dashboards that are part of a larger solution. Remember, your consumers are problem-solvers, and dashboards are tools to aid—not replace—their efforts.

2. **Foster a Data-Driven Culture**

   As a data leader, your responsibility extends beyond building dashboards. You must drive a cultural shift that emphasizes data-informed decision-making. This requires strong influence, visionary leadership, and a commitment to becoming an **inspirational change agent**. Collaborate with your reporting team to create visuals that align with leadership's goals and demonstrate how to achieve them.

3. **Expand Coverage and Depth**

   Analytics teams serve as horizontal functions across IAM services and products. It's crucial to

   - **Expand coverage:** Ensure all divisions and processes are supported with actionable metrics to prevent any group from lagging behind.

- **Provide depth:** Go beyond highlighting what is good or bad. Help users understand what's working and why, so they can drive meaningful change. A dashboard without these insights is merely a static report, not a driver of transformation.

A dashboard's longevity and impact depend on its ability to stay relevant, actionable, and aligned with user needs. Analytics teams must go beyond creating dashboards for one-time successes and focus on building **scalable, problem-solving tools**. By fostering a culture of data-driven decision-making, collaborating closely with stakeholders, and addressing both coverage and depth, you can ensure that your dashboards continue to provide value long after their initial launch.

Step 5: Review and Refresh

IAM (Identity and Access Management) is a critical component of enterprise risk management. But what is risk? Simply put, **risk is uncertainty**. With ever-evolving threat vectors and advancements in tooling, the risks associated with IAM are constantly changing. A metric or concern that seemed critical last month might become irrelevant tomorrow.

For example, before the adoption of cloud computing, one of the most critical concerns—apart from security—was the scalability of platforms. Today, with cloud-native autoscaling features, scalability has largely become a non-issue.

This constant evolution underscores the need for identity analytics leaders to regularly assess whether their reporting products are addressing the problems their organizations care about. As part of monthly or quarterly business review processes, leaders should establish clear processes for reviewing and refining their reporting efforts. This includes three essential steps.

1. Confirmation

Confirm that new reporting initiatives align with strategic goals.
For example, if the organization is working to reduce reliance on on-premise Active Directory, reporting solutions should focus on monitoring and analyzing active traffic across both cloud and on-premise directories. This ensures alignment with IAM's strategic direction and priorities.

2. Verification

Verify whether existing dashboards are actively used and valuable to leadership and operational teams.

If a dashboard is inactive or not driving actionable discussions, it's likely time to reassess. This often indicates the need for more **empathy sessions** with stakeholders to better understand their needs. Gathering updated requirements and incorporating them into dashboards can enhance usability and relevance, ensuring reporting is meaningful and accessible.

3. Validation

Validate the accuracy and relevance of the metric registry on a regular basis. Metrics often need adjustment after their initial rollout. Changing exceptions or inaccurate calculations are common. For example, after deployment, users might identify false positives or negatives that need to be addressed—either by refining calculations or adding new exceptions. Regular validation ensures the registry reflects current realities and provides reliable insights.

By systematically addressing these three areas—confirmation, verification, and validation—you can ensure that

1. Old metrics are retired in a timely manner.

2. Existing metrics are refreshed to improve accuracy and relevance.

3. New metrics are created to address emerging needs, enabling IAM teams to operate effectively with robust reporting at the launch of new initiatives.

Leading reporting products in IAM are no different from leading software engineering products. You must actively manage customer expectations, iterate on new features, and solve problems for your stakeholders every day. By taking a proactive and iterative approach, identity analytics leaders can maintain reporting systems that are not only accurate and insightful but also central to driving the success of IAM operations.

CHAPTER 4   RISK-AWARE METRICS

Metric Alerting

Meet X, the Head of IAM for a large financial services company. Every day, X arrives at the office at 9 a.m., ready to tackle the day. But before they can even focus on strategic initiatives, they face a common challenge: an overflowing inbox. Their email is cluttered with messages from application owners managed by IAM platforms, leadership teams, control testing groups, insider threat teams, and other risk partners. With such a flood of emails, it's hard to determine what requires immediate attention.

To cut through the noise, X often starts by checking Slack for any direct pings received since they last logged off, prioritizing those over the chaotic email backlog. Despite their efforts, they know there are emails they've missed—possibly ones that matter.

In a leadership meeting, the CISO asks for information on why certain applications are not managing access centrally. As the IAM leader, X has access to over **150 dashboards**, but none clearly answer the CISO's query. Frustrated, X pings their direct reports managing the MFA platforms for help.

The platform owners respond that they'll need at least a week to gather the information. The issue? The dashboards don't include properly configured exceptions, and the last validation was done over a year ago. The delay leaves the CISO unhappy and questioning why, with 150 dashboards available, such a straightforward question remains unanswered.

The story I just shared is fictional, but it reflects the reality in many organizations—even those with dedicated analytics teams. The problem isn't the absence of metrics or reporting; it's the sheer **overabundance** of them, combined with their lack of actionability.

Dashboards are powerful tools that allow teams to slice and dice data, providing insights into various aspects of IAM operations. However, dashboards alone are not enough. Without an accompanying **alerting infrastructure**, the analytics remain passive. Alerting transforms analytics from mere information into actionable signals.

Effective alerting infrastructure enhances the value of analytics by providing proactive notifications. Alerts ensure critical issues are flagged before they escalate, giving leaders the ability to act swiftly. Alerts can be delivered through various channels—emails, direct messages, or even text messages. Many out-of-the-box reporting solutions offer built-in alerting capabilities, but teams can also develop customized frameworks to meet specific organizational needs.

Configuring Alerts: Two Main Approaches

1. **Rule-Based Alerts**

   These are simple, predefined rules based on specific thresholds or attributes. For example:

   - Critical applications within the enterprise fail to send user listings to centralized access management tools for more than ten days.

   - A user exceeds a set number of failed login attempts within a short timeframe.

2. **Machine Learning-Based Alerts**

   These are more advanced and rely on patterns and anomalies detected in logs or data streams. For example:

   - Authentication rejection rates for critical applications deviate by three standard deviations from the norm.

   - Behavioral anomalies in user access patterns suggest potential insider threats.

Advanced ML-based alerts can incorporate complex algorithms to identify subtle or evolving risks, providing organizations with a sophisticated layer of monitoring.

In addition to alerts, I recommend creating a **"Signal View"** specifically for leadership. This is a consolidated summary page that distills information from all dashboards into a single, actionable view. As illustrated in Figure 4-2, the "Signal View" could include

- **KPIs Breaching Thresholds:** A summary of key metrics across domains that have breached their thresholds, including the extent of the deviation

- **Internal Audit Activities:** A concise overview of ongoing internal audits and their key highlights

- **Trending Control Ineffectiveness:** A snapshot of controls that are increasingly flagged as ineffective

CHAPTER 4   RISK-AWARE METRICS

- **Critical Application Failures:** Identification of critical applications failing to integrate or centralize with IAM platforms

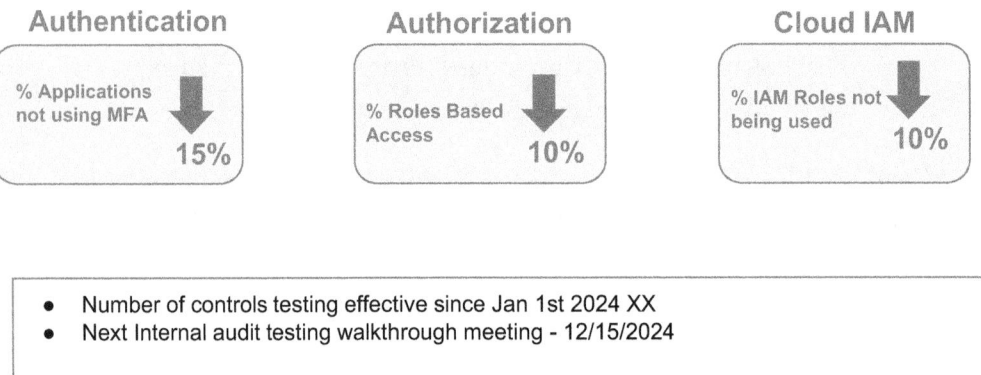

Figure 4-2. Executive Overview

This "Signal View" is not a traditional dashboard but a **distilled, high-impact summary** designed to give leadership clear direction. Before diving into emails, X can review this summary page to quickly identify where they need to focus their attention.

By presenting breached metrics and actionable insights in a simplified format, the "Signal View" eliminates the need for leaders to sift through countless dashboards to understand what's happening. It provides a clear and prioritized starting point for decision-making.

Summary

- In this chapter, we explored the critical importance of using the right metrics in managing risk effectively. Using improper metrics can lead to significant failures, as demonstrated by the 2017 Equifax breach and Wells Fargo's "Gr-eight" initiative. These examples underscore how poorly designed metrics can drive unintended behaviors and hinder risk management.

- We emphasized that effective metrics should measure both performance (KPIs) and residual risks (KRIs), ensuring alignment with strategic goals and driving meaningful actions.

- The chapter also delved into key metrics in Identity and Access Management (IAM), categorizing them into domains and identifying the critical metrics within each domain.

- We reviewed the implementation process for a metrics program, outlining the high-level execution flow and discussing the expected outcomes at each stage.

- Finally, in the metric alerting section, we addressed the challenges posed by an overabundance of dashboards and their potential side effects. We highlighted how an effective alerting infrastructure can reduce this burden, transforming metrics from passive data points into actionable insights.

References

1. Irini Kanaris Miyashiro. "Case Study: Equifax Breach." https://sevenpillarsinstitute.org/case-study-equifax-data-breach/

2. "Wells Fargo and the Misuse of Metrics." https://www.from.digital/insights/wells-fargo-and-misuse-metrics/

3. Robin Abernathy. *CompTIA Advanced Security Practitioner (CASP+) CAS-004 Cert Guide*

4. Steve Wexler, Jeffrey Shaffer, and Andy Cotgreave. *The Big Book of Dashboards*

5. David Parmenter. *Key Performance Indicators, 4th Edition*

6. Jason Edwards and Griffin Weaver. *The Cybersecurity Guide to Governance, Risk, and Compliance*

7. John Fraser. *Enterprise Risk Management*

CHAPTER 5

Risk-Based Access Management

Super Secure Inc. is a company that takes its security seriously. As an early adopter of cutting-edge cybersecurity technologies, the organization prides itself on its ability to safeguard assets while fostering a performance-driven culture. Its top-tier talent pool thrives in an environment where employees are encouraged to compete, excel, and make significant impacts.

In this high-achieving workplace, several standout employees have accumulated extensive access to critical systems in their efforts to deliver exceptional results. Managers, eager to empower their teams, readily approve access requests to help employees excel in their roles and expand responsibilities. The company has also invested in robust access controls, conducting regular access certifications multiple times a year to ensure compliance.

It's January, the season for performance reviews. One of the company's star performers, an analytics expert referred to as Employee X, had just completed a record-breaking year. However, X's hopes for a well-deserved promotion were dashed. Frustrated and disheartened, X began downloading massive datasets far beyond their regular responsibilities. Exploiting elevated access privileges, X used this sensitive customer information for illegal trading, hoping to offset the bonuses they had anticipated. Confident they wouldn't be caught, X's actions spiraled into a full-blown security breach.

Although this story is fictional, it illustrates a stark reality. In 2024, **83% of organizations reported insider attacks**, with nearly half noting an increase in such incidents. Knowing what access someone has—or whether it is appropriate—is no longer sufficient. Just because certification was completed for that access does not mean risk is mitigated.

Now, imagine if Super Secure Inc. had implemented a robust risk-scoring system. With such a system, the riskiest users and the most vulnerable assets would have been easier to identify. This insight could have prompted risk mitigation strategies, such as enhanced monitoring of high-risk users or their access patterns. The ability to measure risk transforms access management, enabling leaders to quantify the risk they are willing to accept, define thresholds for intervention, and take action when necessary.

Challenges with Existing Risk-Scoring Solutions

Many Identity Governance and Administration (IGA) solutions offer risk-scoring capabilities, but these often come with significant limitations:

1. **Generic Industry-Based Scoring:** Most models are built on general industry practices, which may not align with an organization's unique processes.

2. **Limited Data Enrichment:** Effective risk scoring requires custom data enrichment that reflects specific industry and organizational contexts. Relying solely on generic solutions can hinder this.

3. **Assumptions About Architecture:** Predefined architectural patterns in vendor solutions might not align with the actual systems and implementations of a company.

Given these challenges, many organizations choose to develop their own methodologies for risk scoring. This chapter delves into the concept of risk scoring in detail, exploring algorithms, step-by-step implementation from scratch, and strategies for enhancing IGA solutions with custom capabilities.

Risk Scoring

The Importance of Risk Scoring

The National Institute of Standards and Technology (NIST) underscores the critical role of risk scoring as a cornerstone for quantitative, risk-based analysis, assessment, and reporting of organizational IT assets. Given that access management systems and their components are fundamental IT assets, they naturally fall within the scope of such risk assessments.

Approaches to Risk Scoring

Risk scoring can be categorized into two primary approaches, each with its own advantages and applications.

Qualitative Risk Scoring

This approach generates ordinal outputs such as Critical, High, Medium, or Low, making it easier for leaders to quickly grasp the severity of risks. These categories are particularly valuable for

- **High-Level Decision-Making**: They provide a simplified view of risks, enabling leaders to focus on priorities without delving into technical complexities.

- **Communication**: Nontechnical stakeholders, such as business executives, can better understand and respond to the presented risks.

While qualitative scoring is less precise than numerical methods, its ability to distill complex risks into understandable categories makes it an indispensable tool for strategic discussions.

Quantitative Risk Scoring

Quantitative scoring assigns numerical values to risks, with higher numbers reflecting greater levels of risk. This method offers

- **Granular Analysis**: By providing precise risk metrics, organizations can delve deeper into the relative importance of various risks.

- **Threshold-Based Categorization**: Numerical scores can be translated into qualitative categories using defined thresholds. For instance:
  - **0–25**: Low risk
  - **26–50**: Medium risk
  - **51–75**: High risk
  - **76–100**: Critical risk

CHAPTER 5   RISK-BASED ACCESS MANAGEMENT

This hybrid approach—combining qualitative clarity with quantitative precision—empowers organizations to strike a balance between simplicity and detail in their risk management strategies.

By integrating both qualitative and quantitative methods, organizations can tailor their risk scoring practices to fit specific needs. This dual approach enables informed decisions, effective communication, and a stronger overall security posture.

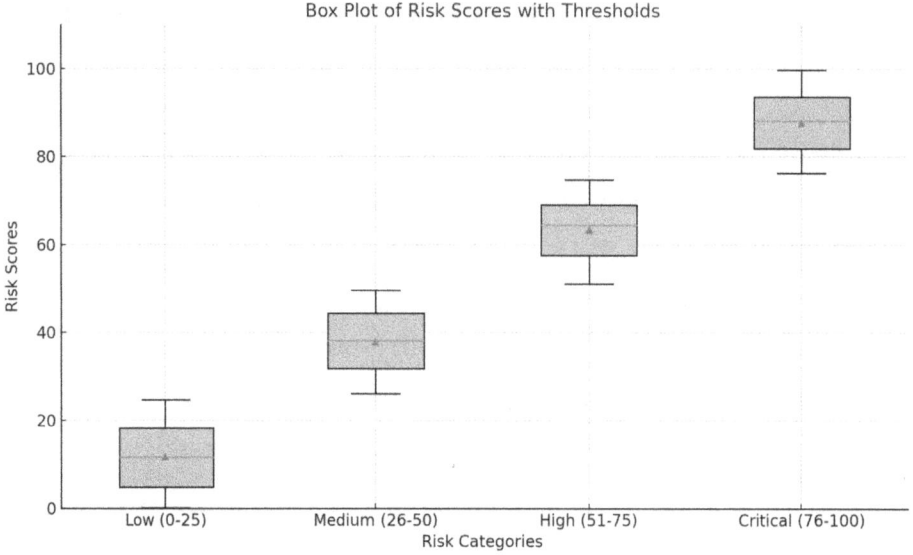

Figure 5-1. *Risk Score Thresholding*

Figure 5-1 shows a box plot of risk scores and illustrates how different ranges of scores can be assigned to risk buckets. This is a mock-up example, so there is little to no overlap between the levels; however, in the real world, overlaps are expected. Any outliers causing overlaps require thorough investigation and should be addressed through parameter tuning or exception handling, both of which must be well-documented for audit purposes.

CHAPTER 5 RISK-BASED ACCESS MANAGEMENT

Risk Scoring Scoping

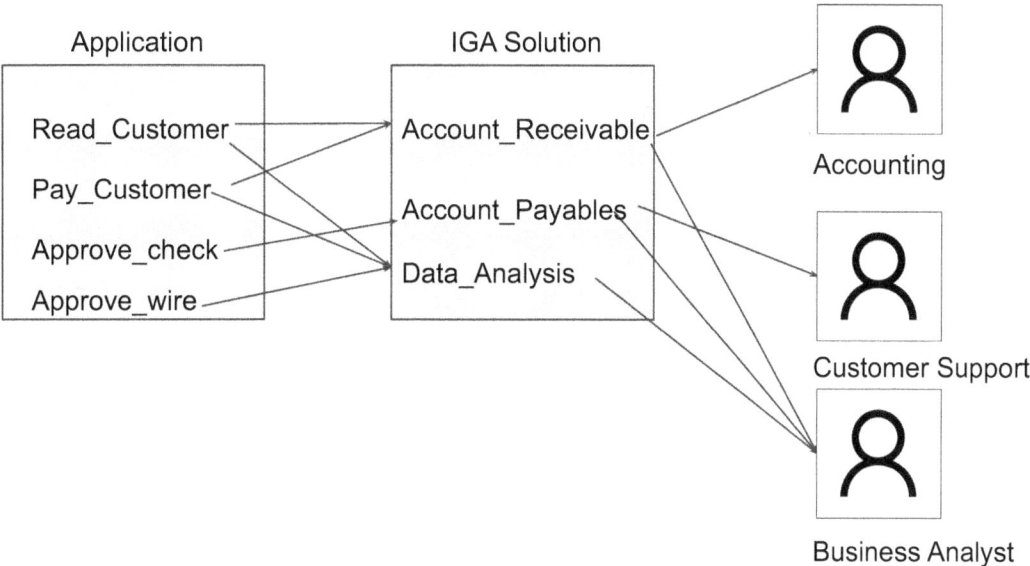

Figure 5-2. *Centrally Managed Access*

Risk scoring is a broad concept, not limited to users alone. It must be applied at a fine-grained level to effectively manage access risks. Figure 5-2 illustrates the key elements of access management. In this example, an application has four roles, referred to as application roles. These roles are assigned unique permissions to fulfill specific responsibilities. An Identity Governance and Administration (IGA) solution manages these application roles by combining them into business roles, which users can request access to.

Users are approved for these IGA-managed roles based on their roles and responsibilities. Risk scoring spans all three tiers—applications, IGA-managed entitlements, and users. Let's explore these in more detail below.

Application-Level Risk Scoring

At the application level, calculating risk scores helps identify critical business applications that require immediate attention from leadership. For instance, if an application contains sensitive customer datasets that can be queried on a large scale, it poses a high risk. Employees with elevated access to such applications could cause significant damage due to the nature of the datasets and architecture.

95

In the example depicted in Figure 5-2, the application handles sensitive tasks such as managing customer datasets, approving payments, and printing checks. Not only does this application process sensitive information, but it also directly impacts the company's financials. Considering its business function and data sensitivity, the application is deemed risky. We will delve deeper into features to use at this level in the implementation section.

IGA-Managed Entitlements

IGA-managed entitlements are those visible to business users in IGA systems. First-line managers approve access requests for these entitlements and review the associated access. Understanding the risk scores tied to these entitlements is crucial for ensuring approvers give them the appropriate attention.

Risk scoring at this level depends on application roles managed by IGA business roles. Additional attributes also influence the risk scores, such as the frequency of access certifications, whether multifactor authentication (MFA) is required, and other security measures. Knowing these factors enables better oversight of IGA-managed entitlements.

User-Level Risk Scoring

Users are evaluated for risk based on their access and responsibilities. For example, users working on critical infrastructure inherently pose higher risks due to their elevated access. Similarly, users in roles that allow them to approve wire payments beyond certain limits are also high-risk and require close monitoring.

In addition to static attributes—such as the access users possess—dynamic attributes play a significant role. For instance, monitoring user behavior in the environment is critical for risk scoring. These dynamic elements provide a more comprehensive view of risk. We will explore this further in the implementation section.

Comprehensive Risk Scoring

By assessing risk at all three levels, it becomes possible to answer critical questions about the risk associated with each access decision. This approach enables detailed access management. Figure 5-3 depicts the key components of an access decision. Understanding who is requesting access, to what they are requesting access, and how they use it allows for monitoring at a granular level, helping to detect any suspicious activity.

CHAPTER 5 RISK-BASED ACCESS MANAGEMENT

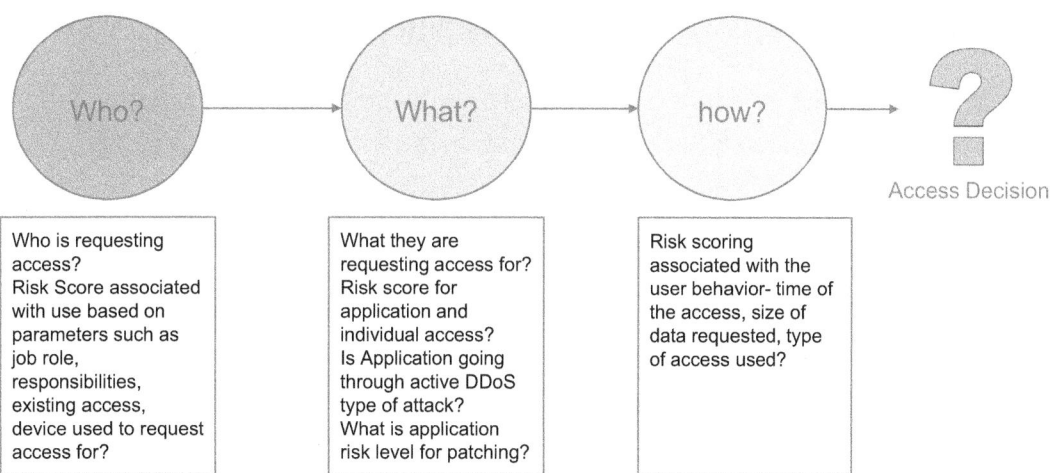

Figure 5-3. Contextualized Access Decision

When risk scores are known for the application, entitlement, and user levels, it's easier to evaluate the overall risk of a user requesting access to a specific asset. This approach facilitates informed decisions about whether the access request is acceptable or requires further scrutiny.

Scenarios to Consider

Here are some scenarios to ponder:

1. Is access risky if a high-risk user requests access to a low-risk application at a usual time?

2. Is access risky if a low-risk user requests access to a high-risk application at an unusual time?

3. Is access risky if a high-risk user requests access to a high-risk application using usual methods and timing?

4. Is access risky if a high-risk user requests access to a low-risk application but a high-risk entitlement in IGA?

These scenarios underscore the importance of implementing a Zero Trust framework, which we will discuss in later chapters.

Risk Scoring Algorithms and Methodologies

Risk scoring in cyber is a really evolving topic; extensive research is being done. We would discuss some of the well-known methods here.

Rule-Based Risk Scoring

Rule-based risk scoring relies on simple, predefined rules that produce binary outputs (e.g., high risk or low risk). These rules are typically created by cybersecurity subject matter experts or architects and are configured to trigger specific actions.

Examples of Rule-Based Implementation
Application-Level Rules

- Applications managing infrastructure access, such as SSH keys or API credentials, are categorized as high risk due to their potential impact on core systems.

- Applications controlling social network handles are considered high risk, as they pose reputational risks to the company.

Entitlement-Level Rules

- Entitlements granting access to customer-sensitive datasets are flagged as high risk because of the critical nature of the data involved.

- Entitlements for birthright applications, such as Slack, onboarding documents, or publicly available corporate information, are classified as low risk due to their limited sensitivity.

User-Level Rules

- Users with access to scheduled conferences or book conference rooms are considered low risk, given the minimal impact of these activities.

- Users with admin-level access to conference management systems, allowing them to view all recordings and bookings, are classified as high risk due to the potential misuse of sensitive information.

Advantages of Rule-Based Scoring

- **Simplicity:** The method is straightforward to implement and easy to understand.
- **Flexibility:** Allows subject matter experts to define rules and their granularity, tailoring the approach to the organization's needs.

Challenges of Rule-Based Scoring

- **Subjectivity:** Rules are highly dependent on expert opinions, making it difficult to achieve consensus across stakeholders.
- **Scalability:** As the access environment grows, the number of rules can become unmanageable, requiring annual reviews and updates to stay relevant.
- **Limited Context:** Rule-based scoring struggles to account for mitigating factors. For example, while admin access to an application is inherently high risk, implementing controls like **multifactor authentication (MFA)** and **just-in-time access** could reduce the risk to a more acceptable level.

Weighted Risk Scoring

Weighted risk scoring calculates cumulative scores by evaluating multiple factors, each assigned a specific weight based on its importance. The sum of these weighted factors determines the overall risk score, which is then compared to predefined thresholds to categorize the asset as high, medium, or low risk.

CHAPTER 5 RISK-BASED ACCESS MANAGEMENT

The formula for calculating a risk score is as follows:

$$Risk\ Score = \sum_{i=1}^{i=N} (Wi * Fi)$$

where:

- Wi: Weight assigned to a specific functional area or factor
- Fi: Score or value for that functional area
- N: Total number of factors considered

Sample Implementation Details
Application-Level Risk Scoring

Risk Factor	Risk Weight
If the application manages Business Critical Functionality	30
If the application access is not managed by a centralized IGA	10
If the application does not use MFA for authentication	20
If the application is behind vulnerability management	50

Example: Let's say we have an application that manages customer receivables, uses MFA for authentication, and access is managed centrally, but behind vulnerability patches.

$$F = (1,0,0,1)$$

$$Risk\ score = 30 * 1 + 10 * 0 + 20 * 0 + 50 * 1 = 80$$

Entitlement-Level Risk Scoring

Risk Factor	Risk Weight
If entitlement is for write access to the databases	50
If entitlement is for read access to the database	30
If entitlement is for SSH access to the servers	50

(continued)

CHAPTER 5 RISK-BASED ACCESS MANAGEMENT

Risk Factor	Risk Weight
If entitlement does go through certification for at least four times a year	40
If entitlement does not need MFA for access	100
If entitlement provides access to sensitive information	100
If entitlement provides admin access to the cloud infrastructure	100
If entitlement provides admin access to the networking security infrastructure	200

Example: An entitlement that provides networking access but does not go through certification and does not require MFA for access.

$$F = (0,0,0,1,1,0,0,1)$$

$Risk\ Score = 50 * 0 + 30 * 0 + 30 * 0 + 50 * 0 + 40 * 1 + 100 * 1 + 100 * 0 + 100 * 0 + 200 * 1 = 340$

An Entitlement is for read access to the database that requires MFA and also goes through certification four times a year.

$$F = (0,1,0,0,0,0,0,0)$$

$Risk\ score = 50 * 0 + 1 * 30 + 50 * 0 + 40 * 0 + 100 * 0 + 100 * 0 + 100 * 0 + 200 * 0 = 30$

User-Level Rules

Risk Factor	Risk Weight
If the user possesses more than 5 admin entitlements	100
If user access is not periodically reviewed	200
If the user is on the insider threat watch list	400
If the user has approved MFA bypass for the access	300
If the user has the authority to approve payment beyond a certain threshold	150

Example: User is a network admin for all firewalls and has MFA bypass.

$$F = (1,0,0,1,0)$$

$Risk\ score = 100 * 1 + 200 * 0 + 400 * 0 + 300 * 1 + 150 * 0 = 400$

Let's combine all these to come up with risk scores for individual authentication. Example:

a. A typical user is trying to write access to the database of a business-critical application that uses MFA and IGA solutions.

   $Total\ Risk\ Score = Application\ Risk\ score + Entitlement\ risk\ score + User\ risk\ score$

   $= F(1,0,0,0) + F(1,0,0,0,0,0,0,0) + F(0,0,0,0,0)$

   $= 30 + 50 + 0$

   $= 80$

b. A network administrator who is on the insider threat watchlist, trying to access sensitive customer applications that are managed by IGA and have MFA enabled.

   $Total\ Risk\ Score = Application\ Risk\ Score + Entitlement\ Risk\ Score + User\ Risk\ Score$

   $= F(1,0,0,0) + F(0,0,0,0,1,0,0,0) + F(1,0,1,1,0)$

   $= 30 + 100 + 650$

   $= 780$

Pros

1. **Simple Yet Effective:** The method is straightforward to understand and implement, leveraging subject matter expertise to guide the calculations.

2. **Numerical Precision:** By providing numerical scores, weighted risk scoring enables greater control over risk thresholds and actions triggered by specific levels of risk.

3. **Comprehensive Evaluation:** This approach combines multiple risk attributes into a unified score, ensuring that diverse factors are considered in the overall assessment.

Cons

1. **Moderate Complexity**: Although simpler than machine learning-based methods, weighted scoring is more complex to implement than rule-based approaches due to the need for precise weights and calculations.

2. **Subjectivity Remains**: Weights and thresholds are still determined by humans, leaving room for bias and debate among stakeholders about their appropriateness.

3. **Limited to Linear Relationships**: This method assumes linear relationships between variables and outputs, which may oversimplify complex risk scenarios.

4. **Regulatory Challenges**: Subjectivity in defining thresholds can make it difficult to justify risk decisions to auditors and regulators, especially when explaining why certain thresholds are deemed acceptable.

Machine Learning-Based Methods

In the methods discussed in the previous sections, we observe a common challenge: managing an overwhelming number of rules. These rules and weights are often subjective, relying heavily on the interpretations of subject matter experts. However, these experts may not be available during regulatory scrutiny, making it difficult for new team members to explain the methods. How can we address this subjectivity and the complexity of maintaining so many rules? This is where machine learning (ML) techniques come into play.

While we have a dedicated section for ML/AI applications in access management, this section provides a high-level overview of how these techniques work.

Supervised Machine Learning Methods

Organizations can leverage the expertise of their cybersecurity teams to label risk scores for existing assets. This labeled data can then be used to train machine learning models to predict risk scores based on these training datasets. Machine learning models are capable of learning generalized rules from the data, effectively encompassing the rule sets outlined in the deterministic methods discussed earlier.

There is a wide array of algorithms available for this purpose, ranging from classical approaches like logistic regression and decision trees to advanced techniques such as XGBoost and neural networks. However, as models become more complex, their explainability tends to decrease. Therefore, it is crucial to involve auditor and regulatory-facing teams during the development process to ensure the approach is well-understood and accepted.

Unsupervised Machine Learning Methods

In scenarios where labeled data is unreliable, unavailable, or expensive to generate, unsupervised machine learning methods can be employed. At a high level, these techniques identify patterns and group data into distinct communities based on similarities. For instance, machine learning models can classify datasets into three categories—high, medium, and low risk—by establishing separation boundaries between these groups.

Like supervised methods, numerous algorithms are available for unsupervised learning. Simpler clustering algorithms such as DBSCAN and K-means can be utilized, along with more advanced techniques like autoencoders and isolation forests.

Hybrid Approach

A significant drawback of weighted risk scoring approaches is the challenge of determining appropriate weights to calculate risk scores. These weights are often hard to justify, making them subject to debate. Statistical methods, combined with machine learning, offer a solution to this problem.

If labeled datasets are available from SOC (Security Operations Center) teams, insider threat teams, or publicly accessible sources, they can be used to train ML models and identify the importance of various features in prediction. These feature importance scores can then guide the determination of weights for calculating risk scores, adding a level of objectivity and reducing debate. We will discuss more details on how to use ML models to decide feature importance in future chapters.

In the long run, **machine learning (ML) approaches** are more effective and provide a scalable framework for implementing automated risk scoring. However, these approaches require labeled data, which is difficult to obtain since risk scores depend not only on inherent risk posture but also on the effectiveness of an organization's mitigation measures. If mitigations are effective, then despite risky activities, the eventual risk label should not indicate high risk. Such analysis, therefore, requires both labeled data and deeper contextual evaluation.

Risk Scoring Implementations

Before we discuss the risk scoring implementations, let's discuss how these scores can be used in access management workflows.

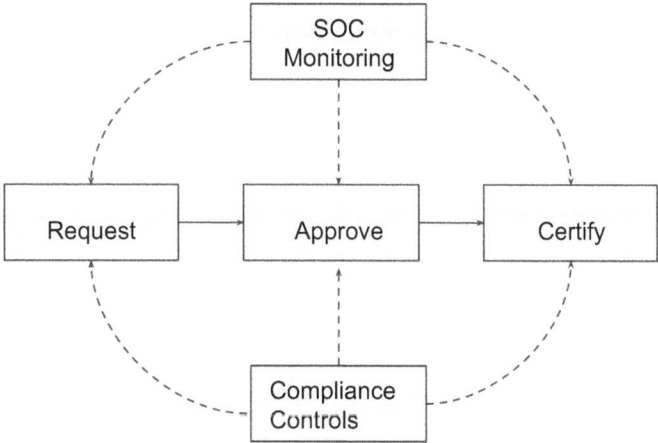

Figure 5-4. *Risk Scoring in Access Management Workflows*

The identity life cycle begins with requesting access, a process that is often handled manually. Users review the access they need based on detailed descriptions of available entitlements. Once the access request is submitted, it moves to the approval stage. Here, the access reviewer evaluates who is requesting access, what type of access is being requested, and whether it aligns with organizational policies. This approval process is also typically manual.

After access is approved, the user begins utilizing it. Periodically, organizations conduct a certification process, which is usually performed two or three times a year. During this review, access approvers assess whether the user still requires the access granted to them. Like the earlier stages, this process is manual. Throughout the life cycle, the Security Operations Center (SOC) monitors activities to ensure the workflow is proceeding as expected and to prevent issues like access creep—the accumulation of unnecessary or unauthorized permissions. Such problems can arise due to system failures or misuse.

Expectations for these processes vary across industries and regulatory frameworks. Consequently, they are governed and monitored by multiple controls to ensure compliance and security.

The Role of Risk Scores in the Identity Life Cycle

Every individual involved in the identity life cycle relies on risk scores to perform their tasks efficiently:

- **Requesters**: Need to understand the risk level associated with the access they are requesting. For example, accessing a system containing sensitive data would typically have a higher risk score.

- **Approvers**: Require insight into the risk associated with both the access being requested and the individual making the request. This information helps them make informed decisions.

- **Compliance Officers**: Need to identify when access requests or approvals deviate from established policies and assess the risk introduced by such deviations.

- **SOC Analysts**: Monitor activities at every stage of the life cycle to detect and address risky behaviors. For instance, they look for patterns like multiple authentication failures or access from high-risk locations.

Risk Scoring: Real-Time or Not?

Revisiting the identity life cycle in detail underscores the critical role of risk scoring at every stage. However, the necessity for real-time risk scoring varies depending on the specific stage. Recognizing this need has profound implications for both the design and implementation of risk scoring systems, as well as the overall system architecture.

1. **Access Request Stage**: Requestors primarily need risk scores associated with the entitlements they seek. These scores depend on factors such as

- The sensitivity of the data in the system
- The criticality of the application
- Operational risks related to managing the application

2. These parameters are generally static, meaning they change infrequently. As a result, risk scores at this stage can be calculated in advance through batch processes.

3. **Approval and Certification Stages**: Approvers and certification reviewers rely on similar static risk metrics. These scores help determine whether access requests or existing entitlements remain appropriate over time.

4. **SOC Monitoring**: The SOC's role involves a mix of static and dynamic risk scoring. While some risks can be anticipated in advance, others depend on contextual factors such as

   - The type of device being used
   - The geographic location of access
   - Patterns of authentication failures or unusual behaviors

5. These dynamic elements require real-time evaluation to adapt to changing conditions and potential threats.

Static vs. Dynamic Risk Scoring

The concept of static and dynamic risk scoring is crucial for managing user and identity risks:

- **Static Risk Scoring**: Based on fixed attributes such as data sensitivity, application criticality, and predefined roles. These scores remain stable and can be calculated ahead of time.

- **Dynamic Risk Scoring**: Incorporates real-time factors like device type, access location, and behavioral patterns. This type of scoring requires ongoing analysis to respond to evolving risks.

Identity Risk Scores

We will go a little bit deeper into how these scores are derived for identity risk scores.

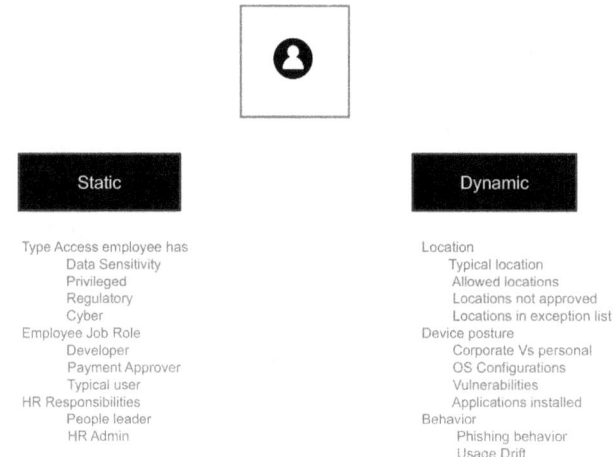

Figure 5-5. Risk Factors

Figure 5-5 depicts typical features that go into calculating risk scores for identities.

Identity Static Risk Scores

These scores are calculated based on the type of access an employee has, their job role, and core responsibilities in high-sensitivity areas such as HR management. These features are not real time in nature, and they do not change that often. Daily calculation for static scores is typically enough or event based, i.e., when something changes in employee data mentioned here is ideal. Again, the list of features I have given is not a definitive list; you can certainly add many things, but it is a good start, and typically, these datasets should be available with little engineering.

Identity Dynamic Risk Scores

Dynamic risk scores can also be called contextual risk scores, as they are calculated based on the context of access being used. These features are mostly derived from the log datasets.

Location-Specific Features: Organizations have certain policies on which geography is considered as an allowed place to use corporate application—mainly based on the locations of offices—and also allowed partner relationships in the industry based on regulators. Hence, though the vendor provides these capabilities in the MFA module, industry-specific solutions might need customization or calculation outside of vendor-based capabilities.

Device Posture Features: If an employee is at low risk and accessing a low-risk application but doing it from a personal device or corporate device that is misconfigured, then that access is actually risky. These risk scores can be calculated based on endpoint logs, or companies can rely on vendors such as CrowdStrike, Microsoft, BeyondCorp, Zscaler, Wiz, etc.

Behavior: Authorized devices and authorized users can do unauthorized activities such as downloading tons of personal information on the laptops and sharing it on the dark web or terminating all servers. These are not made-up examples; these things have happened. Monitoring activities done by users and identifying drift from their normal activities can give us risk scores as well.

System Architecture

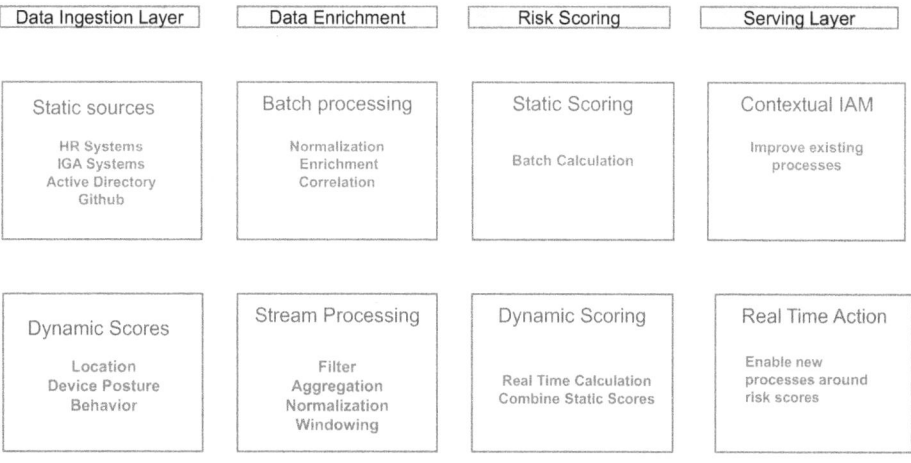

Figure 5-6. High-Level System Designs in Risk Scoring

Figure 5-6 depicts the typical architecture of risk scoring deployment. As every data product, it has four layers: ingestion, enrichment, scoring, and serving.

Data Ingestion Layer

Static risk scoring typically relies on data sources such as HR systems, IGA solutions, and other IAM platforms. These sources provide attributes that define the types of access users hold, the responsibilities they inherit, and the colleagues they collaborate with in their core duties. Because these datasets update infrequently and primarily in sporadic events, batch processing is usually sufficient for handling them.

In contrast, runtime context—such as a user's current location, the device's posture, and user behavior—changes much more frequently. Accurate, real-time awareness of these data points is critical. Log processing systems like Fluentd, Spark Streaming, and Splunk are among many solutions that can manage high-volume, continuous data flows needed for this level of dynamic analysis.

Data Enrichment

As data analysts, we understand the value of working with well-defined datasets—those with clear schemas, minimal duplicates, and attributes tailored for generating actionable insights. In the batch processing layer, our focus is on transforming these datasets to make them more meaningful and easier to analyze. This often includes standardizing timestamps into consistent formats and enriching logs with additional metadata, typically sourced from a Configuration Management Database (CMDB). For example, we might tag a server with the name of the application it supports or identify the engineering team responsible for its maintenance. These enhancements ensure that our data is reliable and comprehensive for downstream analytics.

When we turn to stream processing, many of the same transformations are applied. However, stream processing introduces two critical capabilities: aggregations and windowing. These allow us to process continuous data flows in near-real-time, grouping events and generating insights on the fly—without waiting for the completion of a batch cycle.

Unlike batch data, which operates on a finite and complete dataset, stream processing handles continuous flows of data, requiring incremental updates to keep insights current. Aggregations—such as counts, minimums, maximums, and averages—help us create features essential for subsequent processes, like risk scoring.

For instance, consider user authentication logs. In a batch processing scenario, we might look at historical trends to analyze login failures. However, in stream processing, we monitor authentication failures in real time. The number of failed login attempts within a specific time interval can serve as a key feature to identify whether a user is probing for unauthorized access or attempting lateral movement with elevated privileges. This ability to process and act on data in real time adds a critical layer of responsiveness.

In stream processing, window functions make incremental calculations possible. These functions impose boundaries on the continuous stream of incoming events, grouping them into finite segments based on time intervals, event counts, or user sessions. This segmentation allows us to aggregate and analyze data efficiently.

For example, detecting multiple logins from different devices within a short time frame is often an indicator of suspicious behavior. By using window functions, we can group these login events into specific time frames, calculate aggregated metrics (like the number of unique devices used), and flag them as inputs for machine learning models or threshold-based alerts. This ability to monitor and act on patterns in real time enhances the security and reliability of the system.

Risk Scoring Engine

Like the other layers, risk scoring also comprises two modules: static and dynamic. In most implementations, the static module follows a rule-based approach, with weights derived using advanced statistical techniques. Because the features used in static calculations are well understood, and their importance is relatively clear, insights from subject matter experts—combined with methods like the Analytic Hierarchy Process (AHP) or classical machine learning algorithms—can be applied to determine appropriate weights for these rules.

In contrast, the dynamic module is more involved and requires careful design thinking. These algorithms typically rely on machine learning approaches—such as Isolation Forest or Random Forest-based methods—to detect baselines of normal behavior and identify deviations or drift over time. In the following chapters, we will explore the practical steps involved in implementing these algorithms.

Serving Layer

As discussed in the previous section, static risk scores often play a supportive role in enhancing identity life cycle (IL) procedures. For instance, when an approver is reviewing an access certification, it can be immensely helpful to see a static risk score that reflects how critical or sensitive the access might be. Similarly, a compliance specialist investigating control failures can use these risk indicators to determine the severity level of potential findings.

In contrast, dynamic risk scores are more action-oriented and often feed directly into operational workflows. These scores can be exposed through APIs for Zero Trust platforms, where they may be used during the authentication phase to automatically approve or deny requests based on identified anomalies. Similarly, these real-time risk signals can be integrated into SIEM systems, enabling Security Operations Center (SOC) teams to prioritize and investigate threats more effectively.

Another emerging pattern involves using detected risk "drifts" as triggers to launch targeted certifications for the specific access or behavior in question. If a manager or asset owner cannot verify that a user's access patterns are appropriate, the system can raise an alert for further SOC investigation. This agile approach allows organizations to respond quickly to evolving risks, maintaining a tighter handle on both user activity and potential threats.

Summary

- Risk scoring is crucial for prioritizing security actions. It can be qualitative (e.g., High/Medium/Low) or quantitative (numerical scores) and extends to applications, entitlements, and individual users.

- Effective risk scoring is applied at multiple levels—application, IGA-managed entitlements, and user—enabling finer control and context-specific monitoring.

- Scoring Methods

    - **Rule-Based:** Simple to implement but becomes unwieldy as access needs grow

    - **Weighted Scoring:** Offers more granularity by assigning weights to different risk factors

    - **Machine Learning-Based:** Reduces reliance on large sets of subjective rules by using algorithms to learn from labeled data or detect anomalies in unlabeled data

- **Static vs. Dynamic Scoring**: Static scoring focuses on stable attributes (e.g., application criticality, assigned entitlements), while dynamic scoring leverages real-time data (e.g., user behavior, device posture) for continuous risk evaluation.

- Risk scores feed into identity life cycle processes (request, approval, certification) and SOC monitoring, enabling automated decisions and targeted certifications when unusual activity is detected.

References

1. Josh Nadeau. "83% of Organizations Reported Insider Attacks in 2024." https://www.ibm.com/think/insights/83-percent-organizations-reported-insider-threats-2024

2. NIST. "NIST Cyber Risk Scoring (CRS)." https://csrc.nist.gov/CSRC/media/Presentations/nist-cyber-risk-scoring-crs-program-overview/images-media/NIST%20Cyber%20Risk%20Scoring%20(CRS)%20-%20Program%20Overview.pdf

3. Douglas Hubbard and Richard Seiersen. *How to Measure Anything in Cybersecurity Risk.*

4. Brian Allen, Brandon Bapst, and Terry Hicks. *Building a Cyber Risk Management Program.*

5. Homan Farahmand. "IAM Risk-Based Planning Model and Toolkit for Reducing Operational Risk."

6. Mariano Mattei. *Data-Driven Cybersecurity.*

7. Charles Pfleeger. *Security in Computing, 6th Edition.*

CHAPTER 6

Identity Threat Detection and Response

Digital transformation is a broad term, encompassing initiatives such as cloud transformation, data modernization, process automation, and customer experience enhancements. Organizations leading this change not only survived the pandemic but also significantly expanded their customer base, capitalizing on the rapid shift to digital due to COVID-related disruptions.

However, this digital growth has led to an exponential rise in the number of digital identities. In 2024 alone, 80% of cyberattacks leveraged identity-based attack methods, drastically increasing the blast radius for such organizations.

Despite the high prevalence of identity-based threats, it still takes, on average, 192 days to detect and 64 days to contain these attacks. Why does it take so long? Because most organizations still rely heavily on tools like Security Incident and Event Management (SIEM), Network Detection and Response (NDR), Intrusion Detection and Prevention Systems (IDS/IDP), and Endpoint Detection and Response (EDR) for detection and mitigation. While these tools are effective for monitoring networks and endpoints, they often fall short when it comes to identity-focused threats.

As a result, Identity Threat Detection and Response (ITDR) has gained significant traction—drawing attention from both academic researchers and cybersecurity vendors—as a critical capability in the modern security stack. A question I often hear is, *"Is ITDR just an extension of SIEM?"* or *"Why can't SIEM do what ITDR does?"* These are valid questions—and to address them properly, it's important to first understand what SIEM is designed to do and then explore where it falls short in the identity threat landscape. Only then does the need for ITDR become truly clear.

SIEM: Core Concepts

SIEM aggregates logs from a wide range of data sources—including network devices, endpoints, load balancers, and applications. These logs are correlated to identify suspicious activities and potential security incidents. SIEM enables holistic threat detection across an organization's infrastructure and supports long-term forensic analysis. At its core, SIEM relies on two key components: log ingestion pipelines and correlation engines that analyze patterns and anomalies in real time.

Over the last decade, with advances in computing power and data processing, SIEM has evolved beyond its original role as a log aggregator. Modern SIEMs can now ingest and analyze a much broader variety of log types, allowing them to deliver richer insights and more sophisticated threat detection capabilities. This evolution has led to the integration of additional components into the SIEM ecosystem:

- **Endpoint Detection and Response (EDR)**: This focuses on endpoint assets such as laptops, mobile phones, IoT devices, and servers. Typically, agents are deployed on these devices to collect telemetry data on file activity, memory usage, user sessions, and system behavior. This information is used to identify endpoints exhibiting suspicious activity—such as ransomware infections or the presence of unauthorized software.

- **Network Detection and Response (NDR)**: NDR emphasizes monitoring network traffic through logs from load balancers, virtual private clouds (VPCs), firewalls, and web application firewalls (WAFs). These network logs are inspected and correlated to detect signs of attack, such as unauthorized access attempts or data exfiltration. In many cases, packet inspection is used to identify known malicious signatures or anomalous traffic patterns.

While these capabilities have significantly extended the reach of SIEM, it's important to note that they are still largely asset-centric—designed to protect infrastructure components like endpoints and network devices. These tools excel within their domains, but they struggle when it comes to identity-focused threats.

Identity-based attacks require a different approach. Unlike endpoints or networks, where signatures of malicious activity are well-studied and relatively consistent, identity usage patterns are highly contextual. What is considered "normal" access or behavior can vary dramatically between organizations or even between individuals in the same role. For example, two employees at different pharmaceutical companies may both hold the title of "wire payment approver" in SAP systems yet have entirely different privileges and access paths based on internal policies and configurations. This variability makes identity threats harder to detect using traditional SIEM-based methods.

ITDR: Core Concepts

Identity Threat Detection and Response (ITDR) is a security discipline focused on protecting user and machine identities, as well as the systems that manage them—such as Active Directory (AD), Identity Governance and Administration (IGA), and secrets management platforms.

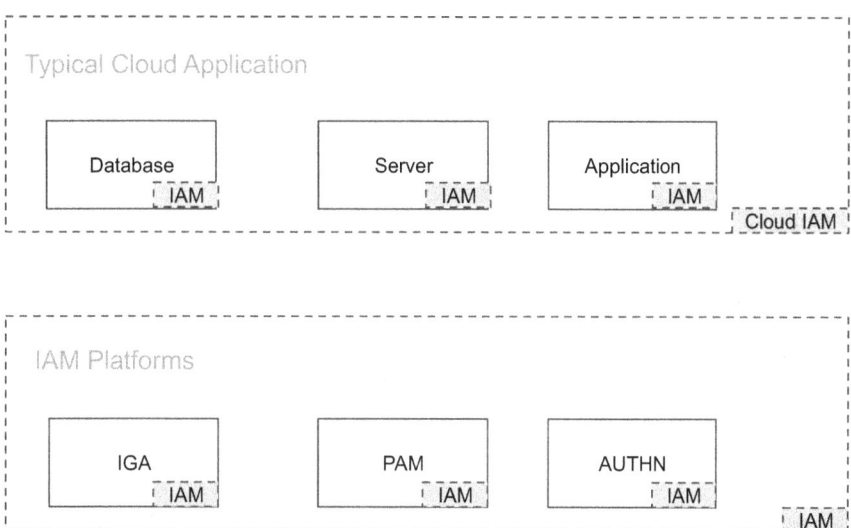

Figure 6-1. *IAM Systems*

We've said a lot in the previous statement, and there's a lot to unpack. Identities are everywhere—refer to Figure 6-1. Modern applications are typically developed in the cloud, using a combination of infrastructure services such as databases, servers, and application layers. Some of these components may be cloud-native or even serverless. Each asset comes with its own identity and access management (IAM) framework, including roles, user inventories, permission models, and logs tied to user activity.

Today, with identity recognized as the new perimeter, organizations are increasingly investing in centralized IAM platforms. These platforms manage access across the environment and include technologies such as

- IGA (Identity Governance and Administration) for managing identity access and conducting access reviews
- PAM (Privileged Access Management) for securing privileged accounts
- AUTHN (authentication solutions) for implementing multifactor authentication (MFA), single sign-on (SSO), and integrations with directories like Active Directory

Each of these platforms has its own access modules and control mechanisms. The roles associated with them are typically highly sensitive, as access to these platforms often translates to access to everything they govern.

This is where Identity Threat Detection and Response (ITDR) comes into focus. The goal of ITDR is to protect identities—not only by securing access to applications and infrastructure but also by safeguarding the access mechanisms within these centralized platforms themselves.

Unlike traditional security monitoring—often handled through SIEMs that focus on infrastructure events—ITDR begins with access. ITDR solutions continuously monitor access-related events such as logins, lockouts, user activity, and access drift across applications and platforms. They establish behavioral baselines and enable detection of suspicious or anomalous activity.

ITDR Implementation Outcomes

Enhanced Security Posture: By focusing on identity threats, organizations can better defend against some of the most common attack vectors. ITDR tools enable quick, in-depth analysis of complex relationships between identities and resources, reducing the attack surface in a meaningful way. They also provide visibility into connectivity between IAM platforms and native application permissions, making it easier to detect access drift.

Improved Incident Response: These mechanisms provide visibility into potential lateral movements, distinguishing between legitimate use cases and scenarios where such movement should not be permitted. By maintaining direct connectivity with

IAM platforms, ITDR tools enable not only the detection of suspicious behaviors but also rapid remediation. This integration significantly reduces risk mitigation SLAs, transforming response times in a material way.

Compliance Support: Compliance frameworks expect IAM programs to enforce the principle of least privilege. ITDR strengthens this mandate by operationalizing preventive and detective controls with full auditability, ensuring that compliance requirements are not treated as a checkbox exercise. In doing so, ITDR platforms transform compliance from a static obligation into a dynamic mechanism for reducing real cyber risk.

ITDR and SIEM Integration

Although ITDR can be deployed as a standalone capability, this does not diminish the importance of SIEM. In fact, integrating the two creates a more comprehensive, end-to-end view of identity-related events. For example, a SIEM might detect that a cloud asset has been exposed to the public internet, leading to a potential data compromise. With ITDR in place, the investigation gains additional depth—shedding light on how the incident unfolded, including which permissions were modified, who made the changes, and when they occurred. This integrated perspective enables security teams to reconstruct the full life cycle of an incident. Beyond faster remediation, such insights contribute to organizational knowledge that helps prevent similar events in the future.

Security Orchestration, Automation, and Response (SOAR) platforms further enhance this ecosystem by automating and orchestrating security operations. They aggregate alerts from SIEM, EDR, NDR, and ITDR systems while also automating responses such as blocking malicious IP addresses or disabling accounts involved in suspicious activity. In addition, SOAR provides visualization and investigation capabilities, allowing analysts to triage alerts efficiently and reducing the reliance on time-consuming manual coordination.

ITDR and UEBA

Gartner defines ITDR as a security discipline that encompasses threat intelligence, best practices, knowledge bases, tools, and processes to protect identity systems. ITDR operates by implementing detection mechanisms, investigating suspicious posture changes and activities, and responding to attacks in order to restore the integrity of the identity infrastructure.

User and Entity Behavior Analytics (UEBA), on the other hand, leverages machine learning and advanced analytics to establish behavioral baselines for identities, detecting threats by monitoring access drift, misuse, or other suspicious activity.

In essence, UEBA is one of the mechanisms within the broader ITDR suite. It serves as the detection engine inside the ITDR toolkit, providing essential behavior monitoring capabilities.

Solution Design for ITDR

At a high level, ITDR functions as a log processing system that correlates events with identities and detects deviations from normal behavior. While there are numerous whitepapers and vendor publications outlining ITDR capabilities and the types of signals they generate, few delve into implementation specifics. This is largely because such details are difficult to generalize—the design of ITDR solutions often depends heavily on a company's specific architectural patterns. As a result, out-of-the-box ITDR signals from vendors are frequently imprecise. Without a clear understanding of an organization's unique permission boundaries, these tools tend to produce a significant number of false alerts.

To provide a more actionable perspective, I've chosen to frame the solution around MITRE ATT&CK tactics, techniques, and procedures—commonly referred to as TTPs. MITRE ATT&CK is a widely adopted, community-driven knowledge base of real-world adversary behaviors, categorized into tactics (the *why*), techniques (the *how*), and procedures (the *specific ways* a technique is carried out). These TTPs offer a structured way to think about threats and align defensive strategies accordingly.

In the context of identity threats, certain TTPs are both highly prevalent and particularly high-risk. For each, I'll outline the types of signals we should aim to detect, as well as the log sources required to support that detection. This approach is intended to give you a practical foundation for designing and implementing ITDR capabilities in your own environment.

Credential Access via Password Spraying/Phishing

One of the most common identity-based attack vectors involves adversaries using password spraying or phishing techniques to gain unauthorized access. In these scenarios, attackers either launch broad phishing campaigns or attempt to log in using previously leaked or commonly used credentials. Once valid credentials are obtained, attackers typically attempt to access cloud platforms and installed applications, often blending in with legitimate user behavior.

Detection Methods

Detection hinges on identifying anomalies in authentication behavior. This includes

- Login attempts from unusual IP addresses or unexpected geographical locations
- Access attempts during abnormal hours or outside typical login patterns
- First-time authentications from previously unseen devices
- Repeated failed login attempts across multiple accounts (indicative of spraying)

Logs Needed

To detect such behavior effectively, it's important to gather

- **Login activity logs** from identity providers (IdPs), including timestamps and outcomes.
- **Device metadata** associated with successful and failed logins.
- **Geolocation data** for each login attempt
- **MFA logs**, if multifactor authentication is in use, are often provided by the same IdP or a dedicated MFA service.
- **Cloud platform logs**, which often include fine-grained authentication details that help track access patterns across services.

Remediation and Response

Once credential misuse is identified, immediate steps include

- **Resetting compromised credentials** and enforcing password policies

- **Revoking session tokens** to log out the attacker
- **Step-up authentication** to re-authentication with additional attributes.
- **Blocking suspicious IPs** or implementing geo-fencing rules

Lateral Movement

After gaining initial access, an attacker often attempts to move laterally within the environment to discover and access other systems. For example, after compromising a server in the cloud, they may explore adjacent systems to which that server is connected—extending their reach and potentially elevating privileges.

Detection Method

To move laterally, attackers typically need to perform reconnaissance—also known as *footprinting*—to understand which assets are available and accessible from the compromised host. Suspicious API calls during this phase can be strong indicators of lateral movement. In cloud environments like AWS, for instance, if an EC2 instance suddenly starts invoking APIs such as DescribeInstances or GetList*, it may signal an attempt to map the environment—behavior not typically expected from standard workloads.

Logs Needed

To detect lateral movement, it's important to monitor

- **Network traffic patterns**, especially new or unexpected connections between systems
- **Cloud API calls** that enumerate resources (e.g., discovery of instances, subnets, or services)
- **Application and infrastructure logs** from cloud components such as VPC flow logs, load balancer access logs, and platform-specific logs (e.g., AWS CloudTrail)

These logs help identify unusual communication paths and behavior originating from compromised systems.

Remediation and Response

Once lateral movement is suspected or confirmed:

- **Isolate the compromised instance** or workload at the network level (e.g., security group or firewall rules).

- **Review and revoke temporary credentials** or roles assumed by the attacker.

- **Harden API access permissions** to follow the principle of least privilege and prevent excessive discovery capabilities.

Data Exfiltration

Data exfiltration occurs when attackers extract sensitive information from databases, cloud storage, or SaaS applications. This often follows unauthorized access gained through misconfigurations, compromised credentials, or overly permissive access controls. A common example is a misconfigured S3 bucket, which may unintentionally expose sensitive data to the public or unauthorized internal users.

Detection Methods

Key indicators of potential data exfiltration include

- **Unusually large volumes of data reads**

- **Frequent access denials**, suggesting probing or unauthorized access attempts

- **High-volume API calls**, especially in SaaS environments where data is typically accessed via vendor-provided APIs

Monitoring these patterns over time can help differentiate between legitimate usage and malicious behavior.

Logs Needed

To detect and investigate potential data exfiltration, the following log sources are essential:

- **Cloud event logs** (e.g., AWS CloudTrail, GCP Audit Logs, Azure Monitor) for access to cloud storage services.

- **Data platform logs** from services like Snowflake, Databricks, and Redshift, capturing read/query events.

- **API logs** from SaaS applications, ideally including request metadata such as payload size and frequency. If API logs provide data volume metrics, this greatly enhances visibility into abnormal data transfer activity.

Remediation and Response

When data exfiltration is suspected:

- **Immediately revoke access** for the compromised identity or application.

- **Restrict access policies** at the storage or database layer (e.g., S3 bucket policies, IAM roles).

- **Enable data loss prevention (DLP) controls** where available to block or monitor future transfer attempts.

Active Directory(AD)

While Active Directory itself is not a TTP, it remains one of the most critical identity infrastructure components—and, therefore, a high-value target for attackers. As the backbone of identity and access management in nearly 90% of organizations, compromising AD can lead to broad, organization-wide damage.

Common attack methods include password spraying, account lockout abuse, and privilege escalation. If attackers gain access to AD administrative accounts, the potential for disruption and data loss becomes immense.

Detection Methods

Indicators of suspicious or malicious activity within Active Directory include

- **Unusual login patterns** or logins from unfamiliar hosts or locations
- **Frequent account lockouts**, often a result of password spraying
- **Unexpected Windows Event Logs**, particularly those associated with authentication or system configuration changes
- **Tampering attempts on the domain controller logs**
- **Unscheduled changes to AD group attributes or memberships**

These behaviors often precede or accompany attempts to gain elevated privileges or disrupt identity services.

Logs Needed

Effective monitoring of AD-related threats requires

- **Domain controller logs**, which capture core AD authentication and administrative events
- **Windows Event Logs** from all servers where AD services are configured
- **Audit logs of AD group changes**, user creations, and privilege escalations
- **Outputs from AD monitoring tools**, such as native Windows auditing or third-party security solutions—these should be integrated into the ITDR pipeline for correlation and enrichment

Remediation and Response

In the event of suspicious AD activity:

- **Investigate account lockouts** to differentiate between user error and credential-based attacks.
- **Temporarily disable or isolate suspicious accounts**, especially those with administrative privileges.
- **Apply stricter login controls** for AD admin privileges.

CHAPTER 6 IDENTITY THREAT DETECTION AND RESPONSE

System Architecture

Now, based on the above discussion, we can understand what types of logs are needed, the system design we need to deploy, and also the mechanisms required to implement remediation and response. Figure 6-2 demonstrates the high-level architecture.

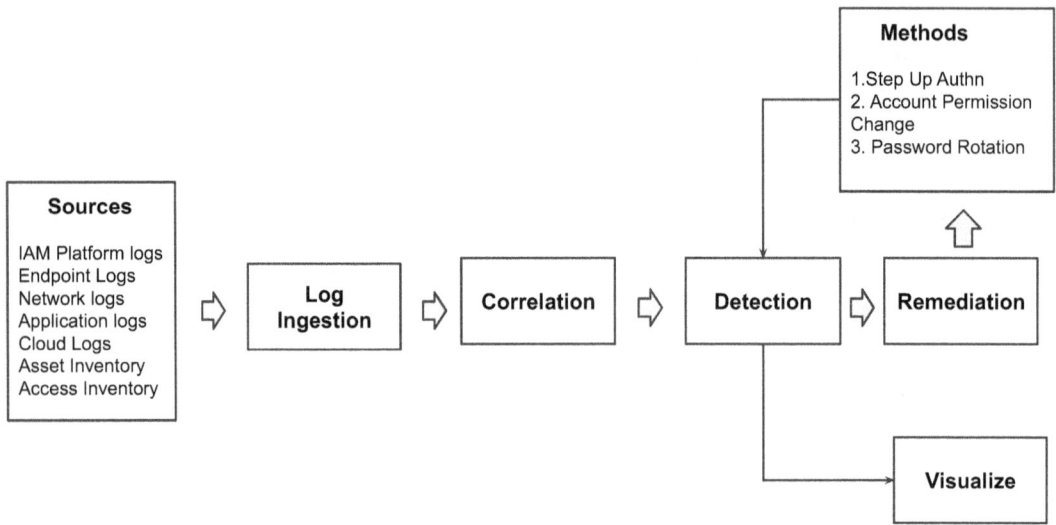

Figure 6-2. High-Level System Architecture

Log Ingestion

To build an effective Identity Threat Detection and Response (ITDR) system, four primary categories of logs are essential. Each plays a distinct role in surfacing identity-related threats, and the completeness of your ITDR capability often depends on how well you collect and process these logs.

Cloud Service and Data Logs

These logs capture **API activity across cloud environments**—such as cloud storage access, infrastructure provisioning, and permission changes. In most organizations, these logs are already being ingested into a SIEM platform. ITDR teams can **leverage existing pipelines**, reducing the need for additional infrastructure and minimizing costs.

IAM Platform Logs

These are critical for understanding how identities interact with the access management layer and are often underutilized in traditional security monitoring.

- **User Logs**: Capture activities like access requests, authentication attempts, admin changes, policy updates in identity governance systems, and secret read/write events. In essence, these reflect how users engage with centralized access platforms.

    These logs are often not integrated into SIEM, as they fall outside the typical security operations focus. ITDR teams will likely need to build custom pipelines to ingest and process them.

- **Administrative Logs**: Generated by developers or admins managing IAM platforms. These logs can include high-risk actions, such as

    - Creating new IGA instances
    - Applying access policies across identities
    - Bypassing MFA for select users

    These logs are highly sensitive and crucial for ITDR. Like user logs, they are often not available in SIEM by default, and identity teams must take ownership of contextual enrichment and ingestion.

Endpoint Logs

These logs provide visibility into user activities at the endpoint level, including

- File access and permission changes
- Execution of administrative commands
- Actions not visible from the IAM layer, such as local role modifications

These logs are often already part of mature SIEM pipelines, especially for organizations with EDR or Sysmon in place. ITDR can leverage these existing streams to enhance visibility and correlate identity activity with endpoint behavior.

Application Access Audit Logs

These logs capture **how users interact directly with applications**—such as accessing sensitive records or executing privileged operations. Unfortunately, this category is the most fragmented:

- Logging formats vary widely across applications.
- No industry-standard exists for how these logs should be structured.

As a result, custom log processing pipelines are often required for each application. SIEM platforms may already ingest some of this data, but in most cases, ITDR teams will need to collaborate closely with the SIEM team to assess existing coverage and enhance it with enrichments tailored for identity analytics.

Correlation

To establish a baseline of normal behavior and effectively detect identity threats, ITDR systems must correlate logs across several key dimensions:

- **Identity**: Activities performed by user or machine accounts
- **Host**: Events occurring at the machine or device level
- **Application**: The applications the host or user is interacting with
- **Entitlements**: Permissions exercised to perform actions on hosts or within applications

Among these, **entitlement-level data** is the most challenging to collect. Only a small number of SaaS applications offer detailed logging at the entitlement level, and most custom-built or legacy applications tend to provide limited visibility into user actions. Despite this, incorporating whatever entitlement data is available significantly improves threat detection accuracy.

Detection

Detection strategies in ITDR should be both **scalable** and **adaptive**, beginning with rule-based approaches and gradually evolving toward machine learning–driven anomaly detection.

Rule-Based Detection
As a starting point, implement simple rules to define expected behaviors and identify deviations. While effective in establishing a baseline, this method often results in false positives. These should be continuously tuned, prioritized by risk, and refined using feedback from security analysts.

Anomaly-Based Detection (Machine Learning)
Once analysts begin labeling alerts from rule-based detections as true or false positives, this feedback becomes **training data** for more advanced machine learning models. These models can then identify subtle anomalies that static rules may miss.

If labeled data is not available, **unsupervised learning methods** can be used to detect outliers. We will explore these techniques in more detail in later chapters.

Respond and Remediate

Detection is only the beginning—**effective response and containment** are what make ITDR truly valuable. According to IBM's *Cost of a Data Breach* report, identity-related attacks take the longest time to contain among all types of security incidents.

Once a compromised identity is detected, the next step is to

1. **Identify affected applications.**
2. **Determine how access is provisioned.**
3. **Take containment actions quickly and precisely.**

Some recommended automated response strategies include

- **Step-Up Authentication**

    Trigger an additional authentication challenge to verify that the activity is authorized. In some cases, a manager approval step can add an extra layer of verification.

- **Session Termination**

    Coordinate with the authentication team (or identity provider) to forcibly end active sessions. Most IdPs provide APIs for this purpose.

    Due to potential operational impact, session termination should be reserved for high-confidence signals, ideally based on deterministic rules or well-trained models.

Visualize

To make ITDR effective, teams must have **clear visibility into access patterns, entitlements, and the relationships between identities and assets.**

Key Considerations

- ITDR should integrate with **CMDBs and entitlement sources** to contextualize access and asset relationships.

- Because identity access relationships often span **multiple layers** (e.g., user ➤ group ➤ role ➤ application), building **access graphs** can be a powerful method to visualize and understand these complex connections.

Visualization plays a critical role not only in investigation and forensics but also in helping security teams design more effective access control and response policies.

Summary

- **Identity Is the New Perimeter:** As digital transformation expands the number of user and machine identities, identity has become the primary target for attackers. Traditional tools like SIEM, EDR, and NDR struggle to detect identity-based threats, highlighting the need for a dedicated ITDR layer.

- **ITDR Complements and Extends SIEM:** While SIEM offers macro-level visibility and log correlation across infrastructure, ITDR adds identity-specific behavioral analysis—tracking access patterns, credential use, and permission drift across applications and platforms.

- **TTP-Based Detection Framework:** Effective ITDR design focuses on real-world adversary behaviors using MITRE ATT&CK TTPs such as credential access, lateral movement, and data exfiltration. These tactics are detected using identity-aware logs, cloud events, API calls, and authentication metadata.

- **Architecting ITDR Requires Specialized Logs and Correlation:** ITDR systems must integrate cloud service logs, IAM platform logs, endpoint telemetry, and application audit logs. Correlation across identity, host, application, and entitlement dimensions is key to establishing baselines and detecting anomalies.

- **Response, Remediation, and Visualization Are Essential:** Detection alone is insufficient. ITDR systems must support rapid response actions like session termination, step-up authentication, and access revocation. Visualizing access relationships and entitlements helps security teams respond decisively and plan proactively.

References

1. Henrique Teixeira, Peter Firstbrook, and others. Gartner. "Enhance Your Cyberattack Preparedness with Identity Threat Detection and Response."

2. Rebecca Archambault, Felix Gaehtgens, and others. "Identity-First Security Maximizes Cybersecurity Effectiveness."

3. Mark Dunkerley. *Resilient Cybersecurity*.

4. Morey J. Haber and Darran Rolls. *Identity Attack Vectors: Strategically Designing and Implementing Identity Security, Second Edition*.

5. Yuri Diogenes and Dr. Erdal Ozkaya. *Cybersecurity - Attack and Defense Strategies, Third Edition*

CHAPTER 7

Analytics for Cloud Access Management

Most chapters in this book start by highlighting the importance of a particular topic and the growing threat landscape that demands immediate attention from identity analytics and IAM leaders. For this chapter, however, let's take a different approach—one grounded in a real-world event that drew significant industry attention: Google's acquisition of Wiz.

In 2023, Google initially attempted to acquire Wiz for $23 billion. That deal fell through due to pricing disagreements, but eventually, both companies reached a mutual agreement—at a much higher price point of $32 billion, nearly 40% more than the original offer. Why did Google—a company with its own robust security suite—value a relatively new player in the cloud security space so highly?

Google justified the move by emphasizing Wiz's unique value proposition. As they put it, *"Wiz is different from the services we offer today—it delivers a seamless cloud security platform that connects to all major clouds and code environments to help prevent incidents from happening in the first place."*

Wiz is part of a growing class of tools known as Cloud-Native Application Protection Platforms **(CNAPP)**. According to industry projections, the global CNAPP market is expected to grow at a compound annual growth rate of over 25% between 2023 and 2028, with 40% of enterprises already adopting such platforms[1]. Despite the native security offerings of cloud providers, there is tremendous investment in third-party CNAPPs, driven by two key factors:

1. **Multicloud and Hybrid Ecosystems**: Modern enterprises rarely operate in a single cloud. Many run core application workloads in AWS, while leveraging Azure or GCP for AI/ML workloads due to their strengths in foundational models. Sensitive workloads may even remain on-premises. In this fragmented world, a unified view across environments is not just helpful—it's essential.

2. **Cross-Cloud Threat Detection**: Cloud-native security services are often built to detect threats within their own ecosystems. But when threats span multiple clouds or bridge into on-prem environments, native tools fall short. CNAPPs fill this visibility gap by stitching together context across disparate platforms.

This leads us to an important question: If CNAPPs can provide such visibility and protection, why is there still a need to discuss cloud access analytics in this book?

It's a fair question. But the reality is that CNAPPs, while powerful, are not a silver bullet. They generate hundreds of alerts—many of which are false positives—not due to flawed design, but because they often lack contextual understanding of enterprise-specific access patterns. For example, what might appear as an overly permissive role could, in practice, be tightly controlled through layered approvals, device restrictions, or limited session scopes. Without recognizing these compensating controls, CNAPPs can trigger misleading alerts.

Another limitation is in regulatory reporting. When asked, *"Who has access to customer-sensitive information?"*, a CNAPP might produce a list of roles and system identities. But regulators often expect to know the actual individuals behind those roles. That requires understanding secondary access patterns, such as federated identities or jump hosts that bridge into cloud environments.

Let's explore two simple but telling examples:

- **CNAPP Alert**: "Critical Violation—Role is overly permissive."

    In reality, that role may be accessible only to a small group of engineers, through a multi-approval process, and only from trusted devices—designed for fast yet controlled response to production incidents.

- **Compliance Inquiry**: "Who has access to customer-sensitive data?"

    CNAPPs may list IAM roles, but without mapping those roles to actual employees—especially across federated access paths—the answer is incomplete.

These examples reflect broader limitations that many CNAPPs face, particularly in answering nuanced, organization-specific questions about access risk and compliance. Risk scoring was discussed in detail in Chapter 5. That's where identity-driven cloud access analytics comes in.

CHAPTER 7 ANALYTICS FOR CLOUD ACCESS MANAGEMENT

This chapter will explore analytics approaches that complement CNAPPs—filling critical visibility gaps and enabling deeper, risk-aware access intelligence. Whether or not your organization uses a CNAPP today, the insights here will help you build stronger foundations for access governance in a multicloud world.

Cloud Access Management

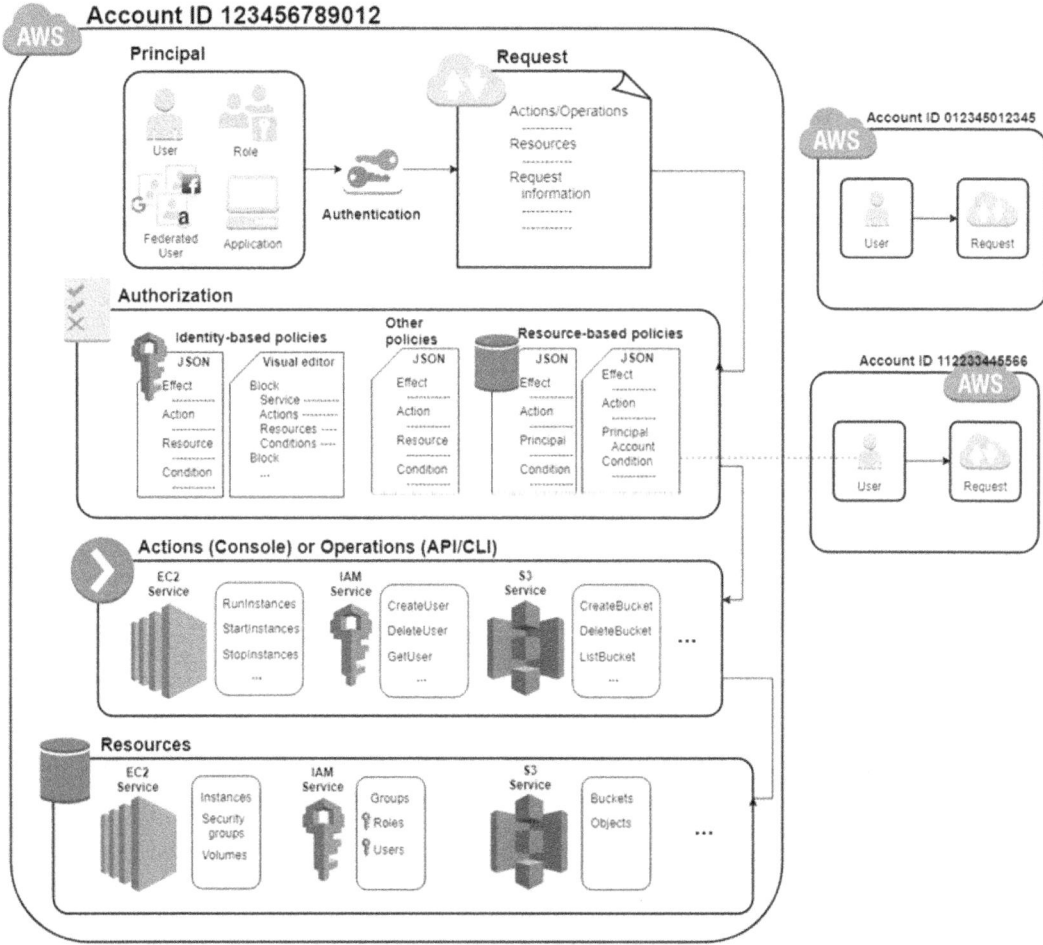

Source: AWS IAM Developer Document

The image above is from the AWS IAM Developer Guide. It illustrates how an access request is processed through authentication and authorization checks before determining whether an identity is granted access to specific resources.

135

Cloud platforms enable fine-grained access control. Access is defined through policies, which are then associated with roles. Policies can also incorporate conditions and tags, enabling Attribute-Based Access Control (ABAC). If an organization uses federated identities, obtaining a complete picture of access requires correlating data from the federated access system with cloud IAM roles and users.

This is not a comprehensive cloud access management book, so I will cover these concepts at a high level. However, it is important for readers to understand the following points:

- With cloud adoption, legacy IGA systems cannot determine who has access to what in the cloud without complete access transparency.

- Similar to IGA and application roles, cloud platforms define their own roles, which are collections of permissions. Unlike traditional IGA systems, where permissions are often coarse-grained (e.g., group memberships), cloud providers encode permissions in JSON objects that must be parsed to understand them.

- As with PAM systems, cloud environments also have privileged access, and providers offer mechanisms such as just-in-time (JIT) access and segregation of duties (SOD) to manage and control these elevated permissions.

As a result, answering access-related questions is no longer straightforward. Looking only at IGA data does not reveal what users can actually do in the cloud. Conversely, examining only cloud data—or even using tools like CNAPP—does not definitively identify which users can assume certain roles and permissions.

This is the gap that this chapter addresses. We will explore how one can design and build a system from scratch to bridge these challenges and provide true visibility into cloud access.

Data Foundation

Before diving into advanced analytics or detection strategies, we must first establish the foundational data models that support both reporting on security posture and detection of policy violations or potential threats. This section will define the core building blocks required to make sense of access patterns in cloud environments.

We'll structure this foundation around three fundamental questions that form the backbone of identity analytics:

1. Who has access to cloud assets?
2. What are those assets?
3. How are those assets being used?

By methodically answering these questions, we can develop a consistent, extensible model for access visibility. This model will not only support compliance reporting and posture management but also act as a critical input to threat detection and incident response workflows.

Each of these questions may seem straightforward on the surface, but in a cloud environment—especially across multiple providers and identity sources—the answers are far from trivial. As we work through this section, we'll explore how identity data, asset inventories, and activity telemetry can be connected to establish a comprehensive and actionable view of cloud access.

Answering Who?

The foundational question in cloud access analytics is deceptively simple: Who has access to what? But in modern cloud environments—especially in multicloud settings—this question is layered, nuanced, and often misunderstood. The complexity arises not just from the number of identities, but from how identity and access are implemented differently across AWS, GCP, and Azure.

Identity Classes in the Cloud

To answer "Who?", we start by classifying identities into three broad categories:

1. **Human Users**

    These are real people—employees, contractors, third parties—usually authenticated through an identity provider (IdP) like Azure AD, Okta, or Google Workspace. These identities typically access cloud resources through SSO or federation into IAM roles.

2. **Machine and Service Identities**

   These are system accounts commonly found in cloud environments, typically used to run scheduled batch jobs or support machine-to-machine orchestration. These identities often take the form of service accounts on EC2 instances or within Kubernetes clusters. They usually inherit the permissions assigned to the underlying compute resource on which they are created, granting them access based on the host's role or policies.

3. **Federated and Indirect Identities**

   These include external identities accessing resources via cross-account roles, federated trust relationships, or jump mechanisms like bastion hosts or service meshes.

Considering AWS is still the largest cloud provider, let's take AWS as an example to understand these identities in more detail.

In Figure 7-1, various user access patterns in a cloud environment are illustrated. To keep the focus on identities, the diagram intentionally omits broader policy types such as Service Control Policies (SCPs), resource-based policies, and Access Control Lists (ACLs). The emphasis here is on how identities interact with AWS resources.

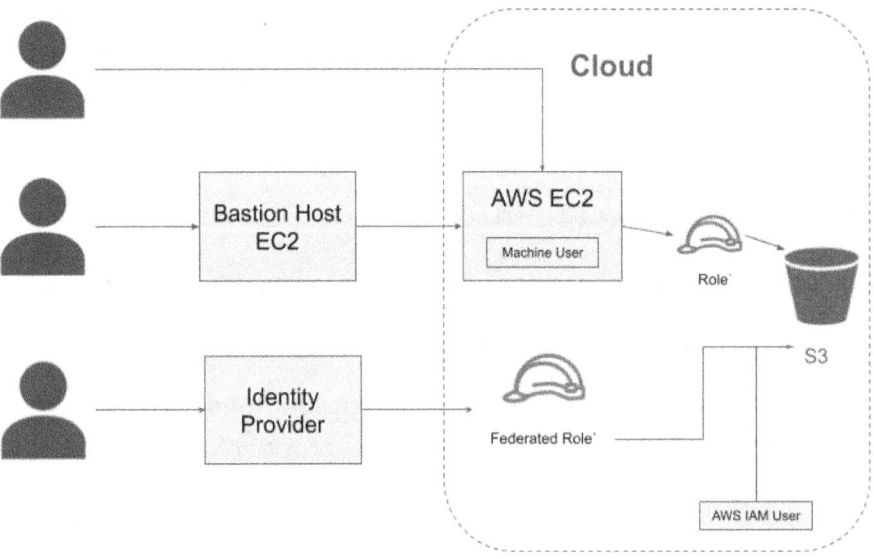

Figure 7-1. Cloud Access Patterns

One common access method is through federated login. A user can authenticate via an identity provider—such as Active Directory, Okta, or any other SAML/OIDC-compatible identity solution—and assume a federated IAM role. This role grants the necessary permissions to access cloud resources, such as the S3 bucket shown in the diagram.

In many enterprises, bastion hosts are used to manage SSH access to EC2 instances. As shown in Figure 7-1, a user first connects to a bastion host in a public subnet, and from there, they can access an EC2 instance hosted in a private VPC. This EC2 instance is assigned an IAM role that authorizes it to access the S3 bucket.

Alternatively, privileged users may connect directly to the private EC2 instance using Privileged Access Management (PAM) tools, bypassing the bastion host. In both cases, the EC2 instance leverages its attached IAM role to interact with the S3 bucket.

From a machine identity perspective, "machine users" can refer to IAM roles or users assigned to cloud-native resources such as EC2. These non-human identities are essential for automation and service-to-service communication.

Therefore, when evaluating "who the users are" in an AWS environment, it's critical to account for all these identity types: federated users, IAM roles assumed by humans or machines, bastion-mediated sessions, and machine identities. Each represents a potential actor with access to cloud resources.

Data Model

Now, let's build a data model that can capture the above identities and their access paths.

Field	Description
identity_id	Unique identifier, this could be an employee ID for humans or an ID for system identity
identity_name	Username, EC2 instance ID, or federated principal name
identity_type	Human vs. machine
identity_source	AWS IAM, federated, EC2 service account
identity_provider	Name of external IdP (if federated), e.g., Okta, AD
role_id	IAM role assigned or assumed

(*continued*)

Field	Description
role_name	AWS role name
role_trust_source	Identities that can assume this role and defined in the trust policy
access_path	JSON or delimited list of access hops (e.g., user ➤ bastion ➤ ec2 ➤ s3)
entry_point	First system touched by the user (e.g., bastion, SSO portal)
account_id	AWS account ID
aws_region	AWS region

With the above identity_access_map table, we can confidently answer complex identity-related questions across the cloud environment. For example:

- Who has access to cloud assets via externally hosted bastion hosts?

  By analyzing the access_path and entry_point fields, we can identify identities entering through bastion hosts and traversing to sensitive resources.

- How many system identities have a particular IAM role assigned?

  Filtering by identity_type = "machine" and grouping by role_id provides clear visibility into how broadly certain roles are used by services or EC2 instances.

- How many identities have access to a specific federated role?

  This helps surface the true human access behind federated roles, giving security teams insight into who can assume roles and access cloud resources through identity federation.

Answering What?

Unlike traditional, non-cloud access patterns—where an IGA solution typically manages entitlements within applications and clearly defines who has access to what—determining access is relatively straightforward. In the cloud, however, it becomes more complex. Simply knowing the list of cloud assets and the permissions assigned to IAM roles is not enough to accurately determine access.

CHAPTER 7 ANALYTICS FOR CLOUD ACCESS MANAGEMENT

For simplicity, let's focus on AWS. As shown in Figure 7-2, an IAM role may have a policy granting access to specific S3 buckets and DynamoDB tables. But understanding the full scope of what that access actually means requires deeper analysis.

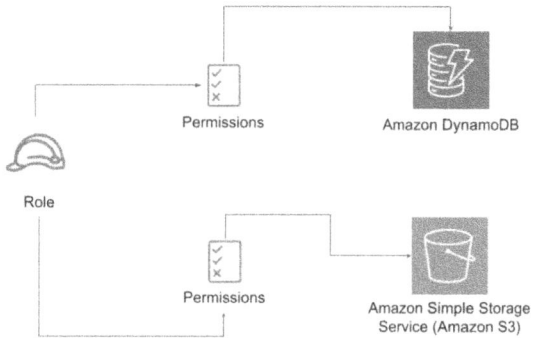

Figure 7-2. *Cloud Roles and Permissions*

If we are asked whether an IAM role has access to the DynamoDB, we can typically answer that by reviewing the permissions attached to the IAM role. However, the same approach doesn't work as reliably for S3 buckets. That's because S3 buckets can also have their own resource-based policies, which operate independently of the IAM role's policies.

Effective access to an S3 bucket is the result of evaluating both the IAM role's permissions and the bucket's resource-based policy together.

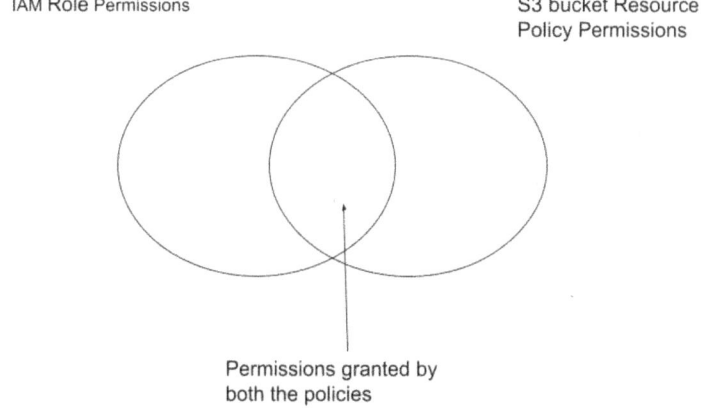

Figure 7-3. *Effective Permissions for S3 buckets*

The visualization illustrates how effective access can be determined. Essentially, we need to examine the permissions assigned to both the IAM role and the S3 bucket, then combine them to evaluate the net permissions the role has on that bucket.

While I've kept things relatively simple here by focusing on the interaction between identity-based and resource-based policies, AWS uses several additional mechanisms that influence access control:

- **Permissions Boundaries**

    These define the maximum permissions an identity can have. They act as guardrails, limiting what identity-based policies can grant.

- **Service Control Policies (SCPs)**

    These are organization-level policies, typically used to enforce whether a particular AWS service is allowed. They apply at the organization, organizational unit (OU), or account level and are useful for governance—for example, enforcing, *"No one can use AWS Glue."*

- **Session Policies**

    These are temporary policies passed when assuming a role via AWS STS. They further restrict permissions for the duration of the session token and are a common mechanism for granting temporary, scoped-down access.

To determine whether a role truly has access to a particular asset, all of these policies—identity-based, resource-based, permission boundaries, SCPs, and session policies—must be parsed and evaluated to compute the effective permissions.

Is this hard to do? It's certainly not easy. Even CNAPP products struggle to accurately replicate AWS's proprietary permission evaluation logic. This is a major reason they often produce false positives, as mentioned earlier.

GCP and Azure follow similar models for access control, with their own variations. Parsing and evaluating effective permissions is equally necessary across these platforms. If the budget allows, I recommend investing in a CNAPP solution and collaborating closely with the vendor to fine-tune access modeling for greater accuracy.

What this pipeline really looks like is shown below.

CHAPTER 7   ANALYTICS FOR CLOUD ACCESS MANAGEMENT

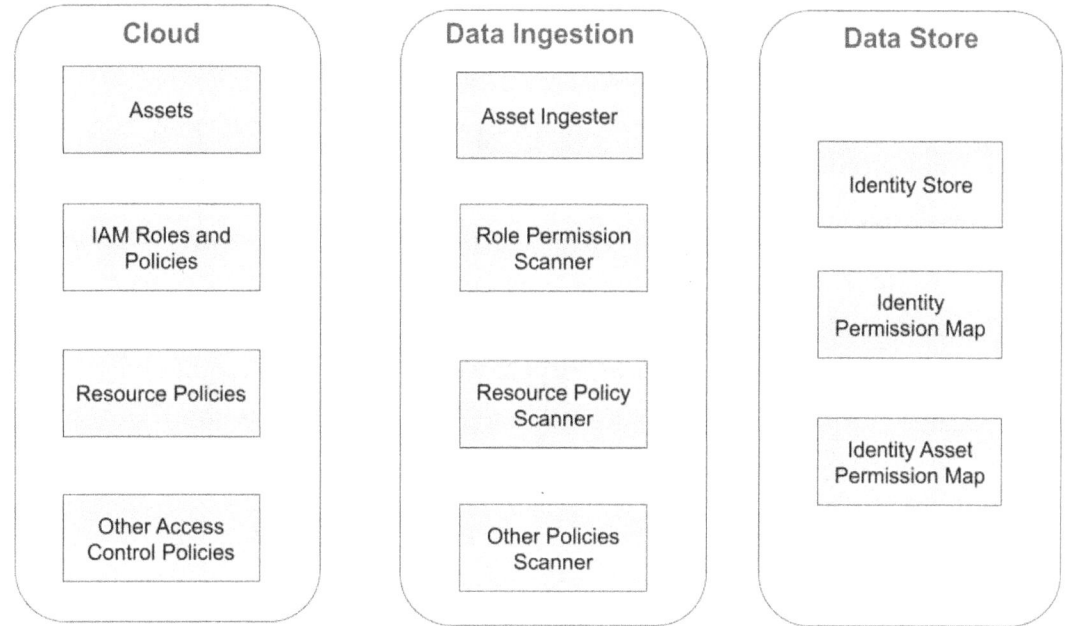

Figure 7-4. *High-Level Data Processing Architecture for Cloud Resources*

Figure 7-4 depicts the possible data pipelines involved in determining effective access. If you are using a CNAPP solution, you can often fetch both the asset inventory and the associated permissions directly from the tool itself.

If not, the following ingestion stages are typically required:

- **Role Permission Scanner**

    In this stage, we scan the policies and permissions associated with IAM roles and users. These permissions are then translated into simplified labels such as read/write. If policies include additional conditions—such as time, device, or specific resources—we capture and include those as well.

- **Asset Inventory**

    Every cloud provider offers an asset inventory service. This ingestion phase collects metadata about cloud assets, including associated tags, to build a comprehensive view of the environment.

- **Asset Policy Scanner**

  For services that support resource-based policies (e.g., S3 buckets in AWS), this component ingests and parses those policies to identify the effective permissions granted at the resource level.

- **Other Policy Scanner**

  As discussed in earlier sections, evaluating effective permissions also requires understanding other access control mechanisms—such as permission boundaries, SCPs, or session policies. This scanner ingests those policies for consideration in the final evaluation.

- **Permission Calculator**

  At this stage, data from all prior ingestors is aggregated and analyzed to compute the effective permissions between identities (roles/users) and assets. This is where we produce the final, actionable permission map needed for our analytics.

It is critical that this entire pipeline operates in near real time. In the cloud, permissions can change frequently. The good news is that cloud providers expose drift-detection or change-tracking services. For example:

- AWS provides AWS Config, which tracks configuration and permission changes across assets.

- GCP offers Cloud Asset Inventory with real-time feeds via Cloud Asset Inventory Feeds.

- Azure uses Azure Resource Graph and Azure Activity Logs to capture changes across assets and configurations.

Data Models

Field Name	Description
identity_id	Unique identifier for the identity (IAM user, role, or service account).
policy_id	Identifier of the attached policy (managed or inline)
policy_type	Type of policy (e.g., identity-based, session, permission boundary, SCP)

(continued)

Field Name	Description
net_permissions	Normalized permissions (e.g., s3:GetObject, dynamodb:PutItem)
access_level	Abstracted permission level (e.g., Read, Write, Admin)
conditions	Any conditions defined in the policy (e.g., IP range, MFA required, time)
resource_scope	Wildcard or specific resources the permission applies to
source	Indicates how the permission was derived (e.g., direct, inherited, STS)
timestamp	When the mapping was last updated

Table: identity_policy_permission_map

Field Name	Description
identity_id	Unique identifier for the identity (IAM user, role, or service account).
asset_id	Identifier of the attached policy (managed or inline)
asset_type	Type of policy (e.g., identity-based, session, permission boundary, SCP)
effective_permissions	Normalized permissions (e.g., s3:GetObject, dynamodb:PutItem)
access_level	Abstracted permission level (e.g., Read, Write, Admin).
permissions_sources	Which policy types contributed (e.g., IAM + resource policy + SCP)
conditions	Any conditions affecting the access (e.g., tags, session limits).

With the above data model, we can answer complex access-related questions that are valuable for both threat detection and compliance use cases:

- **Which identities have access to a specific S3 bucket?**

    This helps identify over-privileged users or unintended exposure.

- **Are there dormant configurations in the infrastructure that could be exploited?**

    For example, roles with unused but dangerous permissions.

- **Which roles grant write access to system users on EC2 instances, potentially bypassing CI/CD controls?**

  This is critical for enforcing least privilege and maintaining pipeline integrity.

- **What threat scenarios are currently going undetected or being incorrectly flagged as false positives by CNAPP solutions?**

  Using effective permission data, we can validate CNAPP findings or uncover blind spots.

Answering How?

Anyone who has worked in identity analytics or cybersecurity for a while will likely agree on one of the most frustrating aspects of the field: the lack of standardized application logging—or, in some cases, the absence of logs altogether. When logs are missing, we have no visibility into whether an application is being used properly. And even when logs are available, if they aren't standardized, it requires significant upfront effort to normalize and transform them before they can be used in any meaningful reporting or analytics platform.

Fortunately, when it comes to cloud infrastructure, we're in a slightly better position. Most cloud environments provide fine-grained access logs that include detailed information about the identity involved, the action taken, and the asset targeted—often in near real time. These logs can generally be categorized into two broad types:

- **Management Events**

  These logs capture actions related to authentication and infrastructure changes. For example, if a user logs into AWS and creates an S3 bucket, the logs will reflect both the login and the resource creation activity. A typical management event log might look like this.

- **Data Events**

  These logs capture data-level activity within the cloud environment. For example, actions such as reading from or writing to an S3 bucket are recorded as data events.

CHAPTER 7 ANALYTICS FOR CLOUD ACCESS MANAGEMENT

What makes these events especially valuable is that they include identity information. This allows us to correlate them with our previously parsed *identity-asset-permission* mapping table to determine when a particular identity last accessed an asset and what action was performed.

Data Model

These are real-time data pipelines, designed to continuously process and correlate identity activity within the cloud environment. A typical pipeline structure is illustrated in Figure 7-5.

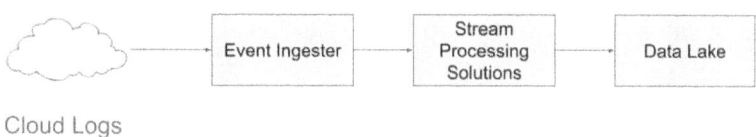

Figure 7-5. Cloud Access Drift Detection

In this setup, real-time logs from the cloud—such as login events and resource actions—are correlated with the permission maps built in earlier modules. This correlation allows us to track identity behavior in context, tying specific actions and login times directly to the permissions that enabled them.

Correlated Identity Activity Table

Field	Description
identity_id	The user or service identity that performed the action
asset_id	The resource being accessed (e.g., an S3 bucket, EC2 instance)
role_id	The IAM role assumed (if any) during the session
action	The specific operation performed (e.g., `s3:GetObject`, `ec2:StartInstances`)
timestamp	When the action occurred
source_ip	IP address from which the action was initiated
session_id	Session identifier (e.g., AWS STS session, Azure token ID)
agent_type	Endpoint device used for access (laptop, phone, tablet)

(*continued*)

Field	Description
auth_type	Authentication type used (e.g., password, access key, federated login)
permissions_granted	The policy or combination of policies that allowed the action
conditions_applied	Any condition (e.g., IP restriction, time, MFA) that was active

These logs can drive a wide range of actions in both security and compliance. With proper correlation and analysis, we can answer several complex questions, such as

- **Which roles have access to many S3 buckets but are only accessing a few?**

    This helps identify over-provisioned roles and potential attack surfaces.

- **Which identities are not using their AWS access?**

    Useful for access reviews and enforcing least privilege.

- **Which identity is attempting to access multiple datastores in a short period—behavior that deviates from the norm?**

    A potential indicator of reconnaissance or malicious automation.

Multicloud Considerations

Although cloud vendors offer broadly similar services at a high level—such as storage, compute, and databases—the way these services are organized, managed, and permissioned differs significantly across providers.

A fundamental point of divergence lies in how cloud assets are organized. In AWS, the core unit of resource containment is the account. All resources—whether they are S3 buckets, EC2 instances, or RDS databases—are created and managed within an AWS account. Permissions are then applied within the context of that account using IAM policies, roles, and user associations.

This organizational model affects how access is granted, how boundaries are enforced, and how multi-account or multicloud governance is implemented. Understanding these structural differences is essential when building identity analytics pipelines that operate across multiple cloud platforms.

Feature	AWS	GCP	Azure
Top Entity	AWS account	Organization	Azure tenant
Resource Hierarchy	Flat within the account	Org ➤ folder ➤ project	Tenant ➤ subscription ➤ resource group

There's certainly more depth to explore, but for the purposes of this discussion, we'll keep it at a high level. Similarly, there are several important differences when it comes to IAM across cloud providers.

Feature	AWS	GCP	Azure
Identity Types	IAM users, roles, and groups	Google accounts, service accounts, Google groups	Users, groups, service principals, managed identities
Policy Attachments	Can be attached to roles, users, and groups	IAM bindings: roles assigned to identities at the resource level	Role assignments at scope (subscription/resource group/etc.)
Cross-Account Access	Supported via trust policies in roles	Supported via IAM policy and workload identity federation	Supported via guest users and B2B in Azure AD

As we've seen, the concepts of deriving identities, permissions, and asset inventories apply across cloud providers. However, while the goals are similar, the logic to parse and evaluate permissions differs significantly between platforms. This means equivalent development effort is needed to extend your analytics pipeline for multicloud environments. Some open source tools can help simplify this process—especially if you don't have a CNAPP solution in place.

The data pipelines and models for ingesting permissions and mapping identities to assets will largely follow the same structure and should support real-time ingestion. However, when working across AWS, GCP, and Azure, you'll need a normalization and standardization layer. This layer ensures that data from all three cloud environments is harmonized and stored in a consistent format—so that downstream consumers of the data don't need to worry about cloud-specific differences. All they need to know is which permissions they want to derive and analyze.

How Does Standardization Work?

When thinking about access management at a high level, permissions can generally be categorized into four types: read, write, delete, and admin. This classification is relatively intuitive when applied to data permissions—such as roles on databases—but the same approach can be extended to cloud permissions. Specifically, cloud API actions can be translated into these effective permission types.

Take AWS RDS as an example.

AWS Actions	Effective Permissions
rds:DescribeDBInstances, rds:ListTagsForResource	Read
rds:CreateDBInstance, rds:ModifyDBCluster, rds:StartDBInstance	Write
rds:DeleteDBInstance, rds:StopDBInstance, rds:RebootDBInstance	Delete

It's possible to write a simple script that parses IAM policy actions and maps them to high-level permissions like read or write. A great starting point for building such logic is the open source project by Salesforce:

Policy Sentry: Access-Level Overrides

There are several key benefits to this approach:

- **Human-Readable Permissions**

    Translated permissions become easier to understand, even for non-cloud experts—significantly helping compliance and security operations teams.

- **Standardization Across Clouds**

    Storing permissions in a consistent format enables cross-cloud querying and analytics without getting bogged down by the specifics of each cloud provider's IAM model.

- **Enforcement of Privileged Access Controls**

    Many infrastructure actions require controls like session management or segregation of duties. By knowing the effective permissions, especially admin-level access, such controls can be applied more accurately and consistently.

Detection Mechanisms

Once we've established a strong foundation of identities, assets, and permissions—alongside real-time activity logs—the next critical step is transforming this data into meaningful security detections. These detections generally fall into three broad categories.

1. Compliance Failure Detections

These detections highlight deviations from established cloud security best practices or internal compliance policies. For example, a detection rule might flag IAM roles that have overly permissive policies such as resource.*, which grants unrestricted access. Most workloads only require a limited set of actions, and such overly broad permissions create unnecessary risk, especially by enabling lateral movement within the environment.

2. Specification-Based Detections

These detections are rooted in expected configurations or policy definitions. For instance, an organization may define that cross-account admin roles should be limited. If the system detects an increase in roles with such permissions, that's a red flag. Similarly, dormant IAM users or roles—those with no activity for an extended period—represent permissions that are unmonitored and potentially exploitable. Specification-based detections help identify such drift from intended access patterns or configurations.

3. Behavioral Detections

These are based on observing deviations in user or system behavior over time. For example, if an account has been inactive for 90 days and suddenly begins generating a large volume of activity, that pattern is suspicious. Likewise, if an identity that previously transferred data between two known applications suddenly begins moving data across several unrelated applications, it may indicate unauthorized or malicious behavior. Behavioral anomalies are strong indicators of potential threats within the environment.

ITDR Integration

Cloud IAM analytics and Identity Threat Detection and Response (ITDR) naturally complement each other. IAM analytics focuses on understanding who has access to what, how permissions are granted, and how access is used over time. ITDR builds on this by detecting and responding to suspicious or risky identity behaviors.

When integrated, IAM analytics provides the baseline and visibility needed for ITDR to be effective. For example, analytics can highlight overly permissive roles, dormant accounts, or unused access paths. ITDR then monitors these insights for real-time behavioral changes—like sudden access from a dormant role or privilege escalation attempts using a broad permission set.

This integration allows for deeper detections, better prioritization of threats, and faster response. Instead of treating identity risk and identity behavior separately, combining IAM analytics with ITDR creates a more complete and proactive identity defense layer in the cloud. Please refer to the previous chapter for more information on ITDR frameworks.

Summary

1. While CNAPPs provide strong visibility and protection across cloud platforms, they often lack contextual understanding of enterprise-specific access patterns and identities—leading to alert fatigue and compliance blind spots.

2. Effective cloud access analytics begins with mapping who has access, what resources they can access, and how those resources are being used. This requires building detailed models of identity types (human, machine, federated), access paths, and role assumptions.

3. Accurate access analysis depends on evaluating all policy layers—including IAM policies, resource-based policies, permission boundaries, session policies, and SCPs. A real-time permission calculator is essential to compute effective permissions in complex environments like AWS, GCP, and Azure.

4. Each cloud provider uses different IAM structures. To support unified analytics, permissions must be standardized (e.g., into read/write/delete/admin levels) across clouds using mapping logic and open source tools like Policy Sentry.

5. Integrating IAM Analytics with ITDR for Real-Time Defense
IAM analytics surfaces latent access risks; ITDR uses that baseline to monitor and respond to active identity threats. Together, they enable real-time, context-rich detection and response workflows focused on identities—the new perimeter in cloud security.

References

1. James Casagrande. "CNAPP Found Identity Problems. How Are You Fixing Them?" https://sonraisecurity.com/blog/whats-next-after-cnapp-bulk-fixes/

2. Kinnaird McQuade. "Salesforce Cloud Security: Automating Least Privilege in AWS IAM with Policy Sentry." https://engineering.salesforce.com/salesforce-cloud-security-automating-least-privilege-in-aws-iam-with-policy-sentry-b04fe457b8dc/

3. Wiz Experts Team. https://www.wiz.io/academy/identity-security-in-the-cloud

4. Eyal Estrin. *Cloud Security Handbook*

5. Charles Pfleeger, Shari Lawrence Pfleeger, and Lizzie Coles-Kemp. *Security in Computing, 6th Edition*

CHAPTER 8

Analytics for Regulatory Reporting

In the previous sections, we covered advanced topics such as insider threat detection, cloud posture management, and configuration drift detection. These are powerful capabilities, but many readers might be thinking: *What if we're not there yet? What if we're still in the early stages—focused primarily on building reporting capabilities to ensure leadership and operational teams can assess whether specific controls are effective?*

It's a common scenario. We often hear, *"This control isn't working—let's build a dashboard for it,"* or *"This is a new control—let's create a dashboard to confirm it's functioning as documented."* Over time, this approach results in analytics teams supporting hundreds of dashboards—many of which have fewer than two or three regular users.

If you're just beginning to build your reporting capabilities, you're in luck. This chapter will provide a robust framework for establishing a solid foundation—one that not only makes it easier to develop new dashboards on top of existing infrastructure but also promotes self-service access to information, reducing the need for dashboards for every small requirement.

And if you already have established reporting capabilities, this chapter will offer practical ideas for optimizing and extending your existing tools to ensure you maximize the return on your current investments.

What Are the Regulatory Requirements?

Regulatory requirements are a broad area, but from an Identity and Access Management (IAM)—and more specifically, an Identity Analytics—perspective, it's important to understand how these mandates shape access policies and reporting expectations. Knowing the underlying reason behind the need to report specific information helps

CHAPTER 8   ANALYTICS FOR REGULATORY REPORTING

analytics and reporting teams go beyond surface-level compliance—enabling them to design reporting mechanisms that not only inform but also improve operational effectiveness.

At a high level, regulatory requirements refer to the rules, laws, or standards imposed by governmental or regulatory bodies that organizations must comply with to operate legally within a specific industry or jurisdiction. These requirements are designed to ensure that organizations meet essential financial, security, privacy, or operational standards. Some are industry-specific, while others apply more broadly across sectors.

For example:

- **GDPR** applies to all organizations operating within the European Union, with strict mandates on data privacy and access control.

- **SOX** governs publicly traded companies in the United States, with emphasis on internal controls, including access governance.

- **HIPAA** applies to healthcare organizations in the United States, requiring safeguards around patient data access.

- **PCI DSS** applies to organizations that handle cardholder data, enforcing strict controls around access to payment systems.

These standards share a common theme: limiting access to only those who need it—and only when they need it. The specific language of the standards may vary, but the intent is consistent: enforce least privilege, verify identity, and monitor access to sensitive systems or data.

Here is a summary of access-related expectations across key regulatory standards:

Regulatory Standard	Access Requirement
GDPR	Article 32 mandates strict access controls and robust identity verification mechanisms.
SOX	Section 404 requires evidence that internal controls—including access controls—are effective.
HIPAA	Requires that access to medical records is limited strictly to individuals who have a legitimate need.
PCI DSS	Requires restricting access to system components and cardholder data based on business need-to-know.

Although the origin and scope of these standards differ, they converge on a foundational principle: access must be justifiable, limited, and auditable.

Implementation approaches may vary depending on the technology stack an organization uses. As systems evolve, so do the reporting requirements—but the fundamental goal remains unchanged: access must be tightly controlled and well-documented.

In addition, the **NIST 800-53** framework provides a comprehensive catalog of security and privacy controls, including detailed requirements for access control. It defines what "securely managed access" means across a wide range of IT environments and serves as a benchmark for federal agencies and organizations seeking to align with best practices.

NIST 800-53 in Depth

NIST 800-53, formally titled *"Security and Privacy Controls for Information Systems and Organizations,"* is a publication developed by the National Institute of Standards and Technology (NIST). It provides a comprehensive catalog of security and privacy controls for organizations. These controls are also referenced in other major frameworks, including the NIST Cybersecurity Framework (CSF), the Center for Internet Security (CIS) benchmarks, and the Federal Risk and Authorization Management Program (FedRAMP).

While the publication covers a wide range of cybersecurity topics, our focus will remain on the key control families most relevant to identity analytics, specifically:

AC: Access Control
These controls focus on managing user and system access permissions.

IA: Identification and Authentication
As the name suggests, these controls center around the authentication and authorization of both human and machine identities.

AU: Audit and Accountability
This control family emphasizes account logging and monitoring for audit and governance purposes.

In the sections that follow, we will explore key controls within each of these families, highlight typical vendor products organizations use to implement them, and outline the reporting needed to ensure these controls are operating effectively.

AC-2 (1–12): Account Management—Manage Identity Life Cycle

Requirements

Automatically disable accounts in response to joiner, mover, or leaver events or when time-based expiration conditions are met.

System Implementation

Most large organizations automate this process using Identity Governance and Administration (IGA) tools such as SailPoint, Saviynt, Okta, or custom-built solutions.

Monitoring Requirements

Although these workflows are typically automated, active monitoring is essential to detect systemic failures. For example, if the IGA system manages database accounts and loses connectivity after a system upgrade, the account may not be disabled—even if the appropriate event is triggered—leading to residual risk. Dashboards showing real-time failures, historical trends, and alert mechanisms can significantly reduce such operational gaps.

AC-2 (13): Account Management—Manage Identity Life Cycle (High-Risk Accounts)

Requirements

Disable accounts of individuals who present a significant security or privacy risk. This includes individuals with credible indicators of intent to misuse access or those being targeted by adversaries.

System Implementation

Implementing this control is complex, as identifying authorized users engaged in unauthorized behavior is nontrivial. It requires integrating ITDR (Identity Threat Detection and Response) and insider threat detection solutions with IGA systems to automate the remediation workflow.

Monitoring Requirements

Reporting should cover the outputs of ITDR tools and the full life cycle of detected threat events. Key metrics include false positives, true positives, time to remediate, and any systemic IT failures—all of which help assess the effectiveness of this control.

AC-5: Separation of Duties (SOD)

Requirements

Prevent conflicting roles from being assigned to the same user. For example, the individual approving a wire payment must not be the one initiating it.

System Implementation

This control is challenging to implement, as SOD can be enforced either within the application or through access provisioning. For example, distinct entitlements can be created for initiators and approvers, and the IGA system can enforce policies to prevent assignment of both to the same user. Alternatively, SOD enforcement can be handled within the application workflow rules, independent of the access management layer.

Monitoring Requirements

Monitoring typically focuses on SOD policies enforced by IGA tools. These tools should prevent users from obtaining conflicting access. Monitoring must ensure that SOD policies are complete, accurate, and functioning as intended. Regulators may also request a full inventory of SOD policies. Reporting capabilities should address: what policies exist, what should exist, and how to remediate any gaps.

AC-6: Least Privilege

Requirements

Apply the principle of least privilege, granting only the access necessary for users (or processes acting on their behalf) to perform their assigned tasks.

System Implementation

This area continues to evolve. Most organizations rely on access reviews and usage monitoring to validate access restrictions. However, there is a growing trend toward reducing reliance on traditional access reviews, as they are often error-prone and ineffective—users may lack the time or knowledge to make accurate decisions during reviews.

Monitoring Requirements

Access review monitoring must address questions such as

- Is every required access included in the certification process?
- Are access revocations being processed as expected?
- Are there certifiers who consistently demonstrate negligence?

In environments using dynamic policies for access control, additional monitoring is needed to ensure those policies enforce true least privilege and that access is granted only temporarily, as claimed.

IA-2: User Identification and Authentication

Requirements

Enforce unique user identification and multifactor authentication (MFA) for all users.

System Implementation

This requirement is typically implemented using identity and authentication platforms such as PingID, Okta, Azure AD, and similar solutions.

Monitoring Requirements

Monitoring for this control operates at two levels:

- **Users:** Identify users who, for any reason, have been granted MFA bypass.

- **Applications:** Detect applications that are unable to support MFA or where the MFA workflow is broken due to technical issues.

Maintaining an up-to-date inventory of all applications eligible for MFA and verifying that they have MFA correctly configured is critical for assessing and mitigating associated risks.

IA-5: Authenticator Management

Requirements

Organizations must enforce strong management of authenticators, including passwords, tokens, cryptographic keys, smart cards, and certificates. This encompasses issuance, life cycle management, complexity enforcement, rotation, revocation, and recovery procedures.

System Implementation

This control is implemented using identity and authentication platforms such as PingID, Okta, Azure AD, CyberArk, and similar solutions.

Monitoring Requirements

Monitoring for this control is also performed at two levels:

- **Users:** Detect users with weak passwords, credentials that haven't been changed within the required timeframe, or expired authentication tokens. Reporting should also include insights into the types of devices used for authentication and whether those devices comply with organizational policies.

- **Applications:** Identify systems using soon-to-expire or self-signed certificates. Ensure all application certificates and cryptographic keys are vaulted and compliant with enterprise standards.

AU-2: Audit Events

Requirements

Organizations must define and document which user actions and identity-related events must be logged. This includes events such as successful and failed login attempts, account creation, privilege modifications, and session terminations.

System Implementation

This control is typically implemented within the SIEM (Security Information and Event Management) ecosystem, which includes real-time analytics tools and log data processing pipelines.

Monitoring Requirements

From an identity analytics perspective, monitoring should focus on two key areas:

- **Log Format Validation:** Ensure logs are in the correct format to support correlation with other activities. Logs should clearly indicate "who did what" to enable actionable insights.

- **Log Coverage and Completeness:** Confirm that all logs relevant to identity-related activities are being ingested into the system.

Without proper formatting and comprehensive ingestion, the sheer volume of logs within a SIEM will not be sufficient to monitor controls associated with identity and access management activities effectively.

CHAPTER 8 ANALYTICS FOR REGULATORY REPORTING

System Design Reporting

Analytics remains an underdeveloped area within many IAM teams. Typically, analytics resources are brought in to address critical audit findings, leading to the creation of a few dashboards meant to resolve specific, point-in-time issues. These dashboards often see heavy short-term use, but the team quickly shifts focus to the next urgent issue—resulting in a reactive, fire-drill-driven approach.

IAM platforms manage thousands of assets from an access perspective. In large organizations, this translates to a massive volume of access requests, certifications, secret rotations, and enforcement of hundreds of controls, as discussed in earlier sections. Relying on ad hoc reports to respond to each new audit request is not sustainable. This cycle repeats with every audit, making the reporting effort feel like running on a hamster wheel—constant motion, but little meaningful progress.

Instead, reporting should be treated as a product, following a typical product maturity life cycle. As with any product, this involves grooming requirements, prioritizing features through stakeholder consultation, and delivering the most critical functionality first.

The development of this reporting product should begin with clear objectives. For our context:

- The reporting system must monitor key and high-risk controls from NIST in near real time.

- It should provide historical trends to evaluate whether processes are operating optimally over time and to track progress.

- Reports must be capable of detecting anomalies, misconfigurations, and errors.

- The infrastructure should support alerting and remediation capabilities.

- All underlying data should be queryable, as access-related datasets are frequently needed across the enterprise.

Figure 8-1 depicts the high-level architectural components in this product.

CHAPTER 8　ANALYTICS FOR REGULATORY REPORTING

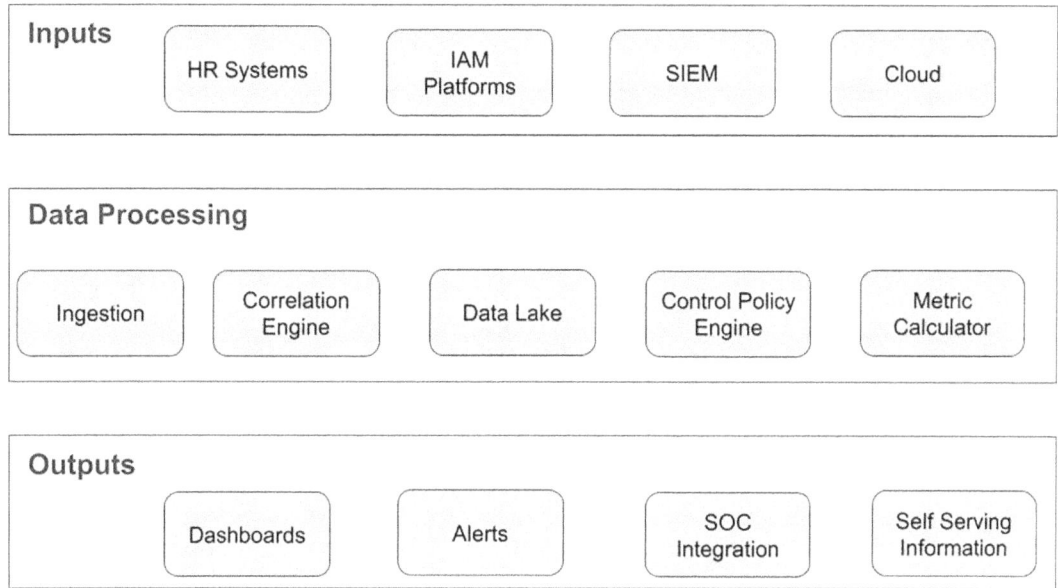

Figure 8-1. High Level System Design

Inputs

It should come as no surprise that we observe similar data and control requirements across related areas such as ITDR. In this section, I'll outline the additional elements we prioritize beyond what has already been discussed in earlier chapters.

HR Systems

As described in the controls section, we focus on events related to identity life cycle—namely, joiners, movers, and leavers. In addition, organizational datasets such as reorgs and structural changes are important to track. These changes often impact access policies that rely heavily on reporting lines or business unit mappings, and it's critical to ensure those policies remain accurately configured.

IAM Platforms

Most of the activities covered under control expectations are executed via IAM platforms. These platforms contain essential data on how systems leverage access workflows and where exceptions exist. For identity analytics, we require fine-grained life cycle event data—for example, access review datasets should include

- All certifiers involved
- The contents of each certification
- Decisions made and the time taken to reach them
- Whether those decisions were implemented
- The time elapsed between the decision and the actual access revocation

For machine identities, we need visibility into ownership, last password rotation, any changes in ownership, how those identities are used, and whether session monitoring tools (like Session Manager) are used to validate the legitimacy of their activity.

SIEM

As outlined in the controls section, SIEM platforms are crucial for identifying inactive accounts and ensuring they are disabled if unused. Logs are also used to detect risky behavior. For instance, we rely on MFA logs to verify

- Whether a device used for login is company-owned
- The geographic location of the login attempt
- The number of failed password attempts

All of these signals require robust log collection and normalization through the SIEM.

Cloud

Beyond NIST, several cybersecurity frameworks guide cloud access governance. While the underlying intent remains the same—ensuring access is restrictive—the implementation differs slightly in cloud environments. As discussed in the section on cloud access analytics, metadata and logs related to cloud identities are essential for monitoring controls in this space.

Data Processing

Ingestion

Most identity-related controls require daily execution and monitoring. While building real-time data pipelines is not strictly necessary for this purpose, having them in place can significantly enhance other areas of identity analytics. Batch ingestion is sufficient for most compliance needs, but real-time ingestion provides added value for anomaly detection and proactive response.

Correlation Engine

This is often the most overlooked component in the early stages of building IAM reporting capabilities. A well-designed correlation engine allows teams to join diverse data sources in a way that answers essential questions such as

- Who has access?
- Who is using the access?
- How is that access being used?

This correlation capability is fundamental to supporting many NIST controls and enables actionable identity insights.

Data Lake and Warehouse

Most identity controls operate continuously throughout the year but are typically audited only a few times annually. Control testers often request evidence of control execution going back 12 months or more. Therefore, retaining these datasets for at least one year is a minimum requirement—though some cybersecurity frameworks recommend longer retention. Cloud-based data lakes offer a cost-effective and scalable solution for storing this historical data efficiently.

Control Policy Engine

Many of the controls outlined in NIST can be expressed and enforced through policy logic. For example, implementing AC-2(13) might involve a policy that flags users logging in from prohibited geographies—such as an associate logging in from a country where carrying company-issued devices is not allowed. While some controls can be enforced through straightforward policies, others are more complex programs—for instance, validating whether access reviews were scoped correctly based on intended coverage.

Metric Calculations

Leaders need visibility into how well controls are functioning. This includes understanding control failure rates, identifying trends over time, and analyzing historical performance. A metric calculation layer enables tracking these key performance indicators, helping leadership assess both the effectiveness and reliability of implemented controls.

Outputs

Dashboards

As we streamline reporting requirements by control family, we begin to identify synergies across various controls. For example, while the NIST framework outlines over 13 key requirements for account management, many of these can be addressed through a single, well-structured data warehouse. Rather than building 13 individual dashboards, most of the insights can be visualized in just one or two dashboards—provided the underlying data model is designed to support multiple use cases. Without this strategic alignment, teams often end up creating numerous one-off datasets and single-purpose dashboards, leading to inefficiencies in both development and maintenance.

Alerting Mechanisms

IAM organizations are often at the center of enterprise operations, supporting every user and application across the company. When something breaks, IAM is usually the first point of escalation. Without built-in alerting mechanisms, the burden falls on someone manually monitoring dashboards to identify and act on risks. Effective alerting shifts responsibility closer to the source of the issue. For instance, if an application misconfiguration prevents user and role data from syncing with the IGA platform, notifying the application owner—who is best positioned to investigate—is far more efficient. Tools like PagerDuty, ServiceNow, and JIRA provide APIs that can be integrated into alerting workflows, enabling automated detection, notification, and even remediation tracking. These alerts also serve as an audit trail, ensuring accountability for both detection and response.

SOC Integrations

Some control failures pose a higher degree of risk and require immediate escalation. For example, if a cloud root account previously marked as disabled suddenly shows activity, this represents a significant threat. Such events should trigger immediate notifications to the Security Operations Center (SOC). A mature control monitoring system must go beyond issuing alerts—it should provide SOC analysts with context, including what triggered the alert and why it matters. This enables quicker triage and response, reducing the risk exposure window.

Self-Service Information Access

Unlike other cybersecurity domains such as network or firewall logs, IAM datasets are routinely needed by various enterprise teams—not just IAM or security. For example, ERP system owners (e.g., SAP, PeopleSoft) are often required to demonstrate how specific users gained access, especially in SOX-regulated environments. These teams frequently turn to IAM for answers. At scale, this leads to a flood of support requests that can overwhelm IAM reporting teams.

Enabling self-service access is critical to operational efficiency. One approach is to build multipurpose dashboards that answer frequently asked questions. Another is to publish curated datasets for enterprise-wide access. With advancements in GenAI, platforms like Databricks and Snowflake now support natural language querying—allowing users to explore IAM data without needing to submit manual report requests. This represents a major shift, significantly reducing the need for ad hoc reporting and democratizing access to critical identity data.

Summary

- The chapter outlines access-related expectations from key regulations (GDPR, SOX, HIPAA, PCI DSS) and shows how they converge on principles like least privilege, just-in-time access, and auditability.

- Focuses on access control (AC), identification/authentication (IA), and audit/accountability (AU) families—detailing control requirements, implementation strategies, and monitoring approaches using real-world tools like SailPoint, Okta, Azure AD, and SIEMs.

- Advocates treating reporting as a product, not a project—emphasizing structured ingestion, correlation engines, data lakes, and metric frameworks to support both audits and operational risk management.

- Encourages centralized, multipurpose dashboards with automated alerting and SOC escalation, while highlighting the importance of self-service access for enterprise users supported by GenAI-powered querying tools.

- Describes how HR, IAM, SIEM, and cloud platforms must work together to support identity analytics, ensuring both proactive control enforcement and responsive investigation.

References

1. https://cube.global/resources/compliance-corner/what-are-regulatory-requirements-2
2. GDPR Article 32. https://gdpr-info.eu/art-32-gdpr/
3. SOX Section 404 Overview. https://auditboard.com/blog/sox-404
4. HIPAA Security Rule Summary. https://www.cms.gov/files/document/hipaa-basics-providers-privacy-security-breach-notification-rules.pdf
5. PCI DSS v4.0 Requirements Summary. https://www.pcisecuritystandards.org/document_library
6. NIST SP 800-53 Rev. 5. https://csrc.nist.gov/publications/detail/sp/800-53/rev-5/final

CHAPTER 9

Machine Learning Techniques in Identity Analytics

In almost every conference, research paper, and innovation talk, the conversation inevitably turns toward AI—how it can be leveraged or how it is already transforming industries. While classical machine learning (ML) may not sound as cutting-edge compared to the latest AI advancements, it remains highly relevant. In fact, despite the explosive growth of AI technologies, classical ML algorithms continue to drive significant risk reduction at scale, particularly in domains like Identity and Access Management (IAM).

IAM systems generate enormous volumes of data. Although this data often requires cleaning and normalization, it provides a rich foundation for applying ML techniques. Many Identity Governance and Administration (IGA) products now incorporate ML modules to enhance decision-making, risk detection, and automation. For example, SailPoint's IdentityAI leverages ML for anomaly detection, risk scoring, and access recommendations.

Below is an overview of some vendor-specific ML capabilities:

Product	ML Use Cases
SailPoint	IdentityAI: access recommendations, detect anomalies, risk scoring, role mining, and outlier access detections [1]
Saviynt	Saviynt intelligence: access recommendations, role mining, risk scoring [2]
Oracle Identity Governance	Role mining [3]
Omada Identity	Role mining, access recommendations [4]

© Nilesh Bhoyar 2025
N. Bhoyar, *Identity Analytics*, https://doi.org/10.1007/979-8-8688-1745-8_9

This list is not exhaustive, but it highlights a key trend: ML is becoming a core component of modern IGA platforms. The common themes revolve around access automation, risk measurement, and anomaly detection.

This chapter is not intended as a deep dive into the academic foundations of machine learning. Instead, it focuses on applied ML in IAM—examining classical ML algorithms, their applicability to real-world IAM use cases, and the general patterns vendors are attempting to solve. We will also walk through sample implementations, enabling you to evaluate vendor offerings, determine whether to build in-house solutions, or enhance existing tools with your own ML models.

Introduction to Machine Learning

Aurélien Géron, in his popular book *Hands-On Machine Learning with Scikit-Learn, Keras, and TensorFlow*, describes machine learning as *"the science (and art) of programming computers so that they can learn from data."* This ability to learn from data enables computers to identify patterns, make decisions, or assist humans in making better decisions.

When we think of Identity and Access Management (IAM), the typical activities that come to mind are requesting access, approving access, and using that access to perform one's job. At first glance, it may not be obvious where machine learning fits into this picture. However, a deeper look reveals that IAM is inherently a data-intensive discipline. Every day, IAM applications generate vast amounts of data—access requests, approvals, usage logs, authentication events, password failures, and information about devices being used to access systems. Humans, in turn, are constantly making decisions: *Should this access be approved? Do I need this access? Is the password policy sufficient? Are the controls aligned with standards? Are we covering all devices on the network?*

Since machine learning excels at reducing decision fatigue and automating repetitive judgment calls, it is natural to leverage the data produced by IAM processes to improve efficiency and accuracy. This is where key themes of ML applications in IAM begin to emerge. Before we dive deeper, let us first understand the "why" behind this transformation.

Why Machine Learning for IAM?

In the early days of ML adoption for IAM, there was noticeable hesitance across the industry. People preferred deterministic, rule-based approaches—and for good reason. Such approaches provide clear explanations, make it easier to meet compliance expectations, and benefit from a sense of familiarity. However, while these static rules worked well in the legacy world, the new reality is far more dynamic. In fact, an excessive reliance on compliance-driven, rule-based logic can now increase risk rather than mitigate it.

Scale

Over the past six years, factors like digitization, cloud adoption, and AI have caused the number of digital identities to grow exponentially. Modern organizations often manage thousands to millions of identities and entitlements. Consider the complexity of integrating identity life cycle data from native systems to IGA platforms, performing configuration checks, or detecting drift in configurations. Doing this without ML techniques is not scalable and is ultimately unsustainable.

Complex and Fluctuating Environments

In the legacy IAM world, infrastructure was primarily limited to local data centers with much simpler access models. Decisions on whether someone should have access were largely determined by static attributes—such as supporting a specific application or belonging to a particular division. These rules are no longer sufficient in modern, dynamic environments. With shared cloud infrastructure, multi-tenant SaaS platforms, employees using personal devices, and applications outside the organization's direct control, static if-else logic quickly becomes unmanageable. The sheer volume of conditions and frequent changes make access decisioning an ideal ML-enabled problem.

Large Amount of Data

Jeff Dean, a prominent figure in the ML world, famously said: *"In many cases, having more data beats clever algorithms, but the best is to have both."* IAM is a perfect example of this principle. Consider the vast datasets generated every day—access requests, approval/rejection decisions, certification outcomes, and authentication events. These data points are often labeled by humans (e.g., "Approve" or "Deny") or are implicitly labeled as safe through machine decisions. With this abundance of labeled data, IAM becomes a data-rich domain that is ideally suited for machine learning applications.

CHAPTER 9   MACHINE LEARNING TECHNIQUES IN IDENTITY ANALYTICS

Key Machine Learning Techniques in IAM

Machine learning (ML) is advancing at an unprecedented pace, especially since the emergence of generative AI (GenAI) models like ChatGPT. Teaching machines to identify patterns from data can take many forms. In this section, we will focus on key ML techniques already being deployed in production environments. Advanced topics, such as generative AI, will be explored in the next chapter.

Supervised Learning

Supervised algorithms rely on labeled data to train models. They are widely used for classification tasks—such as predicting whether a privileged access session is legitimate—and for regression tasks, like risk scoring entitlements or users based on their permissions. Identity and Access Management (IAM) has no shortage of labeled data. Historical records from access approvals, authentication outcomes, or certification campaigns often serve as strong training datasets. However, not all datasets are equally valuable; it depends on what is being modeled and the desired outcome.

In 2021, NIST published a paper on *Machine Learning for Access Control Policy Verification*, which demonstrated an innovative application of supervised learning. Rather than relying on hard-coded rules, the approach used existing access policies to generate test cases and verify whether policies met defined criteria. Given NIST's leadership in standards, this work highlights how policy and standards bodies are aligning with academia in recognizing the growing role of ML techniques in access management.

Unsupervised Learning

Unsupervised methods work with unlabeled data to uncover hidden patterns or anomalies. This approach is especially valuable in **role mining**, where clustering techniques can reveal natural groupings of entitlements, and in **anomaly detection**, where the system flags deviations from normal access patterns. For example, anomaly detection can identify rogue access permissions or unauthorized use by legitimate users, such as downloading unusually large volumes of data to local machines.

UEBA (User and Entity Behavior Analytics) is an emerging area leveraging unsupervised techniques, where dynamic user behaviors are continuously monitored to detect anomalous insider activities. Several vendors are now offering UEBA-based solutions.

Reinforcement Learning

Reinforcement Learning (RL) represents a more advanced ML paradigm where an agent learns optimal decisions through trial-and-error interactions with its environment. While RL is still emerging in IAM, academic research—such as the paper *Adaptive ABAC Policy Learning: A Reinforcement Learning Approach* from the University of Pittsburgh—has shown its potential. This work introduces a contextual bandit RL framework that enables an **adaptive ABAC (Attribute-Based Access Control)** system to automatically learn authorization policies by interacting with users and administrators for feedback, eliminating the need for fully labeled data. Other research has explored self-learning agents capable of modeling user behavior to determine when to enforce step-up authentication. Though still in early stages, these techniques are gaining attention. Their potential is significant, as they can dramatically reduce the manual effort required to build and verify policies—a process that can otherwise take years in complex environments.

Common Machine Learning Use Cases Across IAM

I have already touched on some common IAM use cases in earlier sections, but here I aim to dive deeper into these scenarios. The focus is on understanding where traditional rule-based approaches face limitations and how machine learning can address these challenges more effectively. While the implementation concepts discussed here are intentionally high-level, they should serve as a blueprint or inspiration for your ML team, offering practical ideas on how to approach these problems in real-world settings.

Role Mining or Rule Mining for Policies

Use Case

Large organizations often manage thousands—or even millions—of entitlements. Without logical grouping of these entitlements, Identity Governance and Administration (IGA) systems are forced to operate at the individual entitlement level. This leads to a high volume of access requests, larger certification campaigns, and countless human decisions that are both time-consuming and error-prone.

Roles or policy rules help by grouping entitlements, making access decisions easier and more efficient. However, roles that are too broad may reduce the number of roles but become overprivileged and risky, defeating the purpose of role-based access control.

Conversely, roles that are too granular increase the total number of roles, creating management overhead as IGA systems must now manage entitlements and an equally large set of roles—adding complexity to already complex systems.

Role mining is a well-established capability in many vendor products, but it remains an evolving field with newer methods and optimizations emerging.

Rule-Based Method

Traditional role mining is done through manual role engineering, where identity experts manually analyze entitlement assignments to define roles and policy rules. In such setups, experts must also design and maintain methods to validate and update the accuracy of these rule sets.

Why It May Not Scale

In large enterprises with thousands of roles and millions of entitlements, manual grouping is time-consuming, labor-intensive, and prone to human error. Manual role definitions cannot be easily verified or systematically automated. Over time, access creep (where users accumulate unnecessary privileges) can persist for years, posing significant security risks.

ML Implementation Ideas

The goal of ML-based role mining is to identify permissions that are commonly assigned together to groups of individuals with similar job responsibilities. Three dominant techniques are often applied to this problem space:

- **Clustering Mechanisms:** Algorithms like *k-means clustering, hierarchical clustering,* or *DBSCAN* group users and entitlements based on access similarity.

- **Matrix Factorization:** Techniques like *Singular Value Decomposition (SVD)* or *Non-negative Matrix Factorization (NMF)* reveal hidden structures and permission groupings.

- **Association Rule Mining:** Algorithms such as *Apriori* or *FP-Growth* discover frequent permission sets that naturally form candidate roles.

Here's the updated **Access Recommendations** section with the **ML Implementation Ideas** heading and sample algorithms added:

Access Recommendations

Use Case

Most IGA (Identity Governance and Administration) vendor products either offer or are developing access recommendation modules. In access request or certification workflows, approvers can view machine-generated recommendations to either **approve or deny** a request. Access decisions are inherently complex: an approver must determine if they are granting the right access, to the right identity, at the right time. Evaluating all the necessary context for every request—such as user role, peer access, application sensitivity, and risk level—is nearly impossible at scale. Managers often have to process **hundreds of such decisions daily**, and machine-generated recommendations that consider all relevant contexts have become an emerging and highly valuable feature.

Rule-Based Method

Baseline approaches rely on **hard-coded rules** to automate approvals under certain conditions. Examples include

- *"Approve if the user is in department X."*
- *"Approve if the user belongs to department X and has peers with access to Y."*
- *"Approve if the user is active and the application's risk score is low."*

Why It May Not Scale

The number of rules required to cover all possible scenarios can become unmanageably large, and even with extensive rule sets, it is impossible to capture all the context and nuances involved in every access decision. Static rules lack the ability to adapt to changing contexts or evolving access patterns, often resulting in inconsistent or inaccurate recommendations. Furthermore, there is a constant trade-off between maintainability and accuracy: too many rules create significant operational overhead, while too few increase the risk of overprovisioning or inappropriate access.

ML Implementation Ideas

Supervised ML models can learn patterns from historical approval and denial data to predict outcomes for new access requests. Key features influencing these decisions often include department, user role, peer group access, risk scores, historical approval trends, entitlement descriptions, employee responsibilities, project details, business justifications, and entitlement sensitivity. Many of these attributes are textual, where advanced deep learning techniques excel at processing natural language elements for feature extraction and modeling.

Algorithms: Models such as *logistic regression, Random Forest,* or *Gradient Boosted Trees* can classify requests as "likely approve" or "likely deny."

Approach: By training on past decisions, the model builds a recommendation engine that evolves as new data becomes available, significantly reducing reviewer effort and decision fatigue.

Access Anomaly Detection

Use Case

Historically, most access controls and monitoring mechanisms have focused on verifying whether preventive access controls are functioning effectively. For example, ensuring that appropriate approval mechanisms were followed when granting access or that access was reviewed for appropriateness at regular intervals. These controls typically evaluate whether access at a point in time, along with its associated metadata, is correct.

Traditionally, the responsibility for detecting whether authorized access is being misused has fallen to security operations centers and related detection capabilities. This is changing, however, as identity has become the new perimeter. More than 70% of cyber events today can be traced back to compromised credentials. Detecting such compromises requires not only analyzing logs across multiple resources but also having a deep understanding of access management tools and their configurations. Increasingly, we see closer alignment between IAM engineering, IAM analytics, and broader cyber threat detection teams.

Effective anomaly monitoring requires detailed identity usage data. We need to understand how a given identity is using existing access and what additional access it is attempting to assume. For human identities, monitoring often begins with endpoint logs. For machine identities, however, the challenge is more nuanced: we must understand how applications use these identities, the compute and data services involved, and the ways in which applications communicate internally and externally.

Rule-Based Method

Most monitoring starts with static, predefined rules. Common examples include

- "Alert if more than three failed logins occur within ten minutes."
- "Flag if downloads exceed one GB in an hour."

- "Trigger an alert if administrative privileges are granted without approval."
- "Detect privilege escalations associated with lateral movement."

Why It May Not Scale

Rule-based methods provide quick traction when first implementing monitoring, and they establish a baseline that advanced methods should surpass. However, as environments grow, rules become too numerous and unwieldy. What is suspicious behavior in one application may be completely normal in another.

For instance, downloading one GB of data in an hour might be inappropriate for a customer support representative but perfectly acceptable for a business analyst analyzing a year's worth of complaints. Similarly, modern GenAI-powered tools have enabled nontechnical roles to perform complex analytics, making previously "unusual" activities more common.

The same applies to machine identities: repeated failed logins within a short time window might simply mean a password was rotated. Over-reliance on rules leads to endless exceptions and a flood of false positives. As discussed in the ITDR chapter, static thresholds often generate excessive false alerts, miss subtle anomalies, and require continuous tuning as user behavior evolves.

Before COVID-19, rules around geo-velocity (e.g., flagging a user logging in from two distant locations within a short time) were widely effective. With the rise of remote and hybrid work, however, such rules now generate far more exceptions than meaningful signals.

ML Implementation Ideas

Anomaly detection is not new to cybersecurity. Network threat detection has long relied on such methods, but identity behavior monitoring is only beginning to mature. Some vendor solutions now offer capabilities that enhance traditional monitoring by establishing behavioral baselines for identities—both human and machine—and then identifying deviations.

For human identities, baselines are established by correlating device logs, user access, application activity, and enriched attributes (such as department or role). For machine identities, this involves correlating identity use with application logs, server activity, and enriched metadata about where and how the identity is applied.

Machine learning techniques such as clustering, outlier detection, and specialized anomaly detection algorithms (e.g., Isolation Forest, UEBA) are increasingly used to automatically learn behavioral patterns and detect deviations.

Although ML reduces false positives compared to rules, it is not immune to them. Newer approaches are showing promise in further reducing noise. One example is **LogGPT**, which applies natural language modeling techniques to logs. By treating logs as text and predicting the next log entry, it can identify unexpected deviations with higher accuracy. Early results suggest substantial improvements in distinguishing true anomalies from benign activity.

Peer Group Analysis

Use Case

Peer group analysis, simply put, compares identity access to understand which users have similar access and which ones stand out as outliers. There are several use cases that drive such analysis:

- **Birthright Access Determination:** There is strong emphasis on improving employee productivity, and a key component of that is effective onboarding. Enabling new employees to become functional as quickly as possible requires giving them the right access at the right time. Understanding peer groups with similar access helps assign the appropriate baseline access to new members of that group.

- **Rogue Access Detection:** Peer group analysis helps detect unusual or excessive permissions by comparing a user's access to that of their peers. If an individual has entitlements that are significantly different from others in similar roles, it may indicate over-provisioning or the potential misuse of access.

- **Policy or Role Definitions:** By analyzing what access certain groups need, organizations can create access policies or define roles that simplify access requests and provisioning.

Rule-Based Method

A typical baseline implementation of peer group analysis is rule-based, where rules are defined based on identity and access attributes. For example:

- "All users in Customer Support should have access to the Customer Relationship Management (CRM) system."

- "All IT support staff should have access to a password management application."

- "Accounts Payable should have access to the Enterprise Resource Planning (ERP) payment system."

Why It May Not Scale

While baseline methods work in simple environments, they fail in complex organizations where individuals often perform tasks outside their primary roles. These methods can introduce excessive privileges. For example:

- **Customer Support Users**: Support teams are often organized by line of business, customer segments, or product types. If permissions are not defined at that level of detail, support staff may end up with access to systems they do not need. Even with fine-grained rules, exceptions exist, such as employees transitioning between roles or learning new modules.

- **IT Support Staff**: IT staff are usually grouped by the applications they support, by geography, or by tier (executive vs. standard). Broad rules granting access to multiple applications create high-risk situations, as these permissions are highly privileged. Ideally, IT staff should be granted **just-in-time access** based on context and with proper approvals. For example, password reset access may only be given when responding to a change order or during an incident.

Static grouping cannot keep up with today's dynamic organizational environments. Too many rules make it harder to manage segregation of duties (SOD) violations, while broad rules lead to over-privileges and access creep. Static rules also fail to evolve with context, limiting the ability of IAM systems to support just-in-time access.

ML Implementation Ideas

Unlike rule-based methods, machine learning approaches can incorporate both static attributes and dynamic data. Clustering techniques can analyze datasets with multiple features to provide personalized access recommendations, identify outliers, and flag risky entitlements—whether due to organizational changes or shifts in user behavior.

Typical algorithms include **clustering (K-means, hierarchical)**, **DBSCAN**, and **graph-based clustering**. These methods allow for more adaptive, context-aware peer group analysis.

Risk Scoring and Prioritization

Use Case

Risk scoring is not new in IAM—it has become a foundational capability. It helps us understand *who* the risky employees are and *what* risky access they hold that makes them risky. Several IAM products offer this capability out of the box. Still, risk scoring is an evolving topic, and companies are trying to make these scores more contextual.

Let's revisit static and dynamic attributes and how risk scoring plays a role.

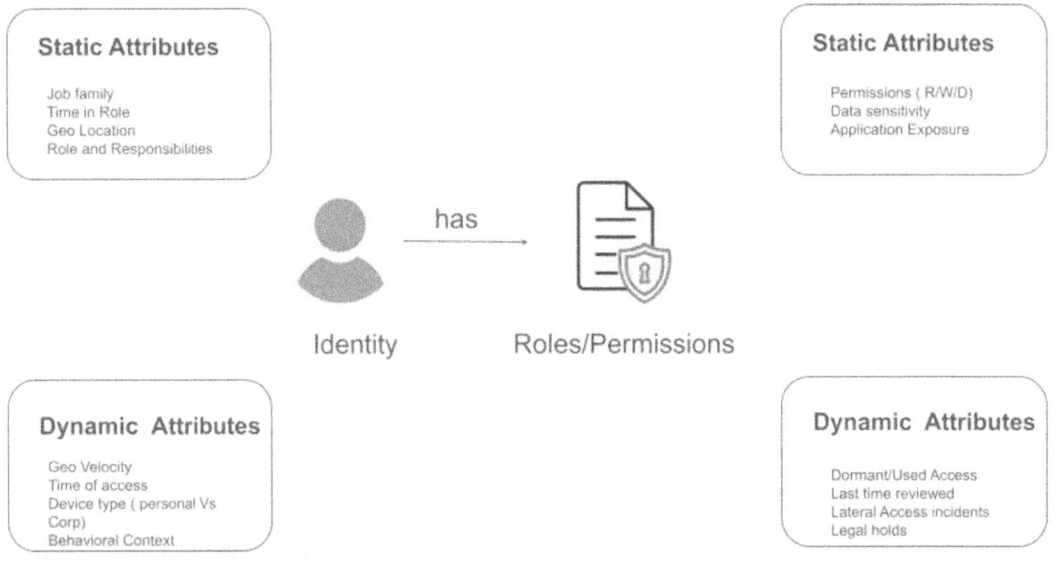

Figure 9-1. *Risk Scoring Factors*

Figure 9-1 illustrates how identity relates to the access it holds, along with examples of static vs. dynamic attributes. A static risk score is pre-calculated based on the attributes associated with identities and roles. Typically, we calculate risk scores for individual permissions, then aggregate and normalize them to determine overall identity risk. The attribute list shown is not definitive—depending on the data collected by the IAM team, additional attributes can be included.

CHAPTER 9   MACHINE LEARNING TECHNIQUES IN IDENTITY ANALYTICS

Net Risk Score = Static Risk Score + Dynamic Score

The net risk score is dynamic—it changes based on user and access behavior. As discussed in Chapter 5, these scores are foundational, and there are several ways they are used:

Informational

- Managers and approvers can see the level of risk tied to an access request before approving it.

- During control failures, investigators and control testers can assess residual risk and prioritize IAM investments accordingly.

Operational

- Net risk scores are used in Zero Trust implementations, where they feed into the decision engine during authentication or authorization workflows.

- Risk scores can drive control design and testing. For example, high-risk entitlements may be reviewed multiple times a year, while low-risk entitlements may only be reviewed once—though always aligned with regulatory expectations.

Rule-Based Method

As discussed in Chapter 5, traditional risk scoring often uses rule-based approaches. Scores are either assigned directly by domain experts or calculated based on weighted values.

Example:

- Database read = 10

- Database write = 15

- Database delete = 20

A database role's risk score is the cumulative sum of these weights, which may then be normalized and classified into high, medium, or low risk tiers.

Why It May Not Scale

While straightforward to implement, rule-based scoring is inherently static and subjective. There are several limitations with this approach:

- Weights are determined by subject matter experts who may eventually leave the company. When regulators later ask for an explanation of how certain calculations were made, it falls to people without prior knowledge to justify these subjective decisions.

- The risk environment is dynamic and multifaceted. For example, the risk associated with a database write is very different if the database supports a mission-critical customer application vs. one that only contains publicly available company information.

- As organizations move toward more fine-grained risk scoring, weights require frequent updates, making the entire program difficult to sustain.

Another part of the puzzle is the risk scoring provided by vendor solutions. Why, despite their availability, should organizations still consider establishing their own risk program?

Vendor solutions vary in maturity—the attributes they prioritize and the methodologies they use differ widely. While these scores can serve as a starting point, merging them in a meaningful way is challenging. Consider the scenario where your provisioning tool flags certain access as low risk, but your certification tool marks the same access as high risk. Which score should you rely on? The choice is still subjective, and in highly regulated environments, it becomes difficult to defend such inconsistencies.

ML Implementation Ideas

Machine learning addresses these shortcomings by enabling us to do three things: consider additional attributes without adding too much maintenance cost, provide an easier way to integrate existing risk scores, and incorporate behavioral attributes more effectively.

Supervised Methods

- Ask business risk groups and other cyber governance bodies to label representative samples—that is, enough data points covering all risk categories (high, medium, low).

- Use existing data from security operations related to insider threats and identity-related investigations, labeling what turned out to be true vs. false positives.

- Combine features from steps 1 and 2 to train classification models that generate risk scores.

Unsupervised Methods

While supervised methods are powerful and often easier to implement, obtaining labeled data is not always feasible—especially for smaller organizations. In such cases, clustering methods can be effective.

- Build features that include both static and dynamic attributes.

- Apply clustering methods, such as Gaussian Mixture Models (GMM), to group data into three clusters.

- Review identity attributes and other features that define each cluster. Subject matter experts should validate whether the features are truly risky, which is usually straightforward. This process will help identify which cluster represents high-risk entitlements vs. medium- and low-risk ones.

- Convert cluster probabilities into usable risk scores.

Incorporating Vendor Risk Scores

A natural question is: What should be done with existing vendor-provided risk scores? They do have merit and should be incorporated into the overall solution. There are two main ways to do this:

1. **As Input to ML Models**

   Vendor risk scores can be used as features within your model. This introduces some double counting—for example, if both your model and the vendor already consider the same attribute. However, this can be managed through techniques such as prior-posterior updates.

2. **As Validation for ML Outputs**

   Vendor risk scores can help validate your model's results. By comparing the overlap between your predictions and vendor scores, you can confirm whether your approach is reasonable. Strong alignment suggests your model is behaving correctly, while significant deviations may highlight areas for review.

CHAPTER 9   MACHINE LEARNING TECHNIQUES IN IDENTITY ANALYTICS

Implementation Details

Figure 9-2 shows a high-level view of how I typically see production implementations come together. This is not a definitive list, but it should give the reader a good sense of what is possible in practice.

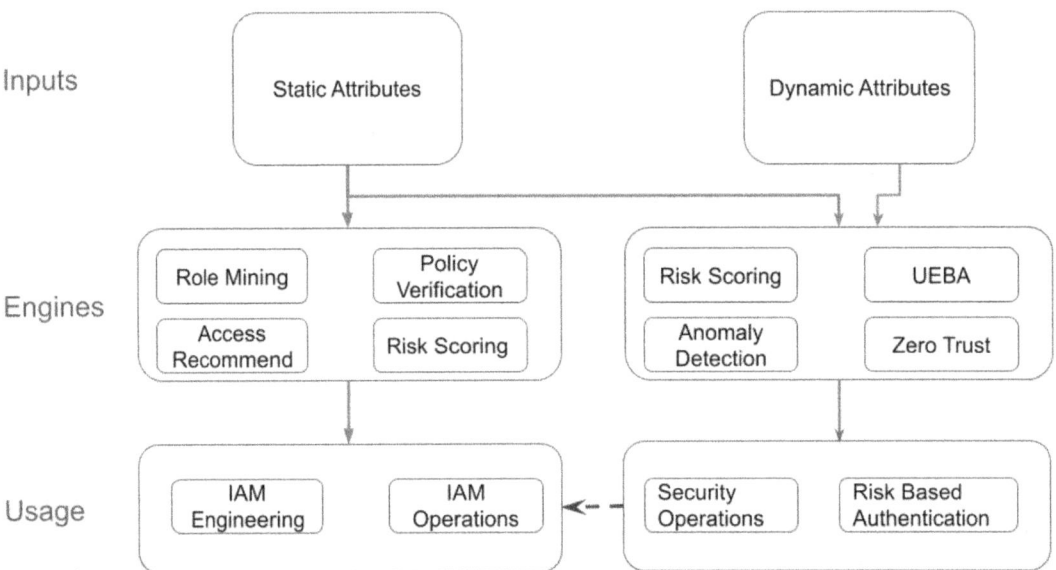

Figure 9-2.   Risk Scores In Action

Inputs

Static attributes are the metadata of identities, access, and assets. These are usually available from IAM products or asset inventories such as Configuration Management Databases (CMDB).

Daily updates via ETL jobs are generally sufficient. While real-time streaming can be built for some applications, many attributes—such as SOD (Segregation of Duties) policies or ownership—do not change frequently.

Some foundational static attributes include

Category	Attributes
Identity	Employment details, roles and responsibilities, organizational details
Asset	Application purpose, asset category, cloud attributes, criticality, exposure, in-house vs. third party, and data sensitivity
Access	Privilege type, effective permissions, SOD rules, and ownership

Dynamic attributes are critical for understanding whether authorized users are engaging in unauthorized activities. These are derived from user activities, application logs, and outputs from systems such as Endpoint Detection and Response (EDR) and Network Detection and Response (NDR).

Large organizations typically provide real-time data processing platforms, which significantly reduce the time and cost of setting up this infrastructure from scratch.

Some foundational dynamic attributes include

Category	Attributes
Identity	Employment change events, login attempts, proxy logs, geo velocity, and lateral access attempts
Asset	Vulnerabilities, configuration drift, network anomalies, and unauthorized data dumps
Access	UEBA systems, last access, access metadata changes, last certification, and anomalous permission changes

Engines

We have already discussed several of these engines and use cases, including risk scoring, which consumes both static and dynamic attributes. Two additional engines worth noting here are **Zero Trust** and **UEBA**.

Zero Trust

We will explore Zero Trust in depth in the next chapter, but here is a brief overview. According to the CISA Zero Trust Maturity Model, at the optimal level, every access request should be evaluated for appropriateness using both static and dynamic context. Once access is granted, sessions should be continuously monitored for anomalies, with remediation actions taken if any drift from normal behavior is detected.

As discussed in earlier chapters, achieving this target state requires a blend of both static and dynamic attributes.

UEBA

User and Entity Behavior Analytics (UEBA) is another important discipline in identity analytics. Its goal is to identify anomalous user behavior using statistical and machine learning techniques. UEBA requires correlating identity metadata with identity activity.

Although many vendors now offer UEBA solutions, significant innovation is still needed. This is mainly due to the cost of correlating massive log volumes and the challenge of operating in environments with little or no labeled data, which makes it difficult to build monitoring systems that generate fewer false positives.

Usage

- **Static Attribute Use Cases**

    These typically focus on (1) building rules to provide access in a timely and appropriate manner and (2) verifying that access rules are accurate. IAM engineering teams, IAM operations teams, and GRC professionals are the primary consumers of this information. Many automation opportunities can be built on top of these foundations.

- **Real-Time Monitoring Use Cases**

    These are threat-driven and usually demand immediate attention from security operations teams. Remediation often involves IAM operations later in the workflow, but the process typically begins with detection and mitigation handled by SOC teams.

Summary

- Traditional rule-based methods have worked well in simpler environments. However, in today's dynamic landscape—with cloud, SaaS, PaaS platforms, AI-enabled automations, and millions of digital identities—these rule-based approaches do not scale and quickly become unmanageable. This is where machine learning techniques start to make a meaningful difference.

- Both supervised and unsupervised methods have matured from early experimentation to production-ready implementations. Throughout this chapter, we discussed several use cases where each method applies. The dominant ML applications in IAM include role mining, peer group analysis, access recommendations, anomaly detection, and risk scoring.

- Static and dynamic attributes both play a critical role, each driving different types of use cases. In particular, most dynamic attribute use cases originate in security operations but often extend into IAM engineering and operations for remediation.

References

1. SailPoint. IdentityAI. https://documentation.sailpoint.com/saas/help/ai/index.html

2. Saviynt. https://saviynt.com/intelligence

3. Oracle Identity Management. https://www.oracle.com/security/identity-management/governance/#rc30p3

4. Omada. Role Mining. https://omadaidentity.com/resources/blog/ai-role-mining-in-iga/

5. Leila Karimi and Mai Abdelhakim. "Adaptive ABAC Policy Learning: A Reinforcement Learning Approach." https://arxiv.org/pdf/2105.08587

6. Xiao Han, Shuhan Yuan, and Mohamed Trabelsi. "LogGPT: Log Anomaly Detection via GPT." https://arxiv.org/abs/2309.14482

7. Cybersecurity and Infrastructure Security Agency. https://www.cisa.gov/sites/default/files/2023-04/zero_trust_maturity_model_v2_508.pdf

8. Exabeam. SIEM with UEBA. https://www.exabeam.com/capabilities/ueba/

CHAPTER 10

GenAI for IAM

If you've attended any cybersecurity or identity conference lately, you've probably noticed that they've all become "AI-fied." Artificial intelligence is now the centerpiece, with nearly every vendor introducing new, innovative features to tackle long-standing challenges in our industry.

The financial momentum behind this shift is equally significant. Consider the recent numbers:

- Google, Amazon, Microsoft, and Meta collectively invested $364 billion in 2025.

- 72% of large enterprises reported deploying AI solutions in 2025.

- US startup funding rose 75.6% in the first half of 2025, with most of that growth attributed to AI.

This represents a massive bet on infrastructure and future growth. Naturally, investors expect returns, which explains the strong push by both startups and big tech for enterprise adoption. It's no surprise that IAM products are also aligning with this innovation curve.

I firmly believe we are on the brink of a major transformation in IAM operations, IAM engineering, and threat detection. That said, not every investment will yield the expected returns. My goals for this chapter are to help readers:

- Understand the differences between ML, AI, and GenAI.

- Learn what real problems AI can solve today in the IAM space.

- Prepare from a governance standpoint if adopting vendor solutions.

- Explore sample implementations of IAM use cases, including what's involved if you decide to build your own.

This is going to be an exciting journey—let's dive in!

CHAPTER 10 GENAI FOR IAM

Understanding ML, AI, and GenAI

Yes, AI is not the same as GenAI, though many practitioners tend to use these terms interchangeably.

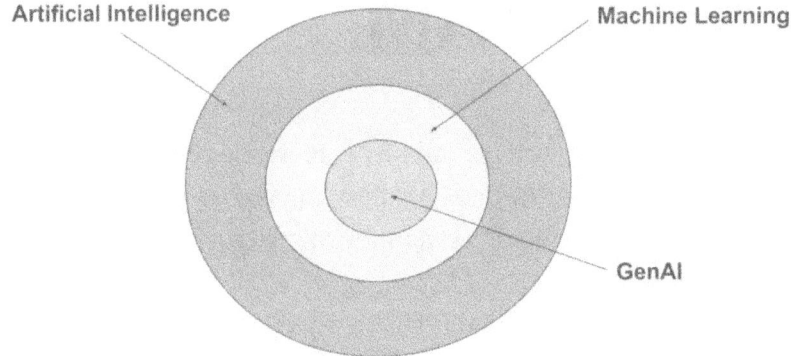

Figure 10-1.

Category	AI	ML	GenAI
Definition	A broad field of computer science that aims to mimic human intelligence and decision-making.	A subset of AI that uses data to teach computers to recognize patterns and improve their performance on tasks without being explicitly programmed.	A subset of ML that not only learns patterns from data but can also generate new content or patterns based on those learnings.
Algorithms	Rule-based Systems, Graph Techniques, ML, computer vision, Natural language processing, robotics.	Supervised learning, unsupervised learning, reinforcement learning and deep learning.	Transformer-based deep learning models- Large language models and Diffusion models.
Few IAM Use Cases	Rule based systems to detect configuration drift on Cloud IAM Roles, and Risk Scoring	Outlier Access Detection, Access Recommendations, UEBA, and Anomaly detection	Generate access policies, Access Chatbot, Natural language querying of access datasets

Figure 10-2. *AI vs. ML vs. GenAI*

Hopefully, Figure 10-2 provides enough clarity for readers to understand how these categories differ. So, when a vendor claims they use AI, don't assume it means ChatGPT-like integration by default—be sure to check what is actually being offered. There are many vendors in this space, but I will highlight only a few that demonstrate key use cases with proven ROI. This is not a preferred list, nor is it exhaustive.

IAM Vendor Perspective on GenAI

SailPoint IdentityAI

Access descriptions play a critical role in the user experience—for both employees requesting access and managers approving it. Unfortunately, neither of these user groups is responsible for writing access descriptions. Instead, the responsibility falls to asset owners. Since asset owners are closest to the system, they typically use minimal words that are sufficient for their own understanding but inadequate for others.

This organizational structure results in poorly written access descriptions. In large enterprises, entitlement catalogs can contain thousands of entitlements, making the issue even more significant. Inadequate descriptions not only create friction in how users request access but also introduce cyber risks, as first-line managers may not fully understand what they are approving.

SailPoint is addressing this problem with a new GenAI feature in its IdentityAI product. The company is leveraging LLMs to generate clear, contextual access descriptions. Early adopters report positive outcomes, with many customers trusting and approving the AI-generated descriptions without edits. Users are also finding it easier to request the correct access, which in turn improves the accuracy of peer-group analysis and other identity analytics, thanks to better-quality data

Veza: AccessAI

Veza is a relatively new player in the IGA space but has gained attention with its access graph technology and deep contextual integrations for fine-grained access management. Despite being new, Veza has already introduced a product called **AccessAI**, which provides assistant-like features to users.

According to their published materials, AccessAI includes a **Universal Search** capability powered by GenAI. This allows any user to query Veza datasets or analyze the access graph without needing to know complex query languages.

Other features support access reviewers by providing context around entitlements, helping them decide whether to approve or deny access. IAM processes are often highly manual, requiring reviewers to apply due diligence across hundreds of decisions. Veza is attempting to reduce this burden with GenAI, addressing one of the most important problem areas in identity governance.

IBM: AskIAM

IBM has launched **AskIAM**, an offering designed to address another major challenge in access management: onboarding applications to IGA and PAM platforms. According to IBM's newsroom, AskIAM accelerates application and privileged access onboarding by guiding application owners and users through the required steps, while also automating identity onboarding and secure access management for PAM tools.

As IT systems grow more complex, onboarding applications to IAM platforms remains a resource-intensive process, often requiring significant domain knowledge and engineering expertise. IBM claims that AskIAM reduces this burden by streamlining workflows and assisting consultants, customers, and application teams. In addition, AskIAM provides features to optimize workflows for access requests and approvals, further reducing inefficiencies.

Okta AI

Okta, one of the leading IAM vendors, has also announced new GenAI-powered features. The company aims to address inefficiencies in access workflows, delays in defining restrictive policies, and the shortcomings of current methods for detecting and mitigating identity threats.

With Okta AI, users can understand threats in natural language and receive proactive recommendations, including suggested new policies to mitigate risks. Developers can also use natural language to generate integration code for Okta's access management products. Additionally, the product can analyze existing configurations and recommend optimizations to streamline access flows.

These assistant-style features benefit both engineering and security operations teams, providing insights that previously required advanced analytical expertise.

Why Highlight These Vendors Now?

Until this chapter, I deliberately avoided focusing on specific vendors and their offerings. Readers might wonder why I am introducing them here and why I am mentioning only these four when there are others with similar capabilities. My intent is not to highlight these specific vendors, but rather to illustrate the **common themes** in how GenAI is being applied in IAM today. These examples help set the stage for the next section, where I will build on these themes to discuss the broader problem spaces GenAI is addressing across the industry.

IAM Use Cases

Almost everyone in an organization interacts with Identity and Access Management (IAM) in some way. Broadly, users can be grouped into four personas, each with distinct challenges.

Enterprise Users
The workforce of a company that performs day-to-day business functions. They typically request access through IGA (Identity Governance and Administration) solutions and then use that access to complete their tasks.

Pain Points

- Difficult to determine what access they need by simply looking at entitlement names.
- Long wait times to receive access.
- Uncertainty about automatically assigned access—employees often do not understand how it supports their role.

First-Line Managers
Managers of enterprise employees, who themselves are also enterprise users with added responsibilities. They must approve access requests and conduct access reviews.

Pain Points

- Entitlement names alone do not provide enough clarity to decide whether access is truly needed.
- Overwhelmed by too many certification items and approvals, often with little supporting context.
- Lack of visibility into how employees are actually using the access they have been granted, since managers typically cannot view activity logs.

Application/Asset Owners

Owners of applications or systems who also approve access requests for their assets. They are responsible for entering access descriptions into the entitlement catalog within IGA systems.

Pain Points

- While they understand their assets, describing entitlements in a way that is meaningful to end users is challenging.

- Frequent system changes and upgrades make it difficult to keep integrations with IGA solutions accurate.

- In cloud environments, restricting access is complicated when applications share accounts.

- With the rise of cloud, agentic AI, and continued reliance on data centers, the cybersecurity responsibilities of asset owners are continually expanding.

Governance and Risk Professionals

These professionals are responsible for understanding the risk landscape, overseeing IAM system integrations, designing controls, and reviewing SOC1/SOC2 reports, cloud service descriptions, and cyber frameworks. Their role requires continuous learning and processing vast amounts of documentation to ensure controls are effective, risks are properly addressed, and regulators remain informed.

Pain Points

- Enormous amounts of information must be analyzed to not only understand general frameworks but also evaluate the organization's specific position.

- Summarizing risks and presenting them to regulators requires synthesizing large volumes of documents and data.

- They must grasp both the technical details and the broader application of technology within the business.

Where GenAI Fits in IAM

Having explored these challenges, and considering the problems that vendors aim to solve, it is clear they are addressing the right issues—though some still persist. Broadly, GenAI applications in IAM fall into two categories.

Assistant Products

These are "know-all" chatbots trained to understand access paradigms, entitlement descriptions, system architectures, cloud service documentation, and company-specific implementation patterns. They can distinguish between risky and non-risky access. Examples include

- **Enterprise Users:** Guided recommendations on what access they need.

- **First-Line Managers:** Assistance in interpreting access requests and determining whether to approve based on business context.

- **Application Owners:** Automatic generation of access descriptions that update dynamically as systems change.

- **Governance and Risk Professionals:** A consolidated assistant to interpret the risk landscape and generate audit-ready regulatory responses.

Automation Products

This category leverages the code-generation capabilities of large language models.

- **Application Owners:** Generate integration code to connect applications with IAM systems.

- **IAM Engineers:** Produce access policies and rules to streamline workflows and ensure employees receive the right access with fewer requests.

- **IAM System Integrators:** Overcome traditional limitations of brittle RPA solutions or manual file uploads when APIs, databases, or SCIM connectors are unavailable. AI-enabled automation and web-driven tools are transforming how IAM systems integrate with such applications.

Sample Implementation Details

IAM systems are rarely straightforward. Many organizations have grown through acquisitions, which often leaves them operating multiple IAM platforms. In fact, it is common to see organizations running different IAM systems for the same use case—for example, using SAP solutions to manage SAP environments while relying on entirely separate tools for non-SAP products.

When companies purchase AI services from multiple vendors to support these fragmented IAM landscapes, costs can quickly become prohibitive. Over time, I suspect most large enterprises will shift toward developing their own AI services tailored to their unique IAM use cases. This section is written with that future in mind.

To illustrate this, I will present two use cases with simple starter code. While the examples are basic, my goal is to give readers a clear idea of how to approach building such solutions.

There are many foundational AI models available, but for the sake of simplicity, I will use OpenAI services in the examples that follow.

Use Case 1: Generate Access Descriptions

As explained above, accurate access descriptions help associates request the right access and enable managers to approve only what is truly needed. While this may seem like a simple use case, it can have a significant impact.

You can apply this access description system in two key scenarios:

- **During Application Onboarding to the IGA Solution:** When entitlements are recorded as requestable items within an application
- **For Existing Application Entitlements:** To enrich or improve their descriptions

Step 1: Collect all entitlement information for which access descriptions are required.

Step 2: Gather metadata about the application, including its type and key attributes describing what each entitlement does.

```
Entitlement: DB_ADMIN
System: Oracle HR
Tags: privileged, sensitive

Entitlement: DB_SYS_ROLE
System: Tableau Dashboards
Tags: readonly
Data Category- NPI
```

Step 3: Use the OpenAI endpoint to generate access descriptions.

```python
import os
from openai import OpenAI

# Get the key from environment variable
api_key = os.getenv("OPENAI_API_KEY")
if not api_key:
    raise RuntimeError("OPENAI_API_KEY not set. Please export it before running.")

# Initialize client
client = OpenAI(api_key=api_key)

prompt = """
You are an IAM assistant. Generate a clear, user-friendly access description
for the entitlement below. The description should explain who needs this access,
what access is for. Generate description in 2-3 sentences.

Entitlement: DB_ADMIN
System: Oracle HR
Tags: privileged, sensitive

Entitlement: DB_SYS_ROLE
System: Tableau Dashboards
Tags: readonly
Data Category- NPI
"""

response = client.chat.completions.create(
    model="gpt-4o",
    messages=[{"role": "user", "content": prompt}]
)

print(response.choices[0].message.content)
```

Step 4: Store the generated outputs in the IGA system.

CHAPTER 10 GENAI FOR IAM

```
print(response.choices[0].message.content)

**Oracle HR - DB_ADMIN Access Description:**

This DB_ADMIN entitlement provides full administrative access to the Oracle HR database system. It is intended for
experienced database administrators who are responsible for managing and maintaining the HR database, including tas
ks such as configuration, performance tuning, and data security, due to its privileged and sensitive nature.

**Tableau Dashboards - DB_SYS_ROLE Access Description:**

The DB_SYS_ROLE entitlement grants read-only access to Tableau Dashboards, specifically for handling Non-Public Inf
ormation (NPI) data. This access is designed for data analysts and reporting specialists who require the ability to
view and analyze dashboards without modifying the data or underlying system configurations.
```

That's it. In this example, we used the OpenAI GPT-4o model to create access descriptions. The model combines its internal knowledge with the provided data to produce descriptions that are ready for production use.

Use Case 2: Access Chatbot for Governance and Risk

The previous case was relatively simple, but it illustrates just how powerful AI models can be for automating back-office activities. Let's now add a bit more complexity. In this example, we will build a chatbot for Governance and Regulatory Response teams.

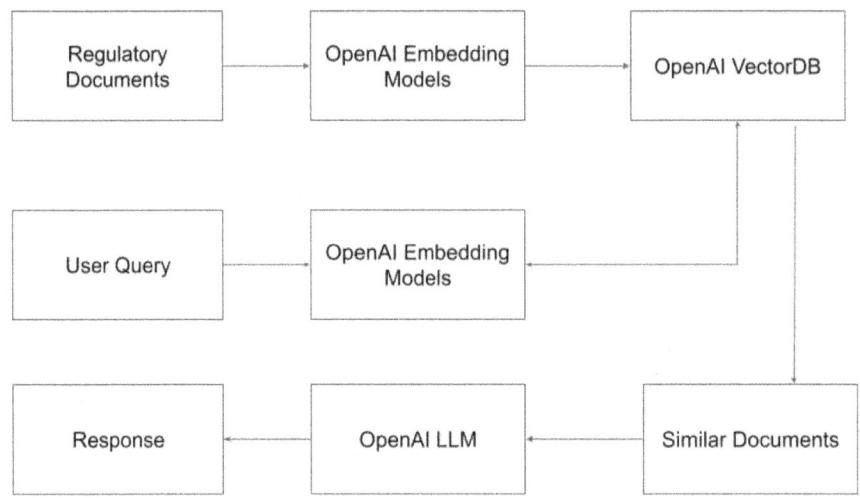

Figure 10-3. *High-Level System Design*

For this solution, I will be using the OpenAI stack end to end. IAM Risk Associates frequently encounter situations where they need to answer questions such as

- *Which NIST guidelines apply to a specific access scenario?*

- *How can we generate responses to regulatory or internal audit bodies explaining why a particular control is effective and how it addresses the referenced risk?*

- *Can prior regulatory responses be reused or adapted to address new concerns?*

In short, we need an AI system that can understand the organization's knowledge base, align it with regulatory standards, and provide accurate, context-aware answers.

Step 1: Create a vector database using OpenAI APIs.

```python
vs = client.vector_stores.create(
    name="nist-800-53r5",
    # expires_after={"anchor": "last_active_at", "days": 1} # uncomment if desired
)
print("Vector store id:", vs.id)

Vector store id: vs_68b4699f4460819192cab698c7be834d
```

Step 2: Download relevant regulatory documents, generate embeddings, and store them in the vector database created in step 1. OpenAI APIs can perform this multistep processing in a single call.

```python
import pathlib

PDF_URL = "https://nvlpubs.nist.gov/nistpubs/SpecialPublications/NIST.SP.800-53r5.pdf"
pdf_path = pathlib.Path("NIST.SP.800-53r5.pdf")

if not pdf_path.exists():
    r = requests.get(PDF_URL, timeout=120)
    r.raise_for_status()
    pdf_path.write_bytes(r.content)

print("Saved:", pdf_path, "Size:", pdf_path.stat().st_size, "bytes")

Saved: NIST.SP.800-53r5.pdf Size: 6073678 bytes
```

```python
# Upload the PDF into OpenAI Files and attach to the vector store in one step
batch = client.vector_stores.file_batches.upload_and_poll(
    vector_store_id=vs.id,
    files=[open(pdf_path, "rb")]
)
print("Ingestion status:", batch.status, "| file_counts:", batch.file_counts)

# Keep the file ids for clean-up later
files_list = client.vector_stores.files.list(vector_store_id=vs.id)
file_ids = [f.id for f in files_list.data]
print("File IDs in vector store:", file_ids)

Ingestion status: completed | file_counts: FileCounts(cancelled=0, completed=1, failed=0, in_progress=0, total=1)
File IDs in vector store: ['file-M4T6bnZrL4rMzmauLAHsUT']
```

Step 3: Process queries by generating embeddings, retrieving similar documents, and passing them to LLMs to generate appropriate responses. Most of these steps are handled directly by OpenAI endpoints.

```python
: q = "What controls are there for dormat accounts? "

resp = client.responses.create(
    model="gpt-4o",
    input=q,
    tools=[{
        "type": "file_search",
        "vector_store_ids": [vs.id],
        # Optional tunables:
        # "max_num_results": 6, "ranker": "auto", "score_threshold": 0.4
    }],
)

print(resp.output_text)
```

Controls for managing dormant accounts, according to NIST SP 800-53, include:

1. **Disabling Accounts**: Accounts should be disabled if they have expired, are no longer associated with a user, are in violation of organizational policies, or have been inactive for an organization-defined period.

2. **Account Management Policies**: Organizations are required to define and document account types and manage accounts according to organization-defined policies and criteria.

3. **Automated Account Management**: Automated mechanisms can be used to manage accounts, which includes notifying account managers of account status changes, monitoring system account usage, and reporting atypical usage.

4. **Inactivity Logouts**: There are requirements for users to log out after a defined period of inactivity.

5. **Usage Monitoring**: System accounts should be monitored for atypical usage, and any atypical usage should be reported.

These controls help organizations to manage the potential security risks associated with dormant or inactive accounts.

Step 4: Delete all temporary data and objects created in this process to avoid unintended charges.

```python
: # 7a) Detach & delete files from the vector store (not strictly required if you delete the store, but explicit is go
for fid in file_ids:
    try:
        client.vector_stores.files.delete(vector_store_id=vs.id, file_id=fid)
    except Exception as e:
        print("Warn(detach):", e)

# 7b) Delete the vector store
try:
    client.vector_stores.delete(vs.id)
    print("Deleted vector store:", vs.id)
except Exception as e:
    print("Warn(vs delete):", e)

# 7c) Delete the underlying File objects so they are not billed or reused elsewhere
for fid in file_ids:
    try:
        client.files.delete(fid)
        print("Deleted file:", fid)
    except Exception as e:
        print("Warn(file delete):", e)
```

Deleted vector store: vs_68b4699f4460819192cab698c7be834d
Deleted file: file-M4T6bnZrL4rMzmauLAHsUT

Key Considerations

As we move toward more advanced use cases with GenAI—such as automating access requests, generating ITDR investigation documentation, and streamlining SOC integration workflows—securing the underlying GenAI infrastructure and models becomes essential. Equally important is ensuring that the data fed into these models remains as close as possible to the original source of truth.

Some of the key considerations are outlined below. A number of these are general best practices that apply to any analytical product, while others are specific to GenAI-driven IAM systems:

- **Data Privacy and Protection:** All data used by GenAI, including user identities and access logs, must be securely stored and transmitted with strong encryption.

- **Access Control and Authorization:** Apply strict access policies so that only authorized personnel can modify or view sensitive configurations.

- **Model Security and Integrity:** Safeguard models against tampering, adversarial attacks, or reverse engineering that could expose sensitive information.

- **Authentication and Identity Verification:** Use robust mechanisms to confirm user identities and prevent impersonation or unauthorized access.

- **Auditability and Transparency:** Maintain detailed logs of AI decisions and actions for compliance, accountability, and forensic review.

- **Bias and Fairness Management:** Regularly test and adjust models to detect and minimize bias in outputs, ensuring fair and nondiscriminatory access decisions.

- **Continuous Monitoring and Threat Detection:** Monitor AI activities to quickly identify anomalies, vulnerabilities, or malicious activity.

- **Secure Deployment Environment:** Protect the AI environment through network segmentation, hardened infrastructure, and timely updates.

- **Data Governance and Compliance:** Align training data and processes with privacy regulations (e.g., GDPR) and industry standards.

- **User Education and Awareness:** Equip stakeholders with training on AI risks, responsible use, and security best practices.

Some of the points mentioned above are general model monitoring capabilities that should be part of any machine learning platform you choose to work with. Author Abi Aryan explores this in detail in the book *LLMOps*, which provides guidance on how to implement these capabilities if you don't already have a platform in place.

While most ML platforms provide many of these core services, one area where model owners must take responsibility is **monitoring model performance**. A lot of focus tends to be placed on building and deploying a specific use case, but monitoring performance is just as important. Unfortunately, monitoring GenAI use cases is not as straightforward as monitoring classification or other supervised ML models. In practice, you will often rely heavily on human feedback to evaluate the accuracy of predictions—and this feedback loop needs to be built into the rollout of the model from the very beginning.

Summary

- GenAI is reshaping cybersecurity and IAM landscapes, fueled by massive investments from big tech and widespread enterprise adoption in 2025.

- We explored how to differentiate AI, ML, and GenAI. While AI and ML focus on detection, pattern recognition, and decision-making, GenAI extends these capabilities to generate content, policies, and contextual responses.

- Leading IAM vendors are embedding GenAI to enhance access descriptions, accelerate onboarding, enable natural language querying, and streamline risk analysis.

- We also examined IAM personas and their pain points, highlighting areas where GenAI can play a significant role.

- Finally, we implemented sample use cases using OpenAI APIs, demonstrating how powerful features can be introduced with minimal effort—provided the right system choices are made.

References

1. https://finance.yahoo.com/news/big-techs-ai-investments-set-to-spike-to-364-billion-in-2025-as-bubble-fears-ease-143203885.html

2. https://www.superannotate.com/blog/enterprise-ai-overview

3. https://www.reuters.com/business/us-ai-startups-see-funding-surge-while-more-vc-funds-struggle-raise-data-shows-2025-07-15/

4. https://www.rackspace.com/blog/distinctions-ai-ml-generative-ai

5. https://www.sailpoint.com/identity-library/gen-ai-entitlements

6. https://veza.com/blog/veza-access-ai-applications-of-gen-ai-for-identity-security-use-cases/

7. https://newsroom.ibm.com/blog-askiam-ibms-new-agentic-ai-for-identity-and-access-management

8. https://www.okta.com/products/okta ai/

9. https://platform.openai.com/docs/api-reference/introduction

CHAPTER 11

Identity Analytics for Zero Trust

Introduction

Most companies still operate in a traditional sense, where security is focused on perimeter defense. Once authenticated, subjects are granted broad access to applications and can often move laterally within the network without further scrutiny.

A well-known example is the **Equifax breach of 2017**:

- Attackers exploited an unpatched vulnerability in the Equifax credit dispute portal to gain initial access.

- Using stolen credentials, they were able to move laterally across the network because credential access was implicitly trusted—once inside, no further verification was applied.

- The attackers discovered additional credentials stored in plain text on servers, expanding their access further.

- Ultimately, they escalated privileges and compromised highly sensitive data.

Had Zero Trust principles related to identity been applied, much of this damage could have been prevented. For example:

- **Real-Time Visibility:** Maintaining an accurate inventory of servers, detecting unpatched vulnerabilities, and quickly isolating or shutting down risky applications.

- **Continuous Verification:** Checking each login attempt for context—where the request originates, what data is being accessed, and whether the activity aligns with normal behavior—rather than assuming access is valid once credentials are presented.

- **Segmentation:** Containing applications within their own network segments to prevent lateral movement.

- **Least Privilege Access:** Implementing fine-grained, time-bound access so credentials grant only what is necessary, limiting an attacker's ability to explore or exploit additional systems.

These mitigations align with the design principles of **Zero Trust architecture (ZTA).**

The key point is that in most traditional environments, organizations do not have clear visibility into *who has access to what* within the network, and authorization controls are static. Once the perimeter is breached, trust is implicit, and static policies cannot prevent unauthorized actions inside the system.

As described in the **NIST Zero Trust paper (800-207):**

"Zero Trust is a cybersecurity paradigm focused on resource protection and the premise that trust is never granted implicitly but must be continually evaluated. Zero Trust provides a collection of concepts and ideas designed to minimize uncertainty in enforcing accurate, least-privilege, per-request access decisions in information systems and services, in the face of a network viewed as compromised."

What Is Zero Trust?

The textbook definition of **Zero Trust** from *NIST SP 800-207* is as follows:

"Zero Trust (ZT) provides a collection of concepts and ideas designed to minimize uncertainty in enforcing accurate, least-privilege, per-request access decisions in information systems and services, in the face of a network viewed as compromised. Zero Trust Architecture (ZTA) is an enterprise's cybersecurity plan that utilizes Zero Trust concepts and encompasses component relationships, workflow planning, and access policies. Therefore, a Zero Trust enterprise is the network infrastructure (physical and virtual) and operational policies that are in place for an enterprise as a product of a Zero Trust architecture plan."

CHAPTER 11 IDENTITY ANALYTICS FOR ZERO TRUST

In summary, Zero Trust assumes that a breach has either already occurred or will eventually occur. It prescribes fine-grained access controls for data and applications so that—even if credentials are compromised—the potential damage is limited. Credentials are short-lived, and active sessions are continuously monitored for anomalies, with access revoked if suspicious activity is detected.

The paper on ssh.com describes the key components of Zero Trust in a clear and succinct manner. The Zero Trust framework enforces the principle of "never trust, always verify," requiring every user or device—whether inside or outside the network—to authenticate and be authorized before gaining access. It further explains core principles such as least privilege access, segregation of duties, microsegmentation, just-in-time access, multifactor authentication, and rigorous auditing and session tracking. Technologies such as authentication, authorization, PAM, encryption, and session recording work together to operationalize Zero Trust in modern enterprise environments.

The Cybersecurity and Infrastructure Security Agency (CISA) has published clear guidelines for evaluating an organization's maturity against the Zero Trust (ZT) framework. Understanding maturity helps leaders identify gaps and prioritize investment in the broader cybersecurity ecosystem.

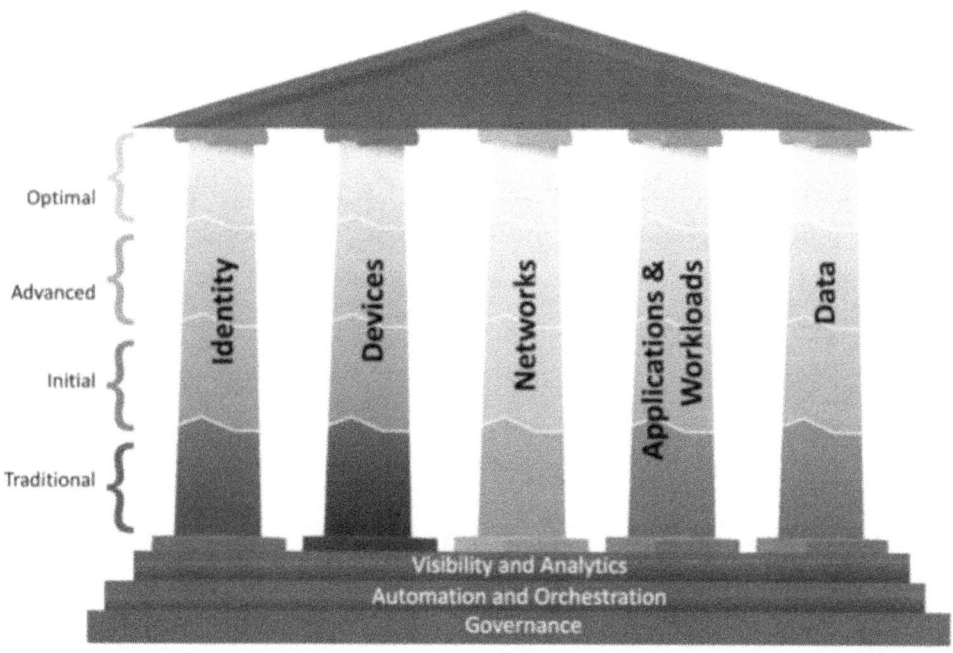

Figure 11-1. CISA Zero Trust Model

CISA describes ZT maturity across five pillars (Figure 11-1): Identity, Devices, Networks, Applications and Workloads, and Data. Each pillar can be evaluated against four maturity levels: Traditional, Initial, Advanced, and Optimal. In addition, three cross-pillar capabilities—such as visibility, automation, and orchestration—are foundational to enabling Zero Trust outcomes. I highly recommend that readers review this paper before continuing with the subsequent sections. I will reference it multiple times to illustrate practical examples of implementing the Zero Trust framework.

Rather than exploring each maturity level in detail, this discussion focuses on the access management capabilities required to enable pillar maturity. While access management is most prominently featured in the *Identity* pillar, it is in fact critical across all pillars. For example, in the *Data* pillar, simply identifying data types and enabling encryption is insufficient; fine-grained access controls are equally necessary to achieve higher levels of maturity.

Role of Identity Analytics in ZT Maturity

In this section, we will discuss the identity analytics capabilities required at the optimal maturity level of each pillar. Once these functional requirements are clear, we can identify the concrete features that need to be developed.

Some readers may wonder: *What if my organization is still at the "traditional" level? Will this discussion be relevant?* The answer is yes. This chapter builds on the foundations covered in earlier chapters. While the future state is described here, even organizations at a traditional level can move incrementally toward it. As emphasized in the CISA ZTMM paper, progress is gradual, and most companies will never reach the optimal state across every pillar. In practice, organizations will operate in a hybrid state—advanced in some areas, less mature in others.

Identity

ZTMM defines identity as

> "An identity refers to an attribute or set of attributes that uniquely describes an agency user or entity, including non-person entities."

At the optimal maturity level, identity capabilities ensure that access grants are automated, context-aware, and just enough to perform duties. Systems interconnect and share context across pillars to inform better access decisions. Capabilities include

- Continuous validation that identities use phishing-resistant MFA, not just at initial login.

- Centralized or tightly integrated identity stores that function as a single source of truth.

- Real-time identity risk scoring, directly influencing access decisions.

- Automated, just-in-time, just-enough access provisioning.

- Correlation of access logs to identities, with ML methods monitoring for behavioral anomalies and drift.

- Access reviews become supplementary, since most access is dynamic and short-lived.

- Automated policies driving access decisions and monitoring with minimal manual intervention.

Device

ZTMM defines a device as

> "A device refers to any asset (including its hardware, software, firmware, etc.) that can connect to a network, including servers, desktop and laptop machines, printers, mobile phones, IoT devices, networking equipment, and more."

While many capabilities are device- or asset-specific, identity analytics must incorporate device context. Key capabilities include

- Automated calculation of comprehensive device risk scores, which also incorporate changes in access permissions—for example, edits to /etc/sudoers, modifications to /etc/ssh/sshd_config, or unauthorized privilege escalations.

- Device posture checks during authentication to ensure logins occur only from authorized devices.

Network

ZTMM defines a network as

> *"A network refers to an open communications medium including typical channels such as agency internal networks, wireless networks, and the Internet as well as other potential channels such as cellular and application-level channels used to transport messages."*

For identity analytics, the network pillar provides critical context. Capabilities include

- Continuous monitoring of network traffic and sharing of anomalies with identity platforms to improve access decisions

- Using network attributes (e.g., IP address, source location, VPC endpoint) in access policies to control asset access

- Encryption of network traffic and effective key management

Applications and Workloads

ZTMM defines this pillar as

> *"Applications and workloads include agency systems, computer programs, and services that execute on-premises, on mobile devices, and in cloud environments."*

Capabilities that intersect with identity analytics include

- Continuous authorization of application access using risk analytics, behaviors, and usage patterns.

- Real-time vulnerability scanning of applications, with scores integrated into access decisions.

- Monitoring of code deployments; if unverified changes bypass SOD processes, access policies become more restrictive until validated.

- Externalized and centrally managed application access, with access enforcement decoupled from the application itself.

Data

ZTMM defines data as

"Data includes all structured and unstructured files and fragments that reside or have resided in federal systems, devices, networks, applications, databases, infrastructure, and backups (including on-premises and virtual environments) as well as the associated metadata."

Since attackers ultimately target data, protecting it is central. Capabilities at optimal maturity include

- Cataloging datastores, enriched with metadata for ABAC and policy-based access control

- Automated, just-in-time, just-enough data access grants

- Encryption of data, with keys accessible only to authorized identities

- Monitoring all data activities (read/write), with logs fed into behavioral analytics systems to detect anomalies

Identity Analytics Capabilities to Support ZT Architecture

Looking across all five pillars and the expectations around access management, we can summarize the foundational identity analytics capabilities required to achieve and sustain high maturity:

- **Cross-Pillar Correlation:** Identity metadata, activities, device posture, and network logs are correlated and enriched into a cross-pillar data warehouse to fuel Zero Trust implementation.

- **Contextual, Risk-Based Decisioning:** IAM systems are transformed to make access decisions based on real-time signals from identity, device, network, applications, and data.

- **Just-in-Time, Just-Enough Access:** Access grants must be provisioned and deprovisioned automatically, in real time. This requires a shift from batch-based IAM systems to event-driven integrations across platforms.

- **Continuous Monitoring and Enforcement:** Access sessions are continuously monitored using UEBA and other techniques to validate that activity remains appropriate. Integrations must be able to terminate sessions immediately if anomalies are detected.

- **Externalized Authorization:** Access controls are standardized and externalized, applied consistently across all applications and systems.

- **Dynamic Policies:** Access policies are adaptive, continuously evaluated for least privilege, and updated based on context and evolving risk.

In prior chapters, we explored many of these building blocks: how to enable a 360-degree identity view with full lineage, the role of continuous monitoring in behavior analytics, common algorithms for anomaly detection, and methods for calculating risk scores in both static and dynamic contexts.

What we have not yet discussed is how to incorporate identity analytics directly into the access decisioning process. That is the focus of this chapter. In essence, this chapter brings together everything we have learned so far and demonstrates how to enable risk-based access decisioning by integrating these advanced identity analytics capabilities.

Let's dive in.

Deep Dive into Dynamic Authorization

Before we deep dive into dynamic authorization, it is important to first understand how access is typically managed today. We call this the **traditional authorization model**.

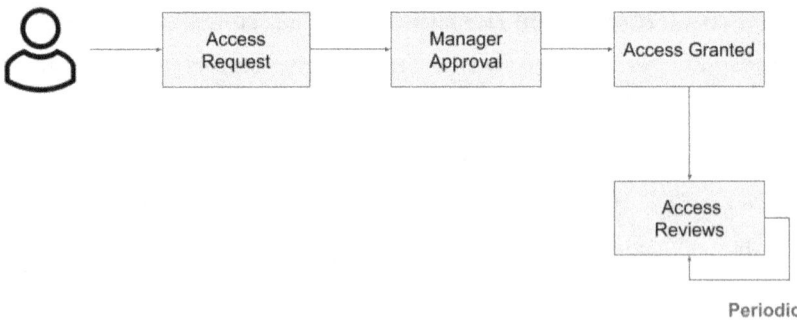

Figure 11-2. Access Request Workflow

CHAPTER 11   IDENTITY ANALYTICS FOR ZERO TRUST

Figure 11-2 illustrates how access is granted to an application. A user requests access, which is then approved by the first-line manager. Depending on regulatory requirements, this step can include multiple levels of approvals. Once approved, access is provisioned—either manually or through Identity Governance and Administration (IGA) solutions.

After the user obtains access, periodic certifications are performed to review its appropriateness. If access is no longer needed, it may be revoked during these reviews. High-risk applications typically undergo quarterly access reviews.

Limitations of Traditional Authorization

This model presents several well-known challenges:

- **Access Persistence**: Once granted, access often remains for years. The only mechanism to revoke it is via periodic access reviews.

- **Lack of Behavioral Integration**: Even if an authorized user engages in unauthorized activities, such signals are rarely integrated into IGA systems. This leads to long detection and remediation SLAs.

- **Approval Blind Spots**: Managers approving access requests have limited visibility into the risks of their decisions.

- **Opaque Entitlements**: The mapping of entitlements to fine-grained application permissions is usually known only to developers, limiting broader monitoring and analytics.

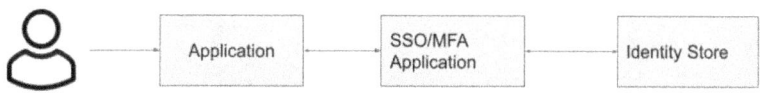

Figure 11-3. Authentication Workflow

Figure 11-3 depicts a typical authentication workflow for MFA-enabled applications. The process works as follows:

1. The user requests access to the application.

2. The application redirects the request to an authentication service.

3. The MFA system verifies the user's identity against identity stores.

4. The application receives an authentication response with user attributes, groups, and metadata.

5. Authorization is then applied according to the access grant workflow described in Figure 11-2.

Once authenticated, sessions are typically long-lived (often lasting at least a day), with little to no continuous monitoring.

Limitations of Traditional Authentication

- **Attribute-Only Checks**: Authentication decisions rely primarily on static identity attributes; broader risk signals are not considered.

- **Loss of Control Post-authentication**: After login, interactions between users and applications fall outside IGA or authentication system visibility.

- **Weak Monitoring of Active Sessions**: Session activity is either unmonitored or entirely dependent on SIEM ingestion. If the application is legacy and logs are incomplete, threats can go undetected.

These weaknesses contribute directly to delays in detecting and managing identity-driven threats.

The answer to these challenges lies in **externalized, continuous, dynamic authorization**.

CHAPTER 11 IDENTITY ANALYTICS FOR ZERO TRUST

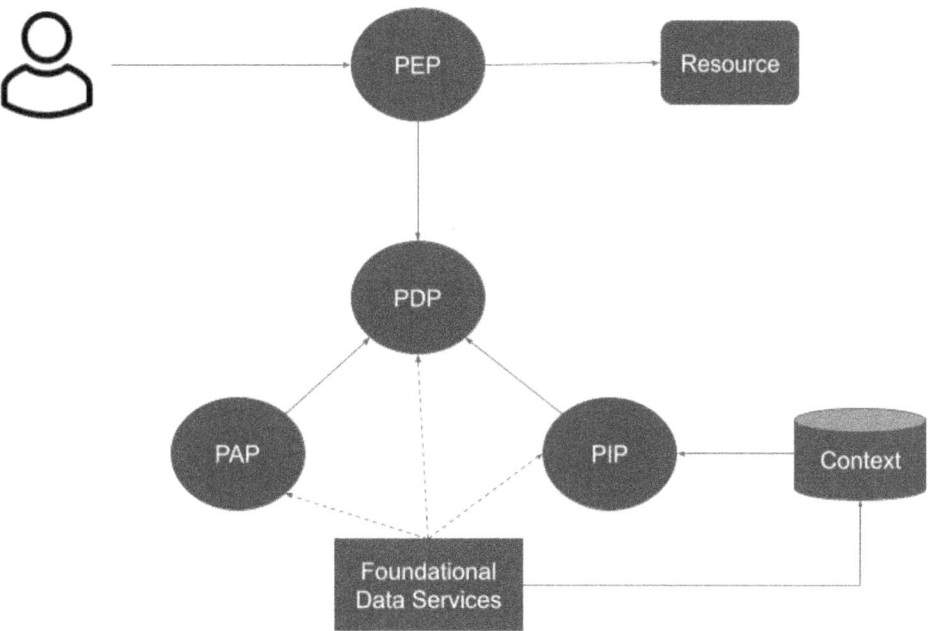

Figure 11-4. *Policy Decisioning*

Figure 11-4 depicts a modern **Zero Trust–aligned authorization model** that introduces policy-driven components:

- **Policy Enforcement Point (PEP):** Intercepts access requests and sends them to the PDP for evaluation. Can be embedded in the application layer or deployed in front of apps via proxies or authentication gateways.

- **Policy Decision Point (PDP):** Evaluates requests and issues allow/deny decisions. This is where authorization is externalized. Policies may include contextual rules (e.g., "Associates can access only during business hours"). The PDP consumes real-time context from the PIP.

- **Policy Information Point (PIP):** Provides contextual data—device posture, network telemetry, identity attributes, LDAP groups, risk and behavior scores—via high-availability data stores to support real-time policy evaluation.

- **Policy Administration Point (PAP):** Enables the authoring and life cycle management of authorization policies consumed by the PDP.

- **Foundational Data Services:** To operationalize this model, supporting services are critical:

    1. **Policy Authoring at Scale**: Tools that translate natural language into enforceable policies help shift decisions closer to business owners.

    2. **Policy Accuracy and Validation**: Policies must be continuously monitored, just as traditional access reviews validate role appropriateness.

    3. **Trust Algorithms and Behavior Monitoring**: "Zero Trust" is a security framework that requires an algorithm to evaluate every access request. This algorithm needs to gather all inputs from the request, fetch additional context, and then decide whether to grant access. Even after access is granted, Zero Trust requires continuous monitoring of active sessions. If an active session exhibits anomalous behavior, the system should trigger an adaptive response, such as session termination. These "trust algorithms" can initially use rule-based logic, similar to the concepts in risk-scoring frameworks. As systems mature and more data becomes available, these algorithms can evolve to incorporate machine learning models for more sophisticated and adaptive decision-making.

        This is the domain where **identity analytics teams play a pivotal role**. Analytics enhance decision accuracy, provide risk context, and support continuous improvement of policy enforcement.

        Understanding the limitations of traditional models and the aspirations of dynamic authorization is essential. Only by seeing where we are today and where we need to go can we design a practical road map toward externalized, intelligent, and adaptive access management.

Foundational Data Services

In this section, I will double-click on the things around foundational services. We will see how identity analytics plays a vital role in each use case I mentioned in the above section.

Policy Authoring at Scale

There are commercial products available for policy authoring that offer solid features. For engineering teams, building the required policies is much easier as they can be generated using command-line tools or an editor. The resulting policies are typically simple.

However, when we talk about externalizing authorization policies, the situation changes. These policies are often authored by business users who have deep knowledge of their applications but aren't coders. For instance, an associate in Accounts Payable who manages a SaaS T&E application like Concur would be responsible for designing the necessary authorization policies. If a policy agent like OPA is used, the policy language is Rego, and building these policies is essentially like writing code, even though UI tools can abstract some of the complexity.

I believe generative AI can play a significant role here. Creating an AI-driven abstraction that generates policies from natural language prompts could eliminate a lot of complexity and help organizations implement policy agents at scale. This agent could also use the output of existing machine learning models to generate policies automatically, with business users only needing to verify their accuracy.

A potential workflow could look like this:

- Analyze employee access to identify peer groups.

- Identify clusters of entitlements that naturally go together using community detection algorithms. Outliers can then be flagged for an analyst to review and determine if they should be explicitly included in a rule.

- Send prompts to a large language model (LLM) to generate Rego policies based on tags associated with these clusters.

The primary issue with rolling out policy-based authorization in large organizations is the sheer number of policies required. This is especially challenging in matrix-based organizations with thousands of applications where roles and responsibilities are constantly changing. Agentic abstraction could make this process much more efficient.

Policy Accuracy and Validation

We've discussed at length why existing certifications, or "access reviews," are inefficient and how decision fatigue makes them risky. You might be wondering, "How are we solving this? Aren't we just going to be reviewing these policies instead?" And if these policies are essentially code, how will non-developers be able to review them?

There are three main types of issues we encounter with policy definitions, and each requires a different approach.

1. Excessive Permissions

    Using analytics, we can identify policies with excessive permissions. A simple yet powerful solution is to correlate the permissions in a policy with usage logs. If certain permissions are never used, the policy is over-privileged. This is a concept similar to AWS Access Advisor.

    Another method involves the access graphs we learned to build in earlier chapters. If a resource node has too many inbound access links, it's a strong sign that multiple, potentially undetected access paths exist, which indicates excessive permissions.

2. Overly Restrictive Policies

    Unfortunately, many enterprises deploy Identity and Access Management (IAM) solutions without thoroughly thinking through the analytics needed to monitor their effectiveness. This strategy is a recipe for failure. Without feedback on how policies are working for users, you're flying blind.

    A great indicator of an overly restrictive policy is the frequency of user complaints about access denials. When users constantly report errors or require manual exceptions, it's a clear sign that a policy is too narrow. Similarly, if you find yourself creating a high volume of policies for the same or similar resources, it often indicates that the existing policies are too restrictive.

To monitor these indicators effectively, a robust reporting infrastructure must be in place from day one. Graph analytics is also useful here, revealing excessively long access paths or even the complete absence of paths to a resource, which points to policies that are too granular and difficult for associates to use.

3. Misused Policies

   As an IAM expert, have you ever seen a non-human identity shared by multiple, distinct applications? Or come across an Identity Governance and Administration (IGA) role that has become bloated with too many permissions, making it overly broad? This type of "access shopping" is common in traditional environments, and unfortunately, access policies are no different. Teams often take the shortcut route of reusing the same policies or expanding existing ones to make them work for new use cases.

   Fortunately, both classical machine learning and LLM-based techniques can be used to identify similarities among policies assigned to different resources. Simple analytics can also provide insight—for example, by tracking which teams created a policy and which applications are using it. NIST publication 8360 also covers various machine learning methods for detecting "access creep" in policies.

Trust Algorithms and Behavior Monitoring

The trust algorithm (TA) is the process the policy engine uses to determine whether to grant or deny access to a resource. As shown in the Figure 11-5, it receives inputs from the requesting system and builds a comprehensive context from several sources:

- Asset management
- Policy rules

CHAPTER 11 IDENTITY ANALYTICS FOR ZERO TRUST

- Identity attributes
- Threat intelligence signals related to the identity, device, and network

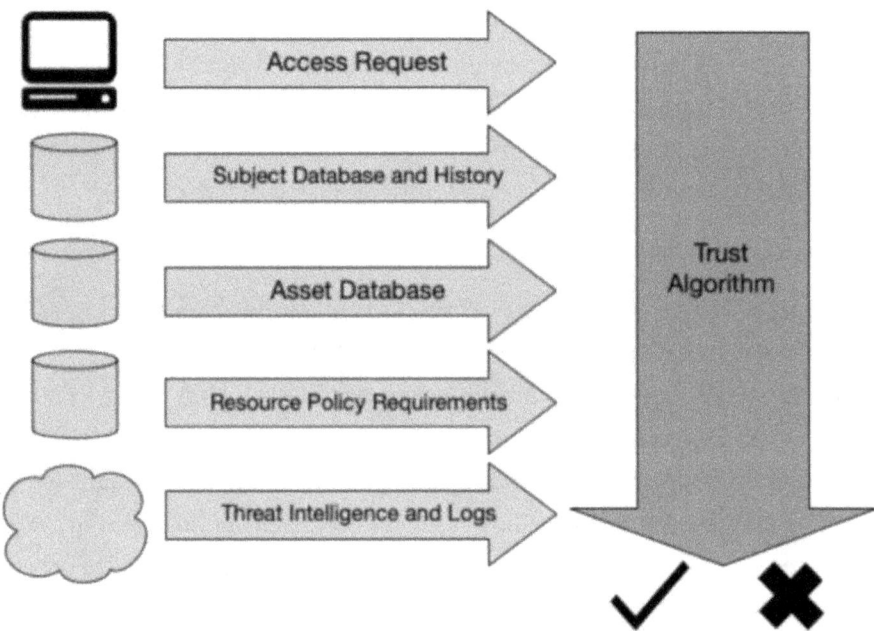

Figure 11-5. *Trust Algorithm (Source: NIST 800-207)*

Using these inputs, the trust algorithm calculates a score that determines if a specific access request should be granted.

Initial implementations often rely on deterministic rules. However, as systems mature, these models evolve into more sophisticated, machine learning (ML)-based scores. These ML models utilize probabilistic scores and thresholds to make more nuanced access decisions. For more ideas on implementation, refer to the chapter on risk scoring.

I've combined the granting of access and the monitoring of ongoing sessions into a single section because they are not distinct problems. In both scenarios, the system must decide if access is valid based on the current context. The chapter on identity threat and detection describes how inputs can be used to monitor user behavior and identify behavioral drift. This drift can be used to make access sessions short-lived or trigger a re-authentication request.

CHAPTER 11 IDENTITY ANALYTICS FOR ZERO TRUST

It's inevitable to have false positives, especially in the early stages of implementation. However, emerging methods using reinforcement learning can help. A feedback loop can be established where user actions—such as a user requesting access through traditional channels after their session was revoked due to a false positive—are used as inputs to improve the model. This continuous input helps the models learn and refine their accuracy over time.

Historically, identity analytics have primarily served a governance function, mainly focusing on building dashboards to pinpoint where core Identity and Access Management (IAM) controls are failing. While this detection-based work is necessary—and something we've discussed in previous chapters—I don't believe it's a truly strategic approach. In this reactive model, you'll always be a step behind hackers who are already exploiting these weaknesses.

In contrast, a Zero Trust (ZT) architecture puts the identity pillar at its core, bringing identity analytics to the forefront. This approach leverages analytics and detection capabilities to enable organizations to make real-time, risk-based decisions, which significantly reduces risk. I have no doubt that we will see a future where credential threats are not only detected but also prevented in real time. Achieving this future requires a significant shift in mindset from leaders. They need to view identity analytics as a strategic solution rather than just a compliance mechanism. There's immense potential in the data your systems generate every day, but it won't be unlocked by simply purchasing vendor software. Consider this a critical investment that will provide your business with a competitive advantage.

For my technical readers, I know this sounds like a hefty expectation. However, while writing this chapter, I came across a new AI tool for cyber vulnerability hunting called CAI, which reportedly detects bugs 3,600 times faster than a human. This makes me optimistic about the future of both identity analytics and the professionals in this field.

A recent paper from MIT highlighted that while 95% of AI initiatives fail, the 5% that generate value are mostly in back-office and IT-enabled process automation. I can't think of any other area in cyber that is as manual as IAM. Just consider the sheer volume of manual tasks involved in your last certification or CMDB review. There is so much to do, and I hope I've provided enough to get you excited about the opportunities and the path to building a solid road map for your team.

CHAPTER 11   IDENTITY ANALYTICS FOR ZERO TRUST

Summary

- Traditional security models rely on a perimeter defense. Once inside, users are implicitly trusted, allowing for lateral movement, as demonstrated by the 2017 Equifax breach. This approach lacks continuous verification and grants excessive privileges, making it vulnerable to breaches.

- Zero Trust assumes that a breach is inevitable, and therefore, trust must never be granted implicitly. It advocates for continuous verification, least privilege access, and network segmentation to limit the damage from a security incident.

- The chapter introduces the CISA ZT Maturity Model, which evaluates an organization's maturity across five pillars: Identity, Devices, Networks, Applications and Workloads, and Data.

- Achieving a high level of ZT maturity requires several key analytics capabilities: cross-pillar correlation of data, contextual and risk-based decisioning, just-in-time, just-enough access, continuous monitoring, and dynamic policies that are constantly evaluated and updated.

- Dynamic authorization uses policy-driven enforcement and evolves from rule-based to ML-driven trust decisions.

- Generative AI and machine learning can simplify policy creation and help detect excessive, restrictive, or misused policies.

References

1. "Equifax Data Breach." https://archive.epic.org/privacy/data-breach/equifax/

2. CISA. "Zero Trust Maturity Model." https://www.cisa.gov/resources-tools/resources/zero-trust-maturity-model

3. "Zero Trust-The Five Pillars of CISA Maturity model." https://www.intersecinc.com/blogs/zero-trust-the-five-pillars-of-cisa-maturity-model

4. CISA. "Executive Order on Improving the Nation's Cybersecurity." https://www.cisa.gov/topics/cybersecurity-best-practices/executive-order-improving-nations-cybersecurity

5. "Machine Learning in Access Control: A Taxonomy and Survey." https://arxiv.org/pdf/2207.01739

6. Access Advisor. https://repost.aws/knowledge-center/iam-access-advisor-access-analyzer

7. "CAI: An Open, Bug Bounty-Ready Cybersecurity AI." https://arxiv.org/abs/2504.06017

8. "Guidance for Modernizing Authorization Architecture." Gartner Approach, by Homan Farahmand.

9. "Improve IAM Architecture by Embracing 10 Identity Fabric Principles." Gartner Approach, by Homan Farahmand.

10. Sheryl Estrada. "MIT Report: 95% of Generative AI Pilots at Companies Are Failing." https://fortune.com/2025/08/18/mit-report-95-percent-generative-ai-pilots-at-companies-failing-cfo/

Index

A

ABAC, *see* Attribute-based access control (ABAC)
AC, *see* Access control (AC)
AccessAI, 191
Access control (AC), 43, 44, 167
Access Control Lists (ACLs), 138
Access request stage, 107
Access shopping, 219
Accounting, 8–10
Account management, 158
ACLs, *see* Access Control Lists (ACLs)
Active directory (AD), 117
    common attack methods, 124
    detection methods, 125
    logs, 125
    remediation, 125
Active Directory groups, 43, 44
AD, *see* Active directory (AD)
Adaptive ABAC (Attribute-Based Access Control) system, 173
Adaptive detection, 128
Ad hoc approach, 16, 27
Ad-hoc dashboard
    data governance, 81
    data ingestion, 80
    data sources, 79
    data system, 81
    energy, 79
    libraries, 80
    monitoring, 81
    performance and risk, 79
    standardized data models, 80
    technology stack, 80
Administrative logs, 127
AHP, *see* Analytic Hierarchy Process (AHP)
AI, *see* Artificial intelligence (AI)
Alerting infrastructure, 86
Analytic Hierarchy Process (AHP), 111
Anomaly-based detection, 129, 172
Apache Flink, 40
Apache Hive, 41
Apache Iceberg, 41
Apache Kafka, 40
Apache Spark streaming, 40
Apache Trino, 41
API integration, 38
Application architecture, 42
Application-level rules, 98
Architecture, 92
Artificial intelligence (AI), 189–191
AskIAM, 192
Asset inventory management, 45, 46
Asset owners, 194
Attribute-based access control (ABAC), 5, 136
AU, *see* Audit/accountability (AU)
Audit/accountability (AU), 167
Audit Events, 161, 162
Authentication, 1–5, 13, 23, 63, 110, 160, 214–216
    device, 40
    logs, 48
Authenticator management, 160, 161

INDEX

Authorization, 1–5, 20, 63, 213, 214
Autoencoders, 104
Automation, 24–26
Autoscaling, 84

B

Back-end services, 42
Behavioral datasets
    data inputs, 40
    data processing layer, 40
    data storage, 41
    deviations, 39
    key types, 40
Birthright access determination, 178
Brute-force attacks, 9
Business outcomes, 62
Business requirements
    stakeholders, 73–75
Bypassing, 43

C

Capability Maturity Model (CMM), 16, 21
    level 1, 17, 18
    level 2, 17, 18
    level 3, 18, 19
    level 4, 19, 20
    level 5, 20, 21
Center for Internet Security (CIS), 157
Centralization, 63
Certification stages, 107
CDC, *see* Change data capture (CDC)
Change data capture (CDC), 38
Change-tracking services, 144
Chatbots, 195, 198–200
ChatGPT, 172
Check printing applications (CPA), 3

CIAM, *see* Cloud Identity and Access Management (CIAM)
CIEM, *see* Cloud infrastructure entitlement management(CIEM)
CIS, *see* Center for Internet Security (CIS)
CISA, *see* Cybersecurity and Infrastructure Security Agency (CISA)
Cloud access management
    annual growth rate, 133
    cloud adoption, 136
    compliance, 134
    data foundation, 136, 137
    data model, 139, 140
    drift detection, 147
    factors, 133
    federated and indirect identities, 138
    identity classes, 137–139
    machine and service identities, 138
    multicloud considerations, 148, 149
    policies, 136
Cloud adoption, 171
Cloud computing, 45
Cloud Identity and Access Management (CIAM), 64
Cloud infrastructure entitlement management(CIEM), 7, 8
Cloud-Native Application Protection Platforms (CNAPP), 133, 134, 142, 146, 152
Cloud transformation, 115
Clustering (K-means, hierarchical), 179
Clustering mechanisms, 174
CMDBs, *see* Configuration Management Databases (CMDBs)
CMM, *see* Capability Maturity Model (CMM)
CNAPP, *see* Cloud-Native Application Protection Platforms (CNAPP)

Columnar Databases, 39
Communication, 93
Compliance support, 119
Configuration Management Databases (CMDBs), 45, 110, 184
Configuring alerts, 87, 88
Confirmation, 84
Conformance, 61
Connectors, 31
Containment, 129
Correlation, 128
COVID-19 pandemic, 177
CPA, *see* Check printing applications (CPA)
Credential access
    detection methods, 121
    lateral movement, 122, 123
    logs needed, 121, 122
    remediation, 121, 123
CRM, *see* Customer Relationship Management (CRM)
Cross-cloud threat detection, 134
CustomerDB, 52, 53
CustomerPayments, 51–53
Customer Relationship Management (CRM), 179
Customer support users, 179
CustomerUpdate, 52
Cyber analysts, 50
Cyber leadership, 73
Cyber modules, 26, 27
Cyber operations, 74
Cybersecurity, 20–22, 26, 28, 29, 45, 59, 61, 82, 91, 146, 157, 164, 177, 189
    exceptions, 78
    paradigm, 206
Cybersecurity and Infrastructure Security Agency (CISA), 207
Cyber vulnerability, 221

D

150 dashboards, 86
Dashboards, 82, 83, 158, 166
Data analytics, 13
Database audit events, 49
Databricks, 167
Data coverage, 29
Data depth, 29
Data enrichment, 92, 110, 111
Data events, 146
Data exfiltration
    detection methods, 123, 124
    logs needed, 124
    remediation and response, 124
Data governance, 81
Data-level activity, 146
Data loss prevention (DLP), 124
Data models, 139, 140, 144, 145
    ever-evolving nature, 79
    standardization development, 80
Data modernization, 115
Data pipelines, 46, 143, 164
Data practitioners, 21, 22
Data preparation
    behavioral datasets, 39–41
    entities, 32–34
    identity attribute data, 36–39
    market disruptors, 29
    requirements, 30, 31
    source code, 54–57
    storage, 38, 39
Data processing, 15
    alerting mechanisms, 166
    control policy engine, 165
    correlation engine, 165
    dashboards, 166
    data lake, 165

Data processing (*cont.*)
   ingestion, 164
   layer, 49, 50
   metric calculations, 165
Data services
   policy authoring, 217, 218
   supporting services, 216
Data serving, 16
Datasets, 31, 35
Data standardization, 49
Data storage, 38, 39, 41, 46, 47, 50
Data stores, 45
Designing performance
   data sources, 77
   exceptions, 78
   frequency, 78
   location, 78
   thresholds, 78
   version, 78, 79
Detection mechanisms
   behavioral detections, 151
   compliance failure, 151
   specification-based, 151
Detection method, 122
Device authentications, 40
Digital representation, 2
Digital transformation, 115
Distributed querying systems, 41
DLP, *see* Data loss prevention (DLP)
Dynamic attributes, 185
Dynamic risk scores, 108, 109
DynamoDB, 81, 141

E

Ecosystem, 31
EDR, *see* Endpoint detection and response (EDR)
Effectiveness, 60
Effective response, 129
Efficiency, 60
Empathy sessions, 85
Employees, 42, 75
Endpoint detection and response (EDR), 115, 116, 185
Endpoint logs, 49
Enforcement, 150
Enrichment, 50
Enterprise Resource Planning (ERP), 179
Enterprise users, 193
Entitlement-level
   data, 128
   risk scoring, 100, 101
   rules, 98
Equifax, 59, 88, 205
Equifax breach of 2017, 205
ERP, *see* Enterprise Resource Planning (ERP)
External audit teams, 74

F

Facebook, 29
File-based integration, 38
Fine-grained access, 146
Fire-drill-driven approach, 162
First-line managers, 193, 194
Fluctuating environments, 171

G

Gaussian Mixture Models (GMM), 183
GenAI, *see* Generative AI (GenAI)
Generative AI (GenAI), 172
   infrastructure, 200
   model performance, 202

GMM, *see* Gaussian Mixture Models (GMM)
Google, 133
Governance frameworks, 8–10
Governance, Risk, and Compliance (GRC), 64
Granular analysis, 93
Graph analytics, 51, 219
Graph-based clustering, 180
GRC, *see* Governance, Risk, and Compliance (GRC)

H

Hard-coded rules, 175
High-impact summary, 88
High-level data processing, 44
High-level decision-making, 93
Human identities, 2, 13, 32, 34, 36

I

IA, *see* Identification/authentication (IA)
IAM, *see* Identity and access management (IAM)
Identification/authentication (IA), 167
IdentityAI, 169, 191
Identity analytics, 14–16, 157
    and automation, 24–26
    cyber modules, 26, 27
    and risk reduction, 23, 24
    three phases, 21, 22
    and value proposition, 22
Identity and access management (IAM), 13, 30, 60, 62, 71, 76, 117, 155, 169, 170, 172, 218, 221
    access management, 2
    accounting and governance, 8–10
    assistant products, 195
    authentication, 1–5
    authorization, 1–5
    automation products, 195
    cloud adoption, 7, 8
    datasets, 166
    escalation, 166
    governance and risk professionals, 194
    human and machine, 3
    identity analytics, 14, 27
    pain points, 193
    platforms, 163
    printing process, 2
    privileged access, 5–7
    questions, 13
    regulatory engagements, 13
    reporting capabilities, 165
    use cases, 193–195
Identity attributes
    data, 36
    data inputs, 36, 37
    data processing layer, 37, 38
    device information, 34
    HR events, 33
    job details, 33
    keystrokes, 34
    risk scores, 34
Identity governance, 43–45
Identity Governance and Administration (IGA), 14, 33, 37, 43, 60, 92, 117, 158, 169, 173, 175, 213, 219
    applications and resources, 46
    risk-scoring system, 95
    tools, 46
Identity life (IL) cycle, 105
    procedures, 111
    risk scores, 106
Identity provider (IdP), 137

INDEX

Identity-related attributes, 31
Identity risk scores
    dynamic, 108, 109
    static, 108
Identity threat detection
    active directory (AD), 124, 125
    data exfiltration, 123, 124
    system architecture, 126, 127
    visualization, 130
Identity Threat Detection and Response (ITDR), 115, 117, 158
    access, 118
    credential access, 120–122
    implementation, 118
    integration, 152
    platforms, 118
    security incident and event management (SIEM), 119
    security monitoring, 118
    solution design, 120
    and user and entity behavior analytics (UEBA), 119, 120
IDS, *see* Intrusion detection systems (IDS)
IDS/IDP, *see* Intrusion Detection and Prevention Systems (IDS/IDP)
IGA, *see* Identity Governance and Administration (IGA)
Implementation
    engines, 185, 186
    high-level, 173
    ideas, 174
    patterns vendors, 170
Incident response, 118
Indicators, 61
Industry-based scoring, 92
Informational risk scoring, 181
Ingestion stages, 143, 144
In-memory storage, 39

Inputs section, 48, 49
Instagram, 29
Internal audit teams, 74
Intrusion Detection and Prevention Systems (IDS/IDP), 115
Intrusion detection systems (IDS), 46
ITDR, *see* Identity Threat Detection and Response (ITDR)

J

JIT, *see* Just-in-time (JIT)
Just-in-time access, 99, 179
Just-in-time (JIT), 136

K

Key data entities, 32
Key identity, 36
Key Performance Indicators (KPIs), 61, 65–70, 76
Key Risk Indicators (KRIs), 59, 61, 62, 65–71, 76, 89
Keystroke data, 40
Keystrokes, 34, 35, 40
KPIs, *see* Key Performance Indicators (KPIs)
KRIs, *see* Key Risk Indicators (KRIs)

L

Lagging indicators, 61
Large language model (LLM), 217
Least privilege access, 206
Linear relationships, 103
LLM, *see* Large language model (LLM)
LogGPT, 178
Log ingestion

INDEX

application access audit, 128
cloud service and data logs, 126
detection, 128, 129
endpoint logs, 127
platform logs, 127
Logs, 47, 48
Logs—to detect deviations, 22

M

Machine-123, 53
Machine identities, 33, 53, 177
Machine learning-based alerts, 87
Machine learning-based methods, 103
    hybrid approach, 104, 105
    supervised, 103
    unsupervised, 104
Machine learning (ML), 169, 190, 191, 220
    access anomaly detection, 176–178
    access recommendations, 175–177
    data-intensive discipline, 170
    identity and access management (IAM), 171–173
    implementation, 175, 177, 178
    implementation ideas, 174
    shortcomings, 182
    supervised method, 182
    unsupervised methods, 183
    use cases, 173, 174
    vendors, 192
    vendor solutions, 182
    vendor-specific, 169, 170
Management events, 146
Measurement phase, 16, 21, 23, 25, 27
Metadata, 196
Metric alerting, 86
Metric consumption
    board presentation, 82

dashboards, 82, 83
Metric implementation
    business requirements, 73
    data professionals, 72
    iterative and continuous, 72
    road map, 72
    thought-provoking, 72
Metrics program, 71
MFA, *see* Multi-factor authentication (MFA)
Micro-Batch Processing, 38
MITRE ATT&CK tactics, 120
ML, *see* Machine learning (ML)
Monitoring phase, 19, 20, 22, 24, 25
Multi-cloud and hybrid ecosystems, 133
Multi-factor authentication (MFA), 1, 4, 16, 22, 24, 61, 63, 96, 99, 118, 160

N

National Institute of Standards and Technology (NIST), 92, 157
NDR, *see* Network Detection and Response (NDR)
Network Detection and Response (NDR), 115, 116, 185
Network devices, 46
Network layer, 42
Network traffic, 48
NIST, *see* National Institute of Standards and Technology (NIST)
NIST 800-53 framework, 157
    AC-5, 159
    AC-6, 159
    AC-2 (13), 158, 159
    AC-2 (1-12), 158
    AU-2, 161, 162
    IA-2, 160
    IA-5, 160

INDEX

NIST Zero Trust paper, 206
NMF, *see* Non-negative matrix factorization (NMF)
Non-cloud access patterns, 140
Non-human identities, 2
Non-negative matrix factorization (NMF), 174
NoSQL database, 52
Numerical precision, 102

O

Okta AI, 192
OpenAI, 196–198, 202
Operational analytics, 64
Operational risk scoring, 181
Overabundance, 86

P

PAM, *see* Privileged access management (PAM)
PAP, *see* Policy Administration Point (PAP)
Parsing, 142
PaymentsDB, 52, 53
PBAC, *see* Policy-based access control (PBAC)
PDP, *see* Policy Decision Point (PDP)
Peer group analysis, 178–180
PEP, *see* Policy Enforcement Point (PEP)
Permissions, 218
    boundaries, 142
    calculator, 144
PIP, *see* Policy Information Point (PIP)
Policy accuracy, 218, 219
Policy Administration Point (PAP), 215
Policy-based access control (PBAC), 5
Policy Decision Point (PDP), 215
Policy Enforcement Point (PEP), 215
Policy Information Point (PIP), 215
Prediction phase, 20, 22, 24, 25, 28
Privilege, 159
Privileged access management (PAM), 5–7, 63, 64, 139
Problem-solving tools, 84
Process automation, 115
Productivity, 60
Proxy logs, 49

Q

Qualitative risk scoring, 93
Quantitative risk scoring, 93–95

R

RBAC, *see* Role-Based Access Control (RBAC)
Real-time data pipelines, 147
Real-time intelligence, 15
Real-time monitoring, 186
Real-time risk scoring, 106, 107
Real-time streaming, 184
Re-authentication, 220
receivepayment, 52
Regulatory challenges, 103
Regulatory reporting, 155
    access-related expectations, 156, 157
    industry-specific, 156
    sensitive systems, 156
Reinforcement learning (RL), 173
Relational databases, 38
Remediation, 123
Restrictive policies, 218, 219
Risk-aware metrics, 64
    metrics in depth, 60–62

Risk-based authentication (RBA), 60
Risk indicators
    calculation method, 77
    domain, 76
    metric ID, 76
    metric name, 76
    metric type, 76
    stakeholder, 77
Risk is uncertainty, 84
Risk management, 6
Risk reduction, 23, 24
Risk scores, 34
Risk scoring, 37, 180–183
Risk-scoring system, 92
    application level, 95
    challenges, 92
    identity governance and administration (IGA), 95
    identity life cycle, 105, 106
    IGA-managed entitlements, 96
    implementations, 105
    qualitative, 93
    quantitative, 93–95
    real-time, 106
    scenarios, 97
    static and dynamic, 107
    user-level, 96
RL, *see* Reinforcement learning (RL)
Robotic Process Automation (RPA), 25
Rogue access detection, 178
Role-Based Access Control (RBAC), 4
Role mining, 172–174
RPA, *see* Robotic Process Automation (RPA)
Rule-based alerts, 87
Rule-based method, 174–176, 178, 181
Rule-based risk scoring, 98
    advantages, 99
    application-level, 98
    challenges, 99
    Entitlement-level, 98
    user-level, 98, 99
Rule mining, 173, 174

S

SailPoint, 169, 191
Sample implementation
    use case 1, 196–198
    use case 2, 198–200
S3 buckets, 7, 141, 142
Scalability, 99
Scalable detection, 128
Scale, 171
SCPs, *see* Service Control Policies (SCPs)
Security Incident and Event Management (SIEM), 115, 164
    capabilities, 116
    holistic threat detection, 116
    identity-focused threats, 116
    log types, 116
    wire payment approver, 117
Security operations center (SOC), 16, 74, 104, 105, 107, 112, 113, 166
Security Orchestration, Automation, and Response (SOAR), 119
SIEM, *see* Security Incident and Event Management (SIEM)
Segmentation, 206
Segregation of duties (SOD), 136, 179
Self-service information access, 166
Separation of Duties (SOD), 159
Service Control Policies (SCPs), 138, 142
Session policies, 142
Session termination, 129
Signal View, 87

INDEX

Single-factor authentication, 3, 4
Single sign-on (SSO), 118
Singular Value Decomposition (SVD), 174
SOD, *see* Segregation of duties (SOD); Separation of Duties (SOD)
S&P 500 account, 29
SSO, *see* Single sign-on (SSO)
Stakeholder, 77
Standardization, 150, 151
Startups, 189
Static attribute, 186
Static risk scores, 108
Step-up authentication, 129
Streamline, 75
Stream processing, 40, 49, 50, 111
Structured approach, 71
Subjectivity, 99
Supervised algorithms, 172
Supervised methods, 182
SVD, *see* Singular Value Decomposition (SVD)
System architecture
  data enrichment, 110, 111
  data ingestion layer, 110
  log ingestion, 126–128
  risk scoring, 109
  risk scoring engine, 111
  serving layer, 111, 112
System design reporting, 162

T

TA, *see* Trust algorithms (TA)
Table
  identity_policy_permission_map, 145
Threshold-based categorization, 93, 94
Traditional authorization model, 212
Training data, 129

Translated permissions, 150
Trust algorithms (TA), 219–221

U

UEBA, *see* User and Entity Behavior Analytics (UEBA)
Universal Search, 191, 192
Unsupervised learning, 172, 173
Unsupervised learning methods, 129
User activities, 48
User and Entity Behavior Analytics (UEBA), 39, 120, 172, 186
User devices, 37
User identification, 160
User interactions, 42
User interface, 42
User-level
  risk scoring, 96
  rules, 98, 99, 101, 102
User logs, 127

V

Validation, 85, 183
Value proposition, 22
Vendor
  entitlement assignments, 174
  offerings, 170
  products, 174, 175
  risk scores, 183
Verification, 85
Veza, 191
Virtual private clouds (VPCs), 116
Virtual Private Networks (VPNs), 49
VPCs, *see* Virtual private clouds (VPCs)
VPNs, *see* Virtual Private Networks (VPNs)
Vulnerability, 59

W, X, Y

WAFs, *see* Web application firewalls (WAFs)
Web application firewalls (WAFs), 116
Weighted risk scoring, 99
    application-level, 100
    entitlement-level, 100, 101
    user-level, 101, 102
WhatsApp, 29

Z

Zero copy, 41
Zero trust, 60, 185
Zero Trust architecture (ZTA), 206, 207, 221
Zero trust (ZT) principles
    applications, 205
    applications and workloads, 210
    damage, 205, 206
    data, 211
    definition, 206–208
    device, 209
    dynamic authorization, 212, 213
    framework, 207
    identity, 208, 209
    identity analytics capabilities, 211, 212
    maturity level, 208
    network, 210
    ZTA (*see* Zero Trust architecture (ZTA))

GPSR Compliance

The European Union's (EU) General Product Safety Regulation (GPSR) is a set of rules that requires consumer products to be safe and our obligations to ensure this.

If you have any concerns about our products, you can contact us on

ProductSafety@springernature.com

In case Publisher is established outside the EU, the EU authorized representative is:

Springer Nature Customer Service Center GmbH
Europaplatz 3
69115 Heidelberg, Germany